Islamic Festivals and Their Religious Importance

Islamic Festivals and Their Religious Importance

By

Sharif Ahmed

2008

CYBER TECH PUBLICATIONS
4264/3, Ansari Road, Daryaganj, New Delhi-110002 (India)
Ph.: 011-23244078. Fax: 011-23280028
E-Mail: cyberpublicationsdelhi@yahoo.com

ISLAMIC FESTIVALS AND THEIR RELIGIOUS IMPORTANCE

Sharif Ahmed

First Edition 2008

Published by :

G.S. Rawat for **Cyber Tech Publications**
4264/3, Ansari Road, Daryaganj, New Delhi-110002 (India)
Ph.: 011-23244078. Fax: 011-23280028
E-Mail: cyberpublicationsdelhi@yahoo.com

Printed at : **Amit Enterprises**, Maujpur, Delhi, (9810878184)

Preface

Holy Quran, the divine book is a great treasure of knowledge and wisdom. It is the original source. This Holy book is the original source of inspiration for the whole mankind. Holy Quran stands for peace-peace for all, not for the Muslims, alone. In fact, Holy Quran, when interpreted, incorporates in its fold, safety and security for the whole mankind. Holy Quran, the divine scripture addresses all human beings, not only the Muslims. Prophet of Islam, Hadrat Muhammad (peace be upon him) is known as the benefactor of mankind. Thus, Islam's message is for the whole universe and Allah (God) is the lord of all the worlds. Islam is universal in its nature, essence, belief, philosophy, ideology, approach and practice.

Truly speaking, Holy Quran addresses all the human beings and not merely Muslims. Islam--despite being the most progressive, logical and scientific religion, on this planet--is also the most misunderstood religion. This confusion about Islam has recently increased due to certain eventual reasons. However, recently, Islam has attracted the minds of people towards it and resulted into a deep interest in knowing Islam. More and more people want to know about Islam, the religion, which has once again stirred the world community. Holy Quran, however, advocates non-violence, peace and fraternity. Holy Quran, from the very first day has raised the banner of reasoning and enlightenment, on the one hand and humanity, equality and fundamental rights on the other.

On may believe it or not, today Islam is the fastest developing religion, which is spreading--through voluntary preaching and invitation--in the whole world and in west, including USA at a faster pace, than ever. Over the past few years, the popularity of Holy Quran and other authentic Islamic books has touched new heights. Islam is perhaps seen as the last bastion of spirituality, mortality, tradition and religious values, leading to real salvation.

For a comprehensive study of Holy Quran, one intelligent reader requires exclusive, authentic and exhaustive books to satisfy their urge, answer their quest and convince them on all counts. This voluminous studies aimed at the same goal. These books are in fact a grand treasure of knowledge and awareness about Holy Quran and as well as a window, leading to Quranic wisdom. Further, it ascertains the honourable status of Holy Quran as a perfect great book, relevant for all times.

The honest intention of the author is focused on projecting Islamic Festivals and their Religious Importance in totality and in nutshell.

—*Author*

Contents

1

Religious Affairs

1. The best portion of the earth in the sight of Allah is that upon which a mosque is raised. The distinctive feature of the devotee of Allah is that he loves the mosque also. On the terrific day of doom when there will be no shade anywhere, Allah will keep that person under the shade of His Heaven whose heart is devoted to the mosque. The Holy Prophet [S.A.W.] has observed:

   "The man whose heart is devoted to the mosque will rest under the shade of Heaven." (Bukhari)

2. Render service to the mosque; keep the house of Allah populated. To render service to the mosque and keep it populated is a sign of faith. Allah affirms:

   "He shall tend Allah's sanctuaries who believeth in Allah and the Day of reckoning." *(Al-Tauba: 18)*

3. Always say your obligatory prayers in congregation in the mosque. Maintain a regular system of congregation and announcement of the Prayer-call in the mosque and correlate your whole life with the mosque. Mosque is the pivot around which the life of a true believer revolves. The Holy Prophet [S.A.W.] observed:

   "There are certain people among the Muslims who stay in the mosque permanently and do not leave the place. They have angels as their companions. If such people disappear from the mosque, the angels go about looking for them. If these people fall ill, the angels enquire after their health and when they are engaged in some task, the angels aid them-A person who sits in the mosque anticipates blessings of the Lord." (Musnad Ahmad)

4. Go to the mosque with eagerness and enthusiasm to say your prayers. The Holy Prophet [S.A.W.] affirmed: "The act of going to the mosque morning and evening is like going to fight in the cause of Allah." And further observed: "The people who go towards the mosque in the dim light of the dawn will be accompanied by full radiance of light on the Day of Doom." In addition, the Holy Prophet [S.A.W.] affirmed: "Each step that a man takes towards the mosque to say his prayers with the congregation, debits one sin and credits one virtue to his account." (Ibn Habban)

5. Keep the mosque clean and tidy. Sweep the place and clean out all dust or filth. Burn incense, especially on Fridays so that the whole mosque becomes fragrant with the aroma of the incense. The Prophet [S.A.W.] observed: "To sweep the mosque; to keep it tidy and clean; to cast out all dust and filth from the mosque; to burn incense in the mosque, especially to make the place fragrant with the aroma of the incense on Fridays- all these are acts which lead to Paradise."(Ibn Majah)

   Moreover, the Holy Prophet [S.A.W.] said: "To clean out the dirt and dust of the mosque is the mehr (dower) of a pretty-eyed Houri." (Tibrani)

6. Go to the mosque in a state of awe and trepidation. Say 'Assalamo 'Alaikum' [peace be on you] on entering the mosque. Sit down quietly and pray in such a manner that your heart should be filled with the awe of the Greatness and Glory of Allah. Those who enter the mosque laughing and talking are careless and impudent. The hearts of such people are devoid of the fear of Allah. Some people in their bid to join the congregation lest they miss any Rakat rush forward into the mosque. This act is contrary to the sanctity of the mosque. Whether you are able to join the 'Rakat' or not, walk in the mosque with poise, dignity and in humility; avoid hurried movement.

7. Sit down in the mosque in peace and avoid worldly talk. To shout or make a noise, to cut jokes and laughter, to discuss bazar rates, to comment on the world affairs or to strike business deals in the mosque is an act of sacrilege. Mosque is a place for Worship; use it for the purpose of offering devotions to Allah only.
8. Do not take such small children with you in the mosque who have not yet attained awareness of the sanctity of the mosque lest they should discharge urine, defecate or spit in the mosque.
9. Do not use the mosque as a thoroughfare. On entering the gate of the mosque it becomes obligatory upon you to say prayers, or sit down and engage in the remembrance of Allah or recite the Holy Quran.
10. If you lose something somewhere else, do not make an announcement of your loss in the mosque. Whenever someone made such an announcement in the mosque of the Prophet [S.A.W.] the Holy Prophet [S.A.W.] was offended and used to remark:

    "May Allah restore not the lost thing to thee!"
11. On entering the mosque put your right foot first in and say 'peace and blessings of Allah be on the Holy Prophet' [S.A.W.] and then say the following prayer. The Holy Prophet [S.A.W.] observed: "Whenever any of you enters the mosque, he should say 'peace and blessings of Allah be on the Holy Prophet' [S.A.W.] and then say this prayer: "O Allah! Open the gates of Thy Mercy for me." (Muslim)

    After entering the mosque, say two Rakat' of supererogatory prayers. These two Rakat are described by the term "Tahiyyat ul-Masjid'. Similarly, whenever you return from a journey, go first to the mosque and say two Rakat of supererogatory prayers and then proceed to your house. On return from a journey, the Holy Prophet [S.A.W.] used to go first to the mosque and offered supererogatory prayers and afterwards proceeded home.

12. On coming out of the mosque, put your left foot out first and say this prayer: "O Allah! I seek your Favour and Blessings."
(Muslim)

13. Maintain a regular system of announcing the prayer-call and holding of congregational prayers. Appoint only such persons as Muaddhin (one who gives adaan i.e. call for prayers) and Imam (one who leads the prayers) as are on the whole better than others in their devotion to religion and possess superior character. If possible try to appoint such people as Muaddhins and Imams who demand no remuneration for their services and are willing to discharge these duties voluntarily in anticipation of the reward in the Hereafter.

14. Say this prayer after hearing the prayer-call. The Holy Prophet [S.A.W.] observed: "The man who after hearing the prayer-call recites the following prayer will thereby acquire a right over me to pray for him on the Day of Doom."
(Mishkat)

"Allah! The Master of this Perfect Call and this Congregation standing for Prayer! Grant Muhammad [S.A.W.] Thy closeness and Excellence and appoint him to that exalted state the promise of which Thou gave him and grant us the favour of Muhammad's [S.A.W.] intercession with Thee on our behalf. Undoubtedly Thou never goes back on Thy promises."

15. When the Muaddhin is announcing the prayer-call, repeat his utterances after him. However, when he says... Hayya 'alassalah and Hayya'alal falah say in reply *La haula wala quwwata illa billahil 'aliyyil 'azim*.1 In the course of announcing the call for dawn prayers when the Muaddhin says. *Assalatu Khairum min-annaum*. (Prayer is better than sleep) say these words in reply *Sadaqta wa bararta*. (You spoke the truth and good).

16. When the announcer of *Takbir* says (*Qadqamatissalah*) says these words in reply *Aqamahallahu wa adamaha*. (May Allah maintain it for ever).

17. The women should say their prayers in the home instead of going to the mosque. On one occasion the wife of

Hadrat Abu Humaid Saadi [R.A.A.] submitted: "O Prophet [S.A.W.]! I cherish a great desire to say prayers in your company." The Holy Prophet [S.A.W.] observed: "I am aware of your eagerness. But it is better for you to say prayers in your room than in the verandah outside your room and saying prayers in the verandah of your house is better for you than saying prayers in the courtyard of your home."

However, the women should try their best to cater to the requirements of the mosque. They should arrange for the supply of water, mats, incense and perfumes and other articles of use in the mosques and should cherish feelings of deep attachment to the mosque in their hearts.

18. Take grown up children with you to the mosque. Mothers ought to persuade their children to go to the mosque so that they may develop eagerness and enthusiasm for prayers. Show tenderness, love and affection to children in the mosque. If they commit any wrong or an act of mischief, do not rebuke or bully them. Make them understand the proper etiquettes with love and affection and instruct them in virtue.

PERFORMANCE OF PRAYERS

1. Observe perfect cleanliness and purity for the purpose of saying the prayers. Brush your teeth (use miswak) also when performing ablutions. The Prophet [S.A.W.] said: "The distinctive mark of the members of my Ummah on the Doomsday will be that their brows and organs of ablution will be glowing with the radiance of Divine Light. Hence it is open to everyone to enhance his share of the Divine Light as much as he wants."
2. Put on clean, neat, respectable civilised and proper dress for observing prayers. The Holy Quran affirms: "O sons of Adam! Adorn yourself properly at each hour of prayer."
3. Say prayers at the prescribed hours.

   The prayer has been made obligatory for the believers to be observed at prescribed hours. Hadrat 'Abdullah b.

Masud [R.A.A.] once asked Holy Prophet [S.A.W.]: "O Prophet of Allah [S.A.W.]! Which deed is the most favourite one to Allah?" The Holy Prophet [S.A.W.] replied: "To say prayer at the proper time." Furthermore, the Holy Prophet [S.A.W.] observed: "Allah has made five prayers obligatory. A person who after performing ablutions carefully observes these prayers in perfect humility at their proper hours acquires a right of salvation by Allah; but he who shows carelessness in prayers has no right to anticipate forgiveness and salvation by Allah. In this case, it is entirely up to the Will of Allah to forgive him or to punish him." (Malik)

4. Always say your prayers in congregation. At times when you miss the congregation for any reason, try to say the obligatory (Fard) prayers in a mosque. However, offering of Sunnah prayers is permissible at home also. The Holy Prophet [S.A.W.] said: "The person who joins the congregation for prayer at the start i.e. first Takbir for forty days at a stretch is secured from the torments of Hell as well as from the evil of discord." (Tirmidhi)

   In addition to this, the Holy Prophet [S.A.W.] also said: "If the people become aware of the rewards and blessings of offering prayers in a congregation, they would hasten to join the congregation for prayer despite a thousand hindrances. The first row of a congregation for prayer is like the row of angels.. It is better for two men to offer prayers together than separately. The larger the congregation the dearer it is to Allah." (Abu Daud)

5. Say prayers with peace of mind. Perform bows (Ruku') and prostrations (Sajda) calmly. Rising from a bow, stand straight with ease and then go into prostration. Keep a suitable interval between two prostrations and in this interval, say the following prayer:

   "O Allah, forgive me, be Merciful to me, set me on the right path, remove my misery, grant me peace and provide for my sustenance." (Abu-Daud)

   The Holy Prophet [S.A.W.] has observed: "The person who observes prayer properly, the prayer itself blesses him with good wishes in these words `May Allah protect thee in the same manner in which they took care of me."

And the Holy Prophet [S.A.W.] also said: "The worst form of theft is the theft of prayer." The people asked: "O Holy Prophet [S.A.W.]! How can one commit a theft in prayer." The Holy Prophet [S.A.W.] answered: "By skipping over the complete performance of bows and prostrations."

6. Start making preparations for the prayer at once on hearing the prayer-call (adaan). Perform ablutions and reach the mosque well before time. Sit down quietly in the line and wait for the congregation to form. It is symbolic of hypocrites to be sluggish, to try and go for the prayers in a languid manner after hearing the prayer-call.

7. Announce the prayer-call with eagerness and zest. A person asked the Holy Prophet: "O Prophet of Allah [S.A.W.]! Tell me a deed that can lead me to Paradise." The Holy Prophet [S.A.W.] said: "Announce the call for prayer." The Prophet [S.A.W.] further said: "Within the extent to which the call of the Muaddhin reaches each man who hears the call will be witness in favour of the Muaddhin on the Day of Judgement. A shepherd who grazes his flock in the pasture and pronounces the adaan in a loud voice at the fixed hour, all things within the radius of the area in which his voice vibrates will stand testimony in his favour on the Day of Judgement."
(Bukhari)

8. If you are acting as an Imam, discharge your responsibility in relation to the saying of prayer with all the manners and rules prescribed by religion. Keep in view the interests of the congregation and perform your duty as a leader well. The Holy Prophet [S.A.W.] said: "The Imams who lead the prayer in a proper manner and entertain a high sense of personal responsibility for the good will obtain reward for the prayers of their congregation also. The Imam's reward in this case will be equal to the combined reward of the congregation.

However, the reward and virtue of the members of the congregation is not curtailed thereby." (Tibrani)

9. Say your prayers with humility in such a state that the heart should be filled with a sense of awe of the Greatness and Glory of Allah and your entire being should be overwhelmed with trepidation and solemnity. It is a great sacrilege to make unnecessary movements of hand and foot, scratching any part of the body, to pass fingers through the beard, to plug the nose with a finger or to fold up your dress. Take the utmost care to avoid such actions.

10. Seek to gain nearness to Allah through prayers. Say prayers in such a state of mind as if you are standing before Allah or at least be mindful that Allah is watching you. The Holy Prophet [S.A.W.] said: "The bondman is nearest to Allah at the moment when he is lying in prostration (Sajdah) before Him. Hence while you are performing Sajdah pray fervently." (Muslim)

11. Say prayers with eagerness and zest. The formal observance of prayers as if prayer were a burden or a compulsion is no genuine form of worship. Having said prayers of one time, look forward to the next hour of prayers with eagerness and fervour. One day after having offered the Maghrib prayers, some people stayed waiting for the hour of 'Isha prayers. The Holy Prophet [S.A.W.] arrived with such hurried steps that he was panting for breath. The Holy Prophet [S.A.W.] observed: "O people! Be happy, your Lord opened a gate of the heavens and showed your view to His angels and said with pride: "Look my devotees have finished one prayer and are awaiting the next hour of worship'." (Ibn Majah)

12. Do not say prayers in a hurried manner with a sense of 'Let us get over with it', like the careless and carefree persons. Remember Allah with a sincere beau and say prayers with complete devotion and a solemn awareness of duty and direct your heart, mind, feelings, passions, thoughts and ideas towards Allah. Prayer, in ord r to become a genuine form of worship, must contain

remembrance of Allah. The prayer of the hypocrites is always devoid of the remembrance of the Lord.

13. Discharge the duty enjoined upon you by prayer even after the prayer and manage your whole life in such a manner that it should fully reflect the injunctions contained in the prayers. The Holy Quran says: "Prayer serves as a deterrent to immorality and contumacy." The Holy Prophet [S.A.W.] elucidated the same point through a deeply impressive simile: The Holy Prophet [S.A.W.] shook a dry branch of a tree briskly so that all the leaves of the branch fell off. Thereupon the Holy Prophet [S.A.W.] observed: "The sins of those who say prayers drop off as the leaves of this dry branch fell off." Afterwards the Holy Prophet [S.A.W.] recited this verse of the Holy Quran: "Establish worship at the two ends of the day and in some hours of the night. Lo! good deeds annul ill deeds. This is a reminder for the mindful." (11: 114)

14. Recite the Quran slowly in the course of prayers and observe other narrations of the prayer at a slow pace with careful attention and devotion of heart and mind. The practice of reciting the Quran and saying other words of the prayer with understanding augments your fervour and the prayer then attains the form of genuine worship.

15. Observe prayers regularly and don't ever miss any prayer. It is the basic attribute of the believers to be regular and punctual in observing prayers: "Save worshippers who are constant at their worship." (70: 22-23)

16. Along with regular observance of obligatory prayers, you should offer supererogatory worship and offer praises to Allah frequently. The Holy Prophet [S.A.W.] said: "Any man who offers twelve Rakats (supererogatory prayers) during a period of day and night in addition to the five obligatory prayers, Allah ordains a dwelling to be built for this man in Paradise." (Muslim)

17. Say your supererogatory prayers (Sunnah and Nawafil) off and on in your homes also. The Holy Prophet [S.A.W.] has said: "Offer some supererogatory prayers at home after saying obligatory prayers in the mosque. Allah shall bestow goodness in your homes as a reward for these prayers." (Muslim). The Prophet of Allah [S.A.W.] himself frequently offered Sunnah and Nawafil at home.

18. When you set out from the house for dawn prayers, say this prayer: "O Allah! Make Light in mine heart, Light in mine eye, Light in mine ear, Light on my right, Light on my left, Light above me, Light beneath me, Light before me, Light behind me, and make thou for me Light. Light in my tongue, Light in my sinews, Light in my flesh, Light in my blood, Light in mine hair, Light in my body, Light in my soul and magnify for me Light! O Allah bestow upon me Light! (Hisn, Hasien)

19. When you have finished the performance of dawn and evening prayers, repeat the following prayer seven times before engaging in conversation.

    "O Allah! Protect me from the Fire."

    The Holy Prophet [S.A.W.] said: "After the dawn and evening prayers, repeat the following prayer seven times before engaging in conversation. If perchance you die in the course of that day or night, you shall certainly be saved from Hell." (Mishkat)

20. After each prayer, repeat Astaghfirullah three times and then say this prayer: "O Allah! Thou art the peace and from Thee is the peace. Blessed art Thou, O Lord of Majesty and Glory." (Muslim)

    Hadrat Thauban [R.A.A.] reports:. "The Holy Prophet [S.A.W.] used to repeat (I seek forgiveness from Allah) three times after finishing each prayer and afterwards said this prayer." (Muslim)

21. Observe proper care in keeping the lines straight for offering the prayer in congregation. Keep the lines perfectly straight and stand shoulder to shoulder close to each other, leaving no space in between. Do not form

lines in the rear unless the front lines are filled. On one occasion in a congregation for prayer, a man was standing in line in such a manner that the position of his chest was inclined forward. On seeing the man standing in this fashion, the Holy Prophet [S.A.W.] warned: "O people of Allah! you must stand in straight lines in a proper manner else Allah shall cause you to stand in opposite directions to each other." (Muslim, Vol. I)

On one occasion, the Holy Prophet [S.A.W.] said: "Any man who arranges the line in a formation, Allah shall bestow Grace on him; and any man who causes disarray in the line, Allah shall cause him to suffer chaos." (Abu Daud, Vol. I)

22. The line of the children must be formed behind the lines of men. Do not let the children stand with their elders. However, in the 'Idgah, where certain difficulties might be faced or where the possibility of the loss of children exists, there is no need to send the children to form lines in the rear. Make them stand with you. The lines of women should be formed either at the farthest rear or separately if a separate enclosure has been built in the mosque for women. Similarly, in the 'Idgah make separate arrangements for the congregation of women.

QURAN'S RECITATION

1. Recite the Holy Quran with eagerness and fervour and put all your heart and soul in the recitation. Be sure that love of the Quran means love of Allah. The Holy Prophet [S.A.W.] said: "The best form of worship for my Ummah is recitation of the Quran."
2. Engage yourself in the recitation of the Quran off and on and never feel weary of reciting the Holy Book. The Holy Prophet [S.A.W.] said: "Allah has ordained that any man who engages himself in the recitation of Quran so oftenly that he finds no time for supplication I shall provide him more without asking than those who ask." (Tirmidhi)

Further than this, the Prophet of Allah [S.A.W.] observed: "The servant gets nearest unto Allah by reciting the Quran." (Tirmidhi)

Advising the people to recite the Holy Quran, the Holy Prophet [S.A.W.] also said: "The man who has studied the Quran and recites it daily is like a basket full of musk whose sweet smell is making the whole atmosphere fragrant. And the man who has studied the Quran but does not recite it is like a bottle full of musk whose mouth has been sealed with a stopper." (Tirmidhi)

3. Recite the Quran with the sole motive of seeking guidance and not for the sake of gaining popularity, or establishing a reputation for good, harmonious recitation or making a name for piety. These are base motives and he who recites the Quran with these motives in mind can obtain no guidance from the Quran.
4. Take care to be completely neat and clean before you sit down for recitation. Do not touch the Holy Book without performing ablution and recite it sitting in a clean and tidy place.
5. Sit cross-legged with your face towards the Qiblah and recite the Quran with your head bowed, with utmost care, complete attention, eagerness of heart and in a proper manner. Allah says: "(This is) a scripture that We have revealed unto thee, full of blessing, that thee may ponder over its revelations, and that men of understanding may get guidance from it." (38: 29)
6. As far as possible recite the Quran in a clear and distinct manner and read the letters correctly and utter the syllables in proper style and recite slowly. The Holy Prophet [S.A.W.] said: "Use your voice and style to recite the Quran in the best manner." (Abu Daud)

   The Holy Prophet [S.A.W.] used to recite each word in a clear and distinct manner and read each verse separately.

   The Holy Prophet [S.A.W.] said: "He who recites the Quran will be told on the Day of Judgement. Recite the

Quran now in the same clear and distinct manner and in the same harmonious style in which you used to recite it with care and propriety in the world and as a reward for the recitation of each verse you shall be elevated one degree higher and your ultimate place is near the end of the final verse."
(Tirmidhi)

7. Do not recite the Quran in an extremely loud or very low voice. Keep your voice at a medium pitch. Allah ordains: "Be not loud voiced in thy prayer nor too low voiced but follow a way between." *(*17.110)
8. Recite the Quran whenever you find time, but do try to recite Quran in the course of Tahajjud prayer at dawn. This recitation of the Quran entails the reward of highest degree and it should be the aspiration of a true believer to attain the apex of excellence in reward for recitation.
9. Do not complete the reading of the whole of the Holy Quran in less then three days. The Holy Prophet [S.A.W.] observed: "He who completes the recitation of the full text of the Quran in less than three days does not understand the meanings of the Quran at all."
10. Keep in mind the glory and value of the Quran and as you observe the etiquette of keeping your person neat and clean while reciting the Quran, so also you must purge your heart of evil thoughts, wicked passions and impure purposes. The heart that is tainted with evil and wicked thoughts and passions cannot appreciate and admire the glory and value of the Holy Quran, nor can the bearer of such an evil heart grasp the meanings and realities of the Quran. Hadrat 'Ikrama [R.A.A.], whenever opened the Quran, he often fainted. He used to say: "These are the words of my Great and Glorious Lord."
11. Recite the Quran with the conviction that on this earth this Book is the only source of guidance for mankind. Meditate and reflect deeply over the meanings of the Quran from this viewpoint and try to grasp the realities

and learn the wisdom contained in this Book. Do not recite it hurriedly but form the habit of reading slowly, distinctly and with careful understanding of the meanings and try to ponder over the message conveyed to us. Hadrat 'Abdullah b. 'Abbas [R.A.A.] often remarked: "I consider it far better to recite small Surahs like Al-Qariah with understanding and care than to read through the longer Surahs of Al-Baqarah and Ali-'Imran speedily without careful understanding of the meanings of the words. The Holy Prophet [S.A.W.] once recited this one verse over and over again all through the night.

"If Thou punisheth them, Lo! they are Thy slaves, and if Thou forgiveth them, Lo! Thou only Thou art the Mighty, the Wise." (5.118)

12. Recite the Quran with full determination to adapt your life to the injunctions of this Holy Book and to reform the pattern of your living in the light of the guidance provided by it. Make constant endeavours to order your life in conformity with the Quranic injunctions and purge your life of all impurities. The Holy Quran like a mirror will clearly reflect each blot and spot on your character. It is entirely your own responsibility to wash off these blots and stains from your life.
13. Feel the full impact of the verses of the Holy Book during recitation. Rejoice and feel happy on reading about the narrations of Divine Mercy, Forgiveness and the Everlasting bounties of Paradise. And on reading about the narrations of the wrath, anger and the terrific punishments of Hell your body should tremble, eyes should flow and the heart should melt with the sentiments of repentance and shame. Your face should glow with the light of happiness on reading about the successes of the pious and faithful people and you should be seized with deep sorrow on reading about the destruction of nations. The study of verses containing warnings and forebodings of torments should make you tremble and your soul should be filled to the brim with

the sentiments of gratitude on reading the verses which bear glad tidings.

14. After reciting the Holy Quran offer a prayer. The words of one of the prayers offered by Hadrat 'Umar [R.A.A.] are as follows: "Allah! Whatever my tongue recites from Thy Book, grant me the favour to reflect upon it. Allah! bestow upon me the understanding of it. Vouchsafe to me the knowledge of its meaning, and spirit, and the vision to see its niceties. Grant me the favour to act according to its injunctions as long as I live. Your Being is without doubt Omnipotent."

FRIDAY MANNERS

1. Take full measures to clean and purify yourself on Fridays. Bathe and adorn yourself in the best possible manner.

   Hadrat 'Umar [R.A.A.] reports that the Holy Prophet [S.A.W.] observed: "The person who comes to offer prayers in the Friday congregation should bathe himself first." (Bukhari, Muslim)

   According to the statement of Hadrat Abu Hurrayrah [R.A.A.] the Holy Prophet [S.A.W.] observed: "Every Muslim owes duty to Allah that he should take bath every week and wash his head and body."

   Hadrat Abu Said Khudri [R.A.A.] relates that the Prophet of Allah [S.A.W.] observed: "It is obligatory upon every adult youth to take bath on Friday and to brush the teeth and use perfume if available."

   (Bukhari, Muslim)

   Hadrat Salman [R.A.A.] states that the Holy Prophet [S.A.W.] said: "Any man who bathes on Friday and takes full care to keep himself neat and clean and uses hair oil and perfume and then reaches the mosque just after mid-day and does not part two men sitting in a line in the mosque and then offers the prayer which Allah had decreed to him and afterwards listens to the sermon seated calmly when the Imam ascends the pulpit, Allah shall pardon all the sins committed by him during the internal between this Friday and the preceding one." (Bukhari)

2. Take care to perform good deeds on Friday such as most frequent remembrance of Allah, recitation of the Holy Quran, prayer, Sadaqa, charity, enquiring after the welfare of the sick, joining the funerals, visit to the graveyard and other pious acts.

   Hadrat Abu Hurrayrah [R.A.A.] reports that the Holy Prophet [S.A.W.] said: "The most important day that ever dawned is the Friday. It was on this day that Adam [A.S.] was created and on this day he was admitted to Paradise and it was on Friday when he was expelled from there (and was appointed the vicegerent of Allah and it is on this day that the Doom will descend." (Muslim)

   Hadrat Abu Said Khudri [R.A.A.] reports that the Holy Prophet [S.A.W.] said: "There are five such acts that if a man shall perform them in the course of a single day, Allah shall write his name among those destined to enter Paradise. These acts are:

   (i) To enquire after the welfare of the sick. (ii) To join a funeral. (iii) To keep a fast. (iv) To offer Friday Prayer. (v) To emancipate a slave." (Ibn Habban)

   It is evident that the performance of all these five acts together is possible only on a Friday.

   In another tradition Hadrat Abu Said Khudri [R.A.A.] reports that the Holy Prophet [S.A.W.] observed: "Any man who recites Surah Kahf on Friday, a radiant light will glow for him in the space between two Fridays." (Nasai)

   And Hadrat Abu Hurrayrah [R.A.A.] states that the Holy Prophet [S.A.W.] said: "Seventy thousand angels beg mercy for the man who recites Surah Ad-Dukhan on Friday night and all of his sins are pardoned." (Tirmidhi)

   The Holy Prophet [S.A.W.] has affirmed: "There is a certain blessed moment in the course of Friday that any prayer said in by a believer is accepted by the Almighty." (Bukhari)

Which blessed moment is this? The opinion of the *'Ulama* is at variance on this point, because of the reason that traditions mention different times in this respect. However, the *'Ulama* agree that two statements are more correct than the others. According to one statements, the intervening time from the moment the preacher ascends the pulpit to deliver the sermon to the end of the prayers is the most propitious one. Another version holds that blessed moment is the end of Friday when the sun is about to set in the horizon. It is advisable, therefore, that you should pass both the times in offering prayers and supplications in utter humility and reverence to the Lord. It is better to add the following prayer with your other prayers:

> *"Allah! You are my Lord. There is no deity except You. You created me. I am Your servant and I hold firm to my promise and allegiance to You as far as it lies in my power. I acknowledge all the bounties and favours that You have conferred on me. I confess my sins; forgive me, for there is no one else except You Who has the power to grant pardon for sins and I beseech protection against the evil effects of my own sins." (Bukhari, Nasai)*

3. Observe Friday prayers according to all the prescribed etiquettes. Friday prayer is obligatory upon every adult, healthy, resident and sane Muslim male. If there be two men beside the Imam present at a place, the Friday prayer must be offered. The Holy Prophet said: "The people ought not to miss Friday prayer under any circumstances or else Allah shall seal their hearts (and having been denied Divine Guidance) they will become one with those who are forgetful (of Religion)." (Muslim)

According to the testimony of Hadrat Abu Hurrayrah [R.A.A.] the Prophet of Allah [S.A.W.] said: "Any man who comes to the mosque for saying the Friday prayer after bathing and washing himself clean and then offers 'Sunnah' prayers which Allah had decreed and then sits quietly till the end listening to the sermon of the Imam and afterwards offers obligatory prayers with the Imam, Allah shall grant him pardon for the sins which he committed between the preceding Friday and this one and the sins committed till three days before."

"Hadrat Yazid b. Mariym [R.A.A.] relates: "I was going to offer Friday prayers when I chanced to meet Hadrat 'Abay b. Rifaah [R.A.A.] on the way. He asked me: "Where are you going?" I said: "I am going to offer Friday prayers". Hadrat 'Abaya [R.A.A.] remarked: "I congratulate you. Every step you move, you move on the path leading towards Allah." The Holy Prophet [S.A.W.] said: "Fire is made unlawful for the man whose feet are soiled with dust while walking along the path of Allah."

4. Hasten towards the mosque the moment you hear the call for Friday prayer. Close your business and stop your other activities at once. Listen to the sermon and say prayers with perfect devotion. Resume your business as soon as the Friday prayer is over. The Holy Quran says: "O ye who believe! When the call is heard for the prayer of the day of congregation hasten unto remembrance of Allah and leave your trading. That is better for you if ye did but know. And when the prayer is over, then disperse in the land and seek Allah's bounty, and remember Allah much, that ye may be successful."

(Al-Jumah 9-10)

These verses contain the following injunctions for the true believers:

(i) A true believer should offer Friday prayers with complete devotion and utmost awareness of the etiquettes of this prayer. He should stop all other engagements on hearing the prayer-call and hasten towards the mosque.

(ii) It is unlawful for the true believer to carry on business or to engage in other worldly interests after hearing the announcement of the prayer-call and thus having forsaken the memory of Allah to turn into a world-loving creature.

(iii) The secret of a pious man's salvation lies in his living as a servant and slave of Allah in this world. Whenever the call of Allah reaches him, he should, as a devoted and obedient servant forsake all interests and set aside all worldly advantage and rush to respond to the call of his Master. He should proclaim by deed that the sacrifice of worldly advantage for the sake of fulfilling the demands of religion does not signify ruin and failure. On the other hand, destruction and failure lies in transgressing the bounds of religion in his lust for gaining worldly interests.

(iv) The theory of renouncing the world altogether is fallacious. Man should not be so much immersed in spiritual pursuits that he should become incapable of dealing with worldly affairs. The Holy Quran, in fact, enjoins upon the faithful to disperse on the earth as soon as the prayer is over and to take full advantage of all the resources and means of livelihood that Allah has provided on the earth. The Quran affirms that the pious should exert all their energies and employ all faculties in the business of earning their share of the subsistence provided by Allah. It is not proper for a true believer to be dependent on others for his needs, nor is it advisable for him to neglect his duty of providing for the needs of his dependents and to cause them suffering and dismay.

(v) The final and important injunction is that the true believer should not be engrossed in worldly affairs so deeply that he should forget Allah. He should remember under all circumstances that the real gain and essence of his life is the remembrance of Allah. Hadrat Said b. Jubayr [R.A.A.] remarks: "The remembrance of Allah is not only announcing the greatness of Allah or uttering praises of Allah but all those are engaged in the remembrance of Allah who are busy ordering their lives in conformity with the Commands of Allah."

5. Try to reach the mosque for the Friday prayer as early as possible to get a seat for yourself in front line.

   According to the statement of Abu Hurrayrah [R.A.A.], the Holy Prophet [S.A.W.] said: "Any man who bathes himself and washes his whole body to cleanse it of all impurities and then reaches the mosque first is like the person who offers the sacrifice of one camel, and he who arrives next to him is like the person who sacrifices one cow (or buffalo) and the one who reaches in the third place is like a person who offers the sacrifice of a horned ram. Coming next to him is like a person who gives away as it were one egg in the way of Allah. Later when the Imam comes forward to deliver the sermon, the angels leave the gate of the mosque and come over to sit in the mosque to hear the sermon and say the prayers." (Bukhari, Muslim)

   Hadrat 'Irbad b. Saria [R.A.A.] states: "The Holy Prophet [S.A.W.] used to invoke mercy of Allah three times upon those who formed the first line and only once upon those who were in the second line." (Ibn Majah, Nasai)

   Hadrat Abu Hurrayrah [R.A.A.] observes: "The people do not know the high degree of reward and blessings reserved for the people who form the first line of prayer. If they knew it, they would start drawing lots for the privilege of joining the first line." (Bukhari, Muslim)

6. Offer your Friday prayers in a Big mosque (Jama Masjid). Take your seat wherever it is available. Do not jump over people's heads and shoulders in an effort to get a seat in front. This causes considerable mental and physical discomfort to the people, disturbs their peace of mind and diverts their attention.

   Hadrat 'Abdullah b. 'Abbas [R.A.A.] relates that the Holy Prophet [S.A.W.] said: "The person who retreats from the first line of prayer and stands in the second line with the intention that his Muslim brother may suffer no inconvenience, Allah will grant such a man reward and blessing twice as much as to people in the first line." (Tibrani)

Hadrat Salman [R.A.A.] reports that the Holy Prophet [S.A.W.] said: "The person who bathes himself on Friday and cleanses and purifies himself as much as he can, and then use oil and applies perfume and reaches the mosque just after mid-day and does not part two men sitting together (in other words he does not commit the error of jumping over the heads and shoulders of people, or making his way through the lines or sitting between two men by pushing them apart, but sits down quietly wherever he finds room) and offers prayer and Sunnah which Allah had decreed upon him and afterwards listens quietly to the sermon when the Imam takes the pulpit, Allah will pardon all his sins which he committed during the period between that Friday and the preceding one." (Bukhari)

7. The sermon should be brief as compared to the prayer. The sermon in fact is meant to induce people to offer devotions and worships and worship to Allah, while prayer is not only worship in itself, but the best worship. Hence it is in no way proper to prolong the sermon and go through the prayer quickly in a shorter period of time. The Holy Prophet [S.A.W.] said:"To prolong the prayer and deliver a brief sermon is an attribute of the wise preacher. Hence say prayers for a longer period of time and make the sermon brief." (Muslim)
8. Listen to the sermon in silence with rapt attention and eagerness in a receptive mood. Make up your mind with all sincerity to act upon the injunctions of Allah and His messenger [S.A.W.] that you have come to know through the sermon. The Holy Prophet [S.A.W.] said: "The man who bathes and comes to offer Friday prayer and says the prayer which Allah has destined for him and then sits quietly and listens to the sermon in rapt attention and with perfect devotion till the preacher has finished the sermon and afterwards says obligatory prayer with the Imam, Allah shall pardon all his sins which he committed during the period between that Friday and the preceding one and his sins even committed during three days before it." (Muslim)

According to another tradition: "When the preacher comes forward to deliver the sermon, then it is improper to say any prayer or engage in conversation."

9. The second sermon must be delivered in Arabic. However, in the first sermon describe some injunctions of Allah and His Messenger [S.A.W.], give some advice, provide guidance and remember Allah in the local language of the participants of the congregation. The sermons which the Holy Prophet [S.A.W.] delivered on Fridays reveal that the preacher should provide advice and guidance to the Muslims in regard to the prevailing circumstances. This purpose can only be achieved if the preacher delivers his sermon to the congregation in the people's own language.
10. It is highly propitious to recite Surah al-Ala and al-Ghashiya or surah Munafiqun and Surah al-Jumah in the obligatory prayers on Friday as was the practice of the Holy Prophet.
11. Make it essential to offer Darood as much as possible and pray for Allah's peace and blessings upon the Holy Prophet on Fridays.

    The Holy Prophet [S.A.W.] has observed: "Recite as much Darood for me as possible on Fridays. The angels join this 'Darood' Prayer and Darood is presented to me.

    (Ibn Majah)

PRAYER FOR THE DEMISED

1. Do join the funeral prayers. The funeral prayer is a petition of mercy for the deceased and this is a duty which every one owes to the dead. If you fear the funeral prayer will be over by the time you have performed ablution, then perform Tayammum and join the prayers at once. The Holy Prophet [S.A.W.] said: "Do say the funeral prayers. May be this prayer induces feelings of sorrow in you. A sorrowful man remains under the shadow of Allah and welcomes every pious deed."

    (Hakim)

The Holy Prophet [S.A.W.] also said: "The deceased whose funeral prayers are offered by three lines of Muslims will certainly be admitted to Paradise."

(Abu Daud)

2. At the time of saying funeral prayers, put the bier on the ground so that the head is towards the north, the feet towards the south and the face of the dead is turned in the direction of the Qiblah.
3. If you are leading the funeral prayer, stand facing the bosom of the dead.
4. The number of lines in a funeral prayer must be odd. A single line would suffice if those present at the funeral prayer are few, but if there are enough present, fall in three. As the number of people increased, form more lines, yet the number of lines should be kept odd.
5. Make a resolve in your mind before starting the funeral prayer that you are saying the funeral prayers to beg Mercy from the Kind and Beneficent Lord for the deceased. The Imam as well as the followers should make this resolve.
6. Whatever the Imam says in the funeral prayer, the followers must repeat the same. The followers should not keep silent. However, the Imam should say Takbirs in a loud voice and the followers should repeat them in a low sound.
7. Say four Takbirs in the funeral prayer. Raise your hands up to the ears while saying the first Takbir and then fold them on you abdomen and offer praise to Allah: "Allah! Thou art Pure and Supreme. High Praise and Thanksgiving is due to Thee. Thy Name is the Most Blessed one and the Bestower of Good. Thy Exaltedness and Glory art Most High. Thy Praise is Great and there is no deity except Thee."

   Now say the second Takbir, but do not raise your hands, nor make a motion of the head. At the end of the second Takbir, recite the Darood: "Allah! May Thy peace and blessings be upon Muhammad and his family, as Thou sent Thy peace and blessings upon Ibrahim and his family. Without doubt Thou possesseth the greatest attributes and art Most High. Allah! May Thy peace and blessings be upon Muhammad and his family, as Thou sent peace and blessings upon Ibrahim and his family. Without doubt Thou possesseth the greatest attributes and art Most High."

Now say the third Takbir without raising your hands and offer a prayer with prescribed supplication to beg mercy from the Lord for the dead. Finally, say the fourth Takbir and say Salam turning the head to right and left.

8. If the deceased is an adult male or female, say this prayer after the third Takbir.

   "Allah! Show mercy to our living, to our dead, to those who are present with us here and to those who are not present, to our youngster, to our elders, to our men and to our women. Allah! Whomsoever it pleases Thee to keep alive among us, keep him alive as faithful of Islam and upon whomsoever it pleases Thee to send death, let him die in faith."

   If the deceased is a minor boy, say this prayer: "Allah! Let this boy serve as a means of Thy grant of salvation to us and let him be a repository of our reward and welfare in the eternal world and let him be our successful intercessor."

   If the deceased is a minor girl, say this prayer. The meaning of this prayer is identical with the prayer offered for the boy.

9. While going along with a funeral procession think over your own end and visualise that as you are proceeding to commit the deceased to earth, in the same way others will be proceeding one day to bury you in the earth. In this pensive and thoughtful frame of mind, you will gain the favour of remembering your ultimate end for some time at least and the worries and cares of the world will vanish from your mind.

Attending the Death-bed

1. When you visit a person whose end is near, keep on reciting the Kalima (There is no god but Allah and Muhammad is His Apostle) in a loud voice. Do not press the patient to utter the Kalima. The Holy Prophet [S.A.W.] said: "When you sit by the death-bed of any Muslim, keep reciting the Kalima." (Muslim)
2. Recite Surah Yasin when the patient is heaving last breaths. The Holy Prophet [S.A.W.] observed: "Recite 'Surah Yasin' by the death-bed." (*Fatawa-e-Alamgiri,* p. 100, Vol. I). When the person has breathed his last, do not recite the Quran near the deceased till his body has been given bath. The man who needs a bath and the woman who is passing through the period of her menses or the after-birth course should not go near the dead.
3. Say ("We are for Allah and we shall return to Him.) "The Holy Prophet [S.A.W.] said: "The following three rewards are conferred on a man who recites (We are all creatures of Allah and we shall return to Him) in the moment of distress: (i) Firstly, blessings and salvation descend on him from Allah. (ii) Secondly, he receives the reward for seeking the Truth. (iii) Thirdly, his loss is compensated and a better reward in lieu of the dead and lost one is conferred on the bereaved person who says: (Tibrani)
4. Abstain from loud lamentations and wailing for the deceased person. However, if the eyes are filled with tears out of grief it is but natural. When the Holy Prophet's [S.A.W.] son Hadrat Ibrahim [R.A.A.] expired, the eyes of the Holy Prophet [S.A.W.] were filled with tears: Similarly, when his grandson, the child of his daughter Zainab [R.A.A.] passed away, the Holy Prophet [S.A.W.] shed tears. The people asked: "O Prophet of Allah [S.A.W.]! How is it?" The Holy Prophet [S.A.W.] said: "This is a blessing which Allah has bestowed upon the hearts of His creatures. Allah shows mercy to those among His creatures who are tender hearted and kind." The Holy Prophet [S.A.W.] further said: "He who slaps

his face, tears his clothes and indulges in lamentation like the pagans, has nothing to do with us."

5. As soon as one expires, straighten out his arms and legs; close the eyes and pass a wide bandage below the chin and tie its ends over the head. Both toes of the feet should be tied together with a strip of cloth. Wrap the body in a shroud and keep on reciting 'In the name of Allah' and according to the custom of the followers of the Prophet of Allah [S.A.W.]. Pass around an obituary notice among the people. At the moment of lowering the corpse in the grave, continue to say the same prayer.
6. Mention the virtues of the dead and avoid narration of his ills. The Holy Prophet [S.A.W.] said: "Do mention the virtues of your dead and keep silent about their vices." (Abu Daud). In addition, the Holy Prophet [S.A.W.] said: "When a man dies and a few of his neighbours testify that he was a good man, Allah observes-"I accept your testimony and I grant him pardon even for those of his acts which remained a secret to you."

   (Ibn Habban)

   On one occasion the companions [R.A.A.] praised the virtues of a dead man in the presence of the Holy Prophet [S.A.W.] whereupon the Prophet of Allah [S.A.W.] said: "This dead person's abode has been made in Paradise. O people, you are the witnesses of Allah on earth. If you testify that a certain man is good, Allah admits him to Paradise and if you bear witness that a certain man is wicked, Allah consigns him to Hell."

   (Bukhari, Muslim)

   And the Holy Prophet [S.A.W.] also said: "When you visit a patient to enquire after his welfare or join a funeral procession, "do utter good remarks, for the angels say 'So be it' (Amin) after each good remark you make."

   (Muslim)
7. Always show patience and fortitude on the death of your near and dear ones. Do not utter any ungrateful remark. The Holy Prophet [S.A.W.] has said: "When a man observes patience on the death of his child, Allah

enquires from His angels, "Did you extract the soul of the child of my servant?" The angels submit: "Yes." Allah then asks: "And what did my servant say?" They submit: "Lord! He offered praise to Thee and recited (We all belong to Allah and to Him shall we return, thereupon Allah ordains the angels: "Build a dwelling in Paradise for this servant of mine and name this dwelling 'Bait-al-Hamd' (House of Thanksgiving)."

(Tirmidhi)

8. Do not delay washing the body of the deceased. It is better to put some leaves of the 'plum tree' in the bath water and heat it a little. Stretch the body on a clean wooden board; take off its garments and wrap a sheet round the lower part of the body. Cover your hand with a cloth and clean the front and back private parts of the body. Take care that the wrapping sheet does not slip off. Then perform ablution on the body. There is no need, however, to rinse the mouth or pass water into the nose of the body during the performance of ablution. When washing the corpse block the ears and nostrils with cotton wool so that water does not enter into them. Then wash the head clean with soap or something else. Turn over the corpse towards the left side and pouring water from the right side bathe the body from head to foot. Similarly, pouring the water from the left side wash the body from head to foot. Take off the water soaked sheet and wrap a dry sheet round the lower part of the body. Now lift the body from the board, and place it in the coffin on the cot. The Holy Prophet [S.A.W.] said: "Allah shall pardon forty capital sins of man who bathes a corpse and conceals the sins of the dead person; and the man who lowers the corpse in the grave, provides, as it were, a home to the deceased to live in until the Day of Doom." (Tibrani)

9. Use a white cloth of average quality as a shroud for the body; don't use a very costly cloth nor a cloth of very low quality. For men the shroud should consist of three garments; one sheet, one 'Tehband' (a sheet for wrapping

round the lower part of the body) and a 'Kafni' or 'shirt' (a covering for the upper portion of the body). The length of the sheet should exceed the stature of the dead in measurement so that its ends may be tied on the side of the head as well as on the side of the feet. The measure of the width of the sheet should be adequate to cover the body well. For women, include an additional apparel 'sarband', a piece of cloth to cover the head and conceal the hair in the coffin. It should be one yard long and measure a little less than a yard in width. A 'Chest Band', a cloth to provide an additional covering from armpits to the knees, should also form part of a woman's coffin. The Holy Prophet [S.A.W.] said: "Allah will provide dresses made of Sundus and Astabraq in Paradise for him who puts the body of a deceased in coffin."

(Hakim)

10. Keep your pace quick while taking the bier to the graveyard. The Holy Prophet [S.A.W.] has observed; "Make haste in the matter of funerals." Hadrat Ibn Masud [R.A.A.] submitted to the Holy Prophet [S.A.W.]: "O Prophet of Allah [S.A.W.]! What should be the pace of our steps while taking the bier to the graveyard?" The Holy Prophet [S.A.W.] said: "Keep the pace of your steps short of running. If the deceased was a good man, carry him to his good end quickly. If he was wicked one, make haste to remove his evil from your midst."(Abu Daud)
11. Accompany the funeral on foot. On one occasion, when the Holy Prophet [S.A.W.] was walking with a funeral procession, he [S.A.W.] saw a few participants riding along. The Holy Prophet [S.A.W.] reprimanded them thus: "Don't you feel ashamed of yourselves! The angels are walking on foot, while you are riding on the backs of the beasts." However, on your way back from the burial, you can use a transport. The Holy Prophet [S.A.W.] went with the funeral procession of Abu Wahidi [R.A.A.] on foot and returned on horseback.
12. Stand on your feet on seeing a funeral approaching and if you do not wish to accompany it, wait till the procession

has moved on to some distance before resuming your journey or other activities. The Holy Prophet [S.A.W.] said: "Stand on your feet on seeing a funeral procession approaching. Those who accompany the funeral procession should not sit down until the bier has been placed on the ground."

13. Do offer funeral prayers. You should also participate in funeral processions and put your shoulder under the bier for sometime. The Holy Prophet [S.A.W.] said: "Every Muslim owes a duty to accompany the funeral procession of a deceased Muslim." The Prophet of Allah [S.A.W.] further said: "A man who participates in the funeral procession and offers funeral prayers will get a reward equal to one Carat. He who attends the burial also after saying the funeral prayers will receive a reward equal to two Carats." Some one submitted: "What will be the size of these two Carats?" The Holy Prophet [S.A.W.] said: "It will be equal to the mass of two mountains." (Bukhari, Muslim)

14. Let the grave be excavated from north to south lengthwise. Keep the body of the deceased turned towards the Qiblah when lowering it in the grave. If the body is light, two men are enough, otherwise three or four men may join in entering a body into the grave. At the moment of internment, untie the knots of the shroud and turn over the body towards the Qiblah.

15. Do observe purdah when interning a female body into the grave.

16. Start filling the grave with earth from the side of the head. Pick up the earth in both hands and throw it into the grave. Repeat the act three times. When throwing in the earth the first time say 'Minha Khalaqnakum, "We created you out of this earth." When throwing in the earth the second time, say. 'Wa fiha nuidukum'. "And We return you to the same earth." And when you throw in the earth the third time, say *'Waminha nukhrijukum taratan ukhra*, "And We shall resurrect you from the same earth."

17. Do not raise the grave very high, nor make it in the form of a square. Fill the grave with the same amount of earth which was excavated from it. Sprinkle some water over the grave after filing it with earth.
18. Stay a while near the grave after burial. Offer prayers begging mercy for the deceased. Recite some verses of the Quran and send its blessings for the departed soul. Ask other people to offer prayers to Allah to show mercy to the dead person. The Holy Prophet [S.A.W.] himself used to offer prayers to Allah for the grant of mercy to the deceased and said to other people: "Pray to Allah that your brother may remain steadfast and beg mercy for him from the Lord as now is he to account for every moment of his worldly life." (Abu Daud)
19. If a bereavement occurs among the kin, relatives, or in the neighbourhood, send cooked food for one or two times to their house, because they will be too overcome with grief to think of cooking meals. 'Jami' Tirmidhi' records that when the martyrdom of Hadrat Jafar [R.A.A.] was reported the Holy Prophet [S.A.W.] commanded: "Prepare some food for the family of Jafar. They are preoccupied with grief today."
20. Do not mourn for the dead for a period of more than three days. However, for a woman whose husband is dead, the prescribed period of mourning is four months and ten days. When Abu Sufyan [R.A.A.], the father of Umm-ul-Mominin Hadrat Ummi Habiba [R.A.A.] expired, the illustrious lady Zainab [R.A.A.] came to offer condolences to her. Hadrat Ummi Habiba [R.A.A.] asked for perfume in which some quantity of yellow saffron had been mixed. Umm-ul-Mominin rubbed that perfume on her slave-woman and then applied some to her own face. She then said: "Allah knows I did not need perfume, but I have heard the Prophet of Allah [S.A.W.] say: "No woman who believe in Allah and the Day of Judgement should observe mourning for more than three days for any man. However, the period of mourning in the case of her husband's death is four months and ten days." (Abu Daud)

21. Offer some charity on behalf of the deceased according to your means. However, strictly avoid performance of unpropitious and improper rites in this case.

Visiting Graveyards

1. Accompany the funeral procession to the graveyard and attend the burial. Do pay visits to the graveyard off and on. These visits remind one of the life Hereafter and induce one to start making preparations for the life after death. On one occasion the Holy Prophet [S.A.W.] accompanied a funeral procession to the graveyard and sitting down beside a grave shaddad so much tears that the earth became wet. Then addressing the companions [R.A.A.], the Holy Prophet [S.A.W.] said: "Brothers! Prepare yourself for this day." (Ibn Majah)

   Once when he was seated near a grave, the Holy Prophet [S.A.W.] said: "Every grave proclaims in the most terrific voice; 'O Progeny of Adam! Have you forgotten me? I am the house of loneliness. I am a strange land of wilderness! I am a hole of mites and worms. I am a place of hardship and trial. Save those fortunate one for whom Allah makes me commodious and wide, I am for all other human beings a tortuous place." In addition, the Holy Prophet [S.A.W.] observed: "The grave is either one of the pits of Hell or a small flower-garden out of the gardens of Paradise." (Tibrani)

2. Take a lesson on seeing the graveyard and form the habit of concentrating your thoughts and imaginative powers on the meditation on life after death. Once upon a time, Hadrat 'Ali [R.A.A.] visited a graveyard. Hadrat Kameel [R.A.A.] accompanied him. On reaching the graveyard, Hadrat 'Ali [R.A.A.] looked at the graves and then addressing the inmates of the graves, said: 'O inmates of graves! O inhabitants of ruins! O those who live in isolation in a land of wilderness! Say, how you are? As regards conditions over here, the assets left over have been divided, the offspring are rendered orphans, the widows have entered into new marriage contracts. This is the state of affairs in our world. Now tell us what

is happening to you." Hadrat 'Ali [R.A.A.] then remained silent for some time and then turning towards Hadrat Kameel [R.A.A.] observed: "Kameel, if the inmates of these graves were allowed to speak, they would say: "Piety is the most valuable treasure." Having said this, Hadrat 'Ali [R.A.A.] wept and continued to weep for a long time. Later Hadrat 'Ali [R.A.A.] remarked: "Kameel, the grave is an enclosure where only deeds matter and as soon as one meets death he realises this fact."

3. Say this prayer on entering the graveyard: "Peace be on you, O pious and faithful inmates of this set habitation. Allah willing, we shall soon join company with you. We pray to Allah for our sake and for your sake, that He may protect us from His torture and Wrath."
4. Don't laugh, crack jokes or engage in wordly talk in the graveyard like careless and carefree person. Grave is the gateway to Eternity. Let the sight of this gateway turn your thoughts to the next world and overcome by feelings of care and remorse. Let your eyes shed tears of repentance. The Holy Prophet [S.A.W.] said: "I had forbidden you to visit graveyards (so that faith in one Allah may take firm roots in your heart). But now if you wish you may go to the cemeteries, for the sight of graves makes one remember the life Hereafter." (Muslim)
5. Avoid building graves of bricks and mortar and do not embellish them. When the Holy Prophet [S.A.W.] was close to the end of his [S.A.W.] earthly life, he was restless with physical pain. In this state, he would sometimes draw the sheet over his holy face and then remove it. While the Holy Prophet [S.A.W.] was in this turbulent condition of restlessness, Hadrat 'Aishah [R.A.A.] heard him uttering the following words: "Allah's curse be on the Jews and Christians. They turned the sepulchres of their Prophet's into places of worship."
6. Do pray that Allah may bestow rewards on the dead and grant them mercy, whenever you visit the graveyard.

Hadrat Sufyan [R.A.A.] states: "Just as the living stand in need of eating and drinking, so do the dead stand in dire need of prayers for their salvation."

Tibrani records the following tradition: When Allah elevates a pious man one degree higher in Paradise, the man submits: "O Creator! How did I come to deserve this reward?" Allah thereupon affirms: "This reward has been conferred upon you by virtue of your son's petitions of mercy on your behalf."

Eclipse of Sun or Moon

1. When the sun or the moon is eclipsed, do engage yourself in the remembrance of Allah. Offer prayers to Him. Praise Him, and give charity. As a blessing for these pious deeds, Allah puts off all trials and calamities. Hadrat Mughira b. Shobah [R.A.A.] relates that the Holy Prophet [S.A.W.] said: "The sun and the moon are the two signs of Allah. They do not go under eclipse on the birth or death of anyone. Do call for the grace of Allah, offer prayers to Him, worship Him when you see the sun or the moon in eclipse and continue to offer devotions to the Almighty until the eclipse clears off." (Bukhari, Muslim)
2. When the sun is under eclipse, offer prayers in a congregation in the mosque. However, do not announce the prayer-call, nor say Iqamat: Call the people together by some other means. When the moon is in eclipse, offer supererogatory prayers (Nawafil). Do not assemble a congregation.
3. When the sun is eclipsed, say two 'Rakats' of supplementary prayers well in a congregation and recite long from the Holy Quran and continue your prayers until the sun is clear. Recite the Holy Quran loudly during the prayers. In the days of the Holy Prophet [S.A.W.] once the sun came under eclipse. The same day Hadrat Ibrahim [R.A.A.], the infant son of the Holy Prophet [S.A.W.] expired. The people began to say to each other that since Hadrat Ibrahim, the son of Muhammad [S.A.W.] has passed away, the sun has

gone under eclipse. The Holy Prophet [S.A.W.] assembled the people in a congregation and led them in prayer consisting of two Rakats. The Holy Prophet [S.A.W.] engaged in long recitation of the Holy Quran in the course of his prayer and read through the whole of 'Surah al-Baqarah'. The Holy Prophet [S.A.W.] then told the people: "The sun and the moon are the two Signs of Allah. They do not go into eclipse on the birth or death of anyone. O People! Whenever such an event occurs, do engage in devotion to Allah. Offer prayers to Him, praise Him, hymn His greatness and oneness. Say prayers and give charity." (Bukhari, Muslim)

Hadrat 'Abdul Rahman b. Samurah [R.A.A.] says: "During the propitious days of the Holy Prophet [S.A.W.] the sun went into an eclipse once. I was at that time practising archery outside Medina. I at once flung away the arrows to see what would the Holy Prophet [S.A.W.] do at the occurrence of this event. So I went to the presence of the Holy Prophet [S.A.W.]. He was occupied in offering praises to Allah and repeating His Attributes and uttering Takbir 5 and Tahlil and observing prayers and making supplications with his hands raised to the Heavens. Then the Holy Prophet [S.A.W.] offered prayer consisting of two Rakats and recited two long Surahs of the Quran in the course of the prayers and continued to offer devotions till the sun cleared off the eclipse."

The illustrious companions [R.A.A.] also used to offer prayers during 'Kusuf' and 'Khusuf. Hadrat 'Abdullah b. Zubayr [R.A.A.] offered prayers on the appearance of an eclipse in Medina. Similarly, on another occasion when an eclipse appeared Hadrat 'Abdullah b. 'Abbas [R.A.A.] assembled the people and offered a prayer in congregation.

4. In the course of the prayer on the occasion of an eclipse of the sun, recite Surah 'Ankabut and Surah Fatiha in the first Rakat and recite Surah al-Room in the second Rakat. It is propitious to recite these Surahs, but not obligatory. Surahs other than those mentioned above may also be recited.

5. If the women wish to join the congregation for prayer on the occasion of an eclipse of the sun and the facility for including them in the congregation exists, do let them join. Persuade the children also to join prayers so that faith in one Allah takes firm roots in their hearts in their early years and no other notions derogatory to the belief in one Allah may infiltrate their minds.
6. If the eclipse of the sun occurs during those hours in which the saying of prayers is forbidden i.e., the hours of sunrise, sunset and the declining hours of the day, avoid offering 'Namaz', Do offer praises to Allah however and give charity to the poor and the destitute. If the eclipse continues even after the hour of sunrise or the declining hour of the day have passed, then say prayers also in addition to performing the above-mentioned deeds.

THE FASTING

1. Start preparing your mind from the month of Shaban for according a befitting reception to Ramadan. Keep fasts frequently before the fifteenth of Shaban. Hadrat 'Aishah [R.A.A.] relates: "The Holy Prophet [S.A.W.] used to keep fasts more often in Shaban than in any other month."
2. Make an effort to sight the Ramadan moon with full attention and eagerness and say this prayer on sighting the moon: "Allah is the greatest! O Allah! Do make the appearance of this moon a token of peace, faith, salvation and Islam (obedience) for us. Do make this moon arise as a favour to us so that we may perform deeds which conform to Thy Will and are dear to Thee. Our Lord and thy Lord is Allah!"

   And say the same prayer on sighting the moon of each month. (Tirmidhi, Ibn Habban, etc.)
3. Do take special interest in offering devotions during the month of Ramadan. In addition to obligatory prayers, make it a point to observe supererogatory prayers (Nawafil) also. Make a firm resolve to win the maximum

favour of Allah. Allah has reserved His special favours and blessings for this great and propitious month. On the final day of Shaban, the Holy Prophet [S.A.W.] in a discourse on the blessings of the month of Ramadan said: "O people! A great and blessed month is going to set in on you. Each night of this month is better than a thousand months. Allah has made fasting obligatory during this month and has ordained Taravih as a supplementary prayer. Any one who performs a good deed during this month of his own free volition will receive a reward equal to the reward for obligatory deeds performed during other months. And any one who performs a single obligatory act during this month, shall receive a reward equal to the reward of seventy obligatory acts during other months."

4. Keep fasts whole of the month with deep eagerness and zeal. Even if you can't observe fast due to some serious illness or for any other reason permissible in Shariah, strictly avoid eating before others out of respect for the sanctity of Ramadan. To all intents and purposes, you must appear as if you are fasting.

5. Make it a point to recite the Holy Quran. The month of Ramadan has a special connection with the Holy Quran. The Holy Quran was revealed in this month and the other Divine Books also descended in the same month. Hadrat Ibrahim [A.S.] received scriptures on the first or the third day of this month. 'Zabur' descended on Hadrat Daud [A.S.] on the twelfth or eighteenth day of this month. Torah was revealed to Hadrat Musa [A.S.] on the sixth day of this propitious month. On the twelfth or thirteenth day of the same blessed month, the Bible was transmitted to Hadrat 'Isa [A.S.]. Hence recite Quran as many times as possible in the course of this month. Hadrat Jibbrail [A.S.] used to recite the Holy Quran to the Holy Prophet [S.A.W.] and also heard recitation of the Quran from the Holy Prophet [S.A.W.] every year during the month of Ramadan. In the final year of the Holy Prophet's [S.A.W.] earthly life Hadrat

Jibbrail [A.S.] completed the whole text of the' Quran twice during the month of Ramadan.

6. Try to recite the Quran distinctly and with understanding. Along with frequent recitation, be careful to grasp the meaning of the Holy Quran with a clear impact of its message on your mind and heart.
7. During 'Taravih' do listen to the recitation of the whole text of the Quran. The Holy Prophet [S.A.W.] used to listen to the whole text of the Holy Quran at least once during Ramadan.
8. Say 'Taravih' prayers with humility, eagerness and devotion. Do not just complete the number of Rakats in a mechanical fashion. Offer prayer with understanding and devotion so that your life may be influenced by the propitious influence of Namaz and your devotion to Allah may become firm and deep. Do offer Tahajjud prayers also by the favour of Allah.
9. Give charity and spend whatever you can in the way of Allah. Look after the needs of the poor, the widows and the orphans and arrange provisions for them for 'Sahri' and 'Iftar'. The Holy Prophet [S.A.W.] has affirmed: "This is a month of Maswat." Hadrat Ibn 'Abbas [R.A.A.] reports: "The Holy Prophet [S.A.W.] was by nature generous and munificent, but his [S.A.W.] munificence knew no bounds during the month of Ramadan. When Hadrat Jibbrail [A.S.] visited the Holy Prophet [S.A.W.] each night and recited the Holy Quran to the Prophet [S.A.W.] and heard the recitation of the Holy Book from the Prophet [S.A.W.], during that period the Holy Prophet [S.A.W.] became even more generous than the blowing wind."
10. Do offer maximum rakats of supplementary prayers during 'Shab-e-Qadr, and recite the Holy Quran. The importance of this night is affirmed by the fact that the Holy Quran was revealed during this night. The Holy Quran says: "Lo! We revealed it in the Night of Power. And do you understand what the Night of Power is! The Night of Power is better than a thousand months. The

angels and the spirits descend therein, by the permission of their Lord with all decrees. (That night is) Peace until the rising of dawn."

The traditions record that 'Shab-e-Qadr' is one among the odd nights in the last week of Ramadan. Say this prayer during this night: "Allah! Forgiveness is Thy Greatest Attribute, for Thou likest to forgive. So forgive me."

Hadrat Anas [R.A.A.] relates that once in the month of Ramadan, the Holy Prophet [S.A.W.] observed: "A month has come upon you people in which there is one night which is better than a thousand months. The person who misses offering devotions in the course of this night deprives himself of all the bliss. And only that person remains deprived of the Grace and Blessings of this month who really deserves deprivation." (Ibn Majah)

11. Observe Itikaf in the last week of the month of Ramadan. The Prophet of Allah [S.A.W.] used to perform Itikaf during the last ten days of Ramadan.

    Hadrat 'Aishah [R.A.A.] reports: "When the last week of Ramadan approached, the Holy Prophet [S.A.W.] used to keep awake during most part of the nights and devoted himself to worship. He [S.A.W.] also decreed the female of the household to remain awake and engaged himself in the worship of Allah with full zeal and perfect devotion."

12. Show utmost tenderness and erection to people in the month of Ramadan. Provide maximum facilities to your employees and supply their needs with extreme liberality. Deal with members of your household with kindness and generosity.

13. Say the maximum Rakats of prayers with humility, zeal and devotion. It is related in 'Durr-e-Munthur' that when the Holy Month of Ramadan came, the pattern of the Holy Prophet's [S.A.W.] life underwent a change. The number of the Rakats of supererogatory prayers offered by him [S.A.W.] increased. He [S.A.W.] observed

deeper humility in prayers and appeared totally overcome with fear of Allah.

The traditions record: "In the month of Ramadan, Allah ordains the heaven supporting angels to give up their supplications and say Amin (So be it!) after the prayers of the fasting persons."

14. Pay 'Sadaqa-tul-Fitr' (charity ordained before Eid prayers and at the end of Ramadan) with a willing heart and give it away before saying 'Eid prayer. If possible pay it well before the 'Eid so that the needy and destitute may also buy necessary provisions for the 'Eid and go to the 'Idgah with everybody else and join in the festivities of the 'Eid. It is reported in the traditions that the Holy Prophet [S.A.W.] made the payment of 'Sadaqa-tul-Fitr' obligatory for his followers for two reasons: first, as an atonement for any improper or licentious deed that the fasting people may have committed unconsciously in the period of their fast; and secondly, 'Sadaqa-tul-Fitr' is to be paid to make provisions of food for the poor and the indigent to afford them to enjoy the auspicious Eid day. (Abu Daud)

15. Besides practising maximum possible piety yourself in the holy days of Ramadan, persuade others also with fervour, zeal, tenderness and tact to do acts of piety, so that the fear of Allah, love of piety and goodness may reign supreme all over the society, and as a whole, may derive the greatest benefit from the limitless blessings of the holy month of Ramadan.

Observing Fasts

1. Keeping in view the great reward and great blessings of Fasting, make arrangement for observing fasts with full zeal and complete earnestness. No other form of worship can serve as an alternative to Fasting. For this reason, Allah made Fasting obligatory for every Ummah (Followers of a Prophet). Allah affirms: "O ye who believe! Prescribed for you is fasting, as it was prescribed for those before you so that you may become God-fearing."

The Holy Prophet [S.A.W.] elucidated this sublime objective of Fasting as follows: "A person who does not renounce false speech and practising falsehood while he fasts, Allah cares not for his abstinence from food or drink."

(Bukhari)

The Holy Prophet [S.A.W.] further observed: "The person who fasts with a perfect sense of devotion to faith and 'Ihtisab' (sense of accountability), Allah will pardon all the sins which he may have committed in his previous life."

(Bukhari)

2. Observe all fasts of Ramadan with full care and miss not any fast save in case of severe illness or on the ground of some religious excuse. The Holy Prophet [S.A.W.] said: "Anyone who misses a single fast during Ramadan except in case of severe illness or on ground of religious excuse cannot make amends for this offence by keeping fasts on all the remaining days of his life."

   (Tirmidhi)

3. Keep yourself busy in your daily occupation and be active and cheerful in work so as to avoid hypocrisy and false appearances during fasting. Do not show weakness or lethargy in your behaviour during the fast. Hadrat Abu Hurrayrah [R.A.A.] remarked: "When a man observes fasts he ought to anoint himself with oil as usual so that the effects of fasting do not show off."
4. Make your best efforts to avoid all forms of evil during the fast, because the very objective of the fast is to purge the life of man of all evil and make it righteous. The Holy Prophet [S.A.W.] has affirmed: "Fast is seen as a shield. When any of you is in a state of fasting, he should take care not to utter any evil speech by his tongue or to start an affray. In case someone starts railing at him or is inclined to start a fight with him, the man who is fasting should reflect that he is in a state of fasting (how can he reciprocate offensive language?)

   (Bukhari, Muslim)
5. Covet the great reward for fasting as reported in the Traditions. Offer a prayer to Allah especially near the

hour of Iftar (breaking the fast). "O Allah! Be gracious to accept my fast and grant me that favour and reward which You have promised." The Holy Prophet [S.A.W.] affirmed: "Those who observe fasts will enter Paradise through a special gateway. The name of this gate is 'Rayyan'. When the entire number of all those who observe fasts have gone in, the gate will be closed and no one will be allowed to enter it afterwards."

(Bukhari)

The Holy Prophet [S.A.W.] also observed: "On the Day of Judgement, Fast will intercede with Allah and say: "O Creator! I restrained this man from eating, drinking and taking other pleasures during the day. O Allah! Be gracious to accept my intercession on behalf of this man." And Allah shall grant this petition." (Mishkat)

In addition, the Prophet of Allah [S.A.W.] observed: "Any prayer which a fasting person offers at the hour of Iftar (time of breaking the fast) is granted and is never refused." (Tirmidhi)

6. Bear the hardships of the fast in good cheer. Do not degrade the sanctity of the fast by complaining of the pangs of hunger or thirst or weakness.
7. If you are unable to observe fast during a journey or because of severe illness, you can forego it, but atone for it on other days. The Holy Quran affirms: "But whosoever among you is sick or on a journey (he is required to observe fast instead of these days) the same number on other days." (2: 185)

   Hadrat Anas [R.A.A.] reports: "On occasions when we went on journeys with the Holy Prophet [S.A.W.], some of the companions observed fast and others did not. However, neither those who had kept fast criticised those who had missed the fast nor the latter objected to the fasting of the former." (Bukhari)
8. Avoid back-biting and casting an evil eye strictly during the fast. The Holy Prophet [S.A.W.] has observed: "The person who keeps fast is in fact offering devotion to

Allah from morning till evening unless, of course, he backbites Etiquette of Life in Islam against someone. When he indulges in backbiting, his fast is broken."

(Ad-Dailmi)

9. Earn a lawful living. No devotion of the body fed on illicit earnings is admissible. The Holy Prophet [S.A.W.] has affirmed: "The body fed on illicit earnings is a proper fuel for Hell-Fire." (Bukhari)

10. Do eat 'Sahri' meal. This alleviates the hardship of fasting as well as safeguards against weakness and lethargy. The Holy Prophet [S.A.W.] has observed: "Do eat the 'Sahri' meal, for the eating of 'Sahri' meal entails blessing." (Bukhari)

    Moreover, the Holy Prophet [S.A.W.] observed: "Eating of 'Sahri' meal entails blessing; Take a few draughts of water, if nothing else. The angels of Allah send peace and blessings upon those who eat the 'Sahri' meal."

    (Ahmad)

    Furthermore, the Holy Prophet [S.A.W.] observed: "Take some rest at noon and get some ease in the night prayers. Eat Sahri meal to obtain nourishment during fast in the day time." (Ibn Majah). 'Sahih Muslim' records: The Holy Prophet [S.A.W.] observed: "The only difference between our fasting and the fasting observed by other people of the Book is that we begin the fast by eating the Sahri meal."

11. Do not delay in ending the fast after sunset, for the main objective of fasting is to inculcate the spirit of submission rather than abstinence from food and drink. The Holy Prophet [S.A.W.] affirmed: "The Muslims will remain in good condition if they hasten to do Iftar (meal taken at sunset to end the fast)." (Bukhari)

12. Say this prayer at the time of Iftar: "O Allah! it is for thee that I observe fast and it is with Thine blessing that I break it." (Muslim)

    After ending the fast, say this prayer: "No more was the thirst, moistened were the veins and reward became due if the Lord so Willed." (Abu-Daud)

13. When you perform Iftar (ending the fast) at the house of some body else, say this prayer: "May it please Allah that the fasting people may perform Iftar at your house and pious people may enjoy the hospitality of food provided by you! May the angels invoke blessings upon you by their prayers!" (Abu-Daud)

14. Do arrange Iftar parties. This act entails a high reward. The Prophet of Allah [S.A.W.] has observed: "Any man who supplied meal to a fasting person to perform Iftar, Allah shall pardon his sins in reward for this act and grant him salvation from Hell-Fire. The man who supplies meal for Iftar to a fasting person will receive an equal reward with him. The reward of the fasting person will not, however, be curtailed.". The people submitted: "O Prophet of Allah [S.A.W.]! Where shall all of us end the wherewithal to make provision for the Iftar of a fasting person and to feed him." The Holy Prophet [S.A.W.] observed: "It is enough to feed a fasting person at Iftar with a date or some quantity of milk or even supply him a single draught of water for Iftar." (Ibn Khuzaima)

ALMS GIVING AND CHARITY

1. Give away in the way of Allah with the sole motive of winning the favour of Allah. Do not waste your virtuous deed by keeping in view some ulterior purpose or motive. Do not expect the beneficiaries of your deed to offer thanks to you or acknowledge your favour or testify to your magnanimity. The true believers anticipate reward for their deeds from Allah only. The Holy Quran expressed the sentiments of the true believers in these words: "We feed you for the sake of Allah only. We wish for no reward nor thanks from you." (76: 9)

2. Avoid display, ostentation and showing off. Hypocrisy destroys the virtue of the best of deeds.

3. Pay Zakat openly, so that others may also be induced to perform their duty. However, offer other Sadaqat (charitable acts) secretly so as to promote feelings of

deep sincerity in your heart. Deeds performed with true sincerity are of great value in the eyes of Allah. On the Day of Judgement in that terrible field where there will be no shade, Allah shall keep under the shadow of heaven that man who spends in the way of Allah in such extreme secrecy that the left hand does not know what the right hand has spent." (Bukhari)

4. After spending in the way of Allah avoid reminding the beneficiaries of the favours you have done to them nor cause them any distress. To administer shocks to the self-respect of the indigent and poor, to injure their feelings by reminding them of favours done to them and to expect that they should acknowledge their obligation to you, that they should always humbly bow to you and regard you as their superiors-such sentiments when you have given away charity in the way of Allah, are wicked and despicable. The heart of the true believers should be free of such notions. Allah ordains: "Ye who believe! Render not vain your alms giving by reproach and injury like him who spendeth his wealth only to be seen of men."

5. Do not take pride or assume an air of arrogance after spending in the way of Allah. Do not advertise your magnanimity among the people. You should rather tremble at the thought whether your sacrifice has been accepted by Allah or not. Allah ordains: "And those who give what they give while their hearts are full of fear that to their Lord they shall return."

6. Show tenderness to the poor and destitute. Do not rebuke them, nor rule over them nor show off your superiority over them. In case you have nothing to give to a supplicant, excuse yourself with extreme humility and politeness, so that he may depart silently invoking blessings upon you even without receiving anything from you. The Holy Quran says: "But if you turn away from them seeking means from thy Lord, for which thou hopest, then speak unto them a reasonable word." (17.28)

And Allah also ordains: "Therefore the beggar drive not away."

7. Spend in the way of Allah liberally with eagerness. Do not spend with a stingy or grudging heart, nor consider it an oppressive fine. Only those people deserve grace and success who forswear miserliness, narrowmindedness and stinginess.

8. Spend only 'Halal' (earned by righteous means) goods in the way of Allah. Allah accepts only those goods which are pure and have been earned through righteous means. How can a believer who is eager to spend in the way of Allah bear that his lawfully earned goods should be mixed with illicit gains? Allah ordains: "Ye who believe! Spend of the good things that you have earned."

9. Give away the best goods in the way of Allah. Allah ordains: "You shall never attain righteousness until you spend of that which you love." (3: 92)

   Goods given away as Sadaqa (charity) are being accumulated for the benefit of eternal life in the Hereafter. How can a believer bear the thought of defective goods for his everlasting life.

10. If you are liable to pay the Zakat (poor-due), do not delay the payment. Pay it at once after careful accounting so that, Allah forbid, nothing remains due in your account.

11. Pay the Zakat (poor-due) under a collective system and spend it under the collective system. Where Muslim governments do not exist, the Muslim citizens can form parties and create a Baitul Mal for the receipt and expenditure of Zakat (poor-due).

HOLY PILGRIMAGE

1. Do not delay or keep putting off the performance of Hajj. Whenever Allah bestows enough means on you for the fulfilment of this interesting obligation set out for Hajj at the earliest opportunity. You do not know how much longer life will last, so why should you keep putting

off the performance of this duty from one year to the next. The Holy Quran affirms: "And the people owe this duty to Allah that whoever has the means to journey to his House should make a pilgrimage to it. And whoever refuses to obey this command should know that Allah needs no favour from any one in the world."

A greater ruination and deprival of man cannot be imagined than that Allah should thus openly proclaim His indifference and disconcern to man. The Traditions relate: "The person who makes up his mind to go on the pilgrimage should make haste to perform this obligation. It is possible that he may be taken ill; or his she-camel may get lost, or perhaps an event occurs which makes it impossible for him to go to the Hajj." (Ibn Majah)

The implication is that when means are available a person should not evade the performance of this duty without sufficient reason, for one never knows if these means, freedom and facility will still be available to him in the near future, Allah forbid, the man may remain deprived of the blessing of performing the Hajj forever. May Allah save every believer from this deprival! The Holy Prophet [S.A.W.] has reprimanded such persons in very strict terms. The Tradition records that the Holy Prophet [S.A.W.] observed: "A man who is not prevented by illness or genuine need or is free from the restraints of a tyrannical and despotic ruler and yet does not perform the Hajj may die a Jew or a Christian for aught we care." (Sunan Kubra, Vol. 4)

Hadrat 'Umar [R.A.A.] was heard as saying. "I wish to summon those who, despite having means, do not perform the Hajj, for they are not Muslims, they are not Muslims at all."

2. Go on a pilgrimage to the House of Allah and perform Hajj to please Allah alone. Do not stain this pure objective with any worldly motives or interests. The Holy Quran affirms: "And hinder not those who are proceeding to the Sacred House seeking the graces and pleasure of Allah." (5: 2)

"And complete the Hajj and 'Umrah for Allah's (sake)." (2: 196)

And the Holy Prophet [S.A.W.] has affirmed: "The reward for the performance of 'Hajj Mabrur, is certainly no less than admission to Paradise."

3. Do not circulate the news of your going to the pilgrimage. Keep your departure for Hajj and your return a private matter. Avoid strictly all those customs and ceremonies which smack of ostentation or display. Even though the real test of righteousness and acceptability of a deed is that it should be performed with the sole intention of pleasing Allah, and that the motive of the act should be free from all taint of any extraneous desire; but this point should be especially borne in mind in the case of Hajj, for Hajj is the last resort for effecting a spiritual revolution and the purification of soul and the moral conduct of man. The 'spiritual patient' who is not successfully cured by this efficacious treatment has no hope of healing by any other means.
4. Even if you have no wherewithal to proceed to the pilgrimage, you should cherish the desire to view the House of Allah, to offer 'salam' (peace and blessing) on the Mausoleum of the Holy Prophet [S.A.W.] and keep the Ibrahimi sentiments of sacrifice which are produced in the souls of the believer by Hajj ever afresh in your heart. The heart which is devoid of these sentiments is not that of a true believer but resembles to a desolate ruin. The Holy Prophet [S.A.W.] has affirmed: "Those who go to perform Hajj or 'Umrah' are the special guests of Allah. Their prayers are granted by Allah and if they supplicate for mercy, He forgives them." (Tibrani)
5. Take the best provisions with you when you go for Hajj. The best provision in this case is fear of Allah. In this journey of righteousness, the man who avoids transgressing the Commands of Allah and who reaps the maximum benefit of the blessings of pilgrimage is the one who fears Allah under all circumstances, and has a burning zeal to win the favour of Allah. The Holy

Quran says: "And take provisions for the journey (to perform Hajj) for verily the best provision is the fear of Allah." (2: 197)

6. Having resolved to go to Hajj, start making preparations with singleminded devotion. Keep the date of the Hajj constantly in view. Reflect upon each article of the obligation of pilgrimage. Try to realise the feelings which Allah intends to promote in the heart of the believer through the observance of these articles of the obligation of Hajj. Like a conscious and knowledgeable believer, observe all the articles of Hajj with full awareness and imbibe the realities contained in the articles of Hajj and endeavour to bring about a righteous revolution in your life in conformity with these realities. It is for this reason that Allah has ordained the performance of Hajj obligatory for the believers. Allah ordains: "And remember Him as He has guided you and verily prior to it you were of those gone astray." (2: 198)

   For this purpose, deeply reflect upon those portions of the Holy Quran which describe the reality, importance and the sentiments created by the performance of Hajj. A careful study of the Traditions of the Holy Prophet [S.A.W.] and those books which deal with the date of the Hajj and discuss the articles of Hajj will also prove useful in this respect.

7. Memorise the propitious prayer which should be offered during the Hajj. These may be found in the Books of Traditions. And in the words of the Holy Prophet [S.A.W.] beg not from Allah than what the Prophet [S.A.W.] himself had asked for.

8. Protect your Hajj from all unpropitious motives or actions. Beware lest you Hajj should become like the Hajj of those who will get no share in the Hereafter, because the latter group shuts its eyes from the rewards of the eternal world and begs exclusively for worldly bliss. When they reach the House of Allah, they offer the following prayer: "Our Lord, give to us in this world. And for such there shall be no portion in the Hereafter." (2: 201)

Make a plea to Allah for grace and success in both worlds by means of the Hajj and pray to Allah in these words: "Creator, I have come to Thy Presence to supplicate for success and the fulfilment of my righteous desires in both this life and the life Hereafter." Keep saying this prayer also: "Allah! Grant us goodness in this world and good in the Hereafter (also) and protect us from the agony of Fire." (2: 201)

9. During Hajj avoid transgression of Allah's commands with extreme sensitivity. The journey to perform the Hajj is in fact a passage to the House of Allah. You are the guests of Allah there. You have gone there to renew your covenant of devotion to Allah. By putting your hand on the 'Hajar-e-Aswad' you are in fact taking a pledge of faith and bondage and when you kiss the stone, you kiss the emblem of submission to Allah, you proclaim your fidelity by chanting repeated Takbir (praises) and Tahlil *(La-Ilaha illa Illah)* of Allah. Imagine, then, that in such an atmosphere how disgusting would be the commission of even a minor vice or the blemish of a small transgression. Allah has warned His servants who present themselves in His Court in these words: "There should be no ungodliness."

10. During Hajj keep away from all sorts of quarrels. In the course of the journey when there is a rush of people everywhere, when you suffer discomforts, when there is a clash of interests at every step, when feelings are injured every moment, it is the duty of the guest of Allah to display large-heartedness and self-sacrifice and show toleration, liberality and kindness to everybody. Abstain from rebuking your servant even. "And there should be no quarrels."

11. Safeguard against sexual matters and continue to be vigilant against carnal sentiments in the course of Hajj. In the course of the journey when there is a greater possibility of provocation of sexual passion or of eyes going astray, you should become more alert against the evil promptings of your passions and the devil and try

to protect your piety at all costs. In case you are accompanied by your spouse, you should not only avoid indulgence in sexual relationship with her, but also shun all that can stir up sexual passion. In order to warn the pilgrims, Allah ordains: "The pilgrimage is (in) the well-known month and whosoever is minded to perform the pilgrimage (let him remember that) there is (to be) no lewdness." (2: 197)

And the Holy Prophet [S.A.W.] has affirmed: "Any man who comes here to perform Hajj in the House of Allah and keeps away from immoral and sexual affairs and has not indulged in ungodly acts returns in that state of purity and innocence in which he was born from the womb of his mother." (Bukhari, Muslim)

12. Pay full reverence to the symbols of Allah. The word 'Shariah' refers to the symbol appointed by Allah to remind and bring home to the people some spiritual or meaningful reality. 'Shaair' is the plural of the above word. All things associated with the Hajj serve as symbols to bring home to you of some reality about devotion to Allah. You should revere them all. The Holy Quran affirms: "O ye who believe! Profane not Allah's emblems nor the Sacred Month nor the garlands nor those repairing to the Sacred House, seeking the grace and pleasure of Allah." 'Surah Hajj' affirms: "And whosoever observes the sanctity of what have been ordained as Symbols of Allah, does so because of the piety of the hearts."

13. Perform the articles of Hajj with utmost humility and adopt an attitude of destitution and helplessness before Allah, for above all Allah likes the virtues of humility, modesty and poverty in man. Someone enquired from the Holy Prophet [S.A.W.], "Who is a Haji?" The Holy Prophet [S.A.W.] observed: "The person who has dishevelled hair and is covered with dust all over."

14. Say Talbih with a loud voice after tying the 'Ihram', after each prayer, while ascending a height or descending a slope, on joining a caravan and on waking up each

morning. The words of the Talbih are as follows: "Here I am O Lord. Here I am, Here I am. No partner hast Thou. Here I am. Behold unto Thee belong the Praise and the Bounty; and also the Sovereignty. No partner hast Thou." (Mishkat)

15. On arrival at the plain of 'Arafat', say the maximum number of prayers for mercy and offer penitence. The Holy Quran affirms; "Then hasten onward from the place whence the multitude hasteneth onward and ask forgiveness of Allah. Verily Allah is Forgiving, Merciful." (Al-Baqarah)

    The Holy Prophet [S.A.W.] has observed: "The day of Arafa is the best of all days in the view of Allah. On this day, the Lord of the Heavens especially turns His attention towards the world and expresses His Pride before the angels on the humility and misery of His pilgrims. Allah observes to the angels: "O angels, look! my servants stand before me in the sun in a helpless state. They have gathered here from afar and the hope of begetting My Mercy has drawn them to this place, although they have not yet seen the agony of punishment." After expressing His pride, Allah then ordains that these people have been granted salvation from the torments of Hell. On no other occasion are such a greater number of men granted salvation as on the day of 'Arafa'." (Ibn Habban)

16. On reaching Mina, offer sacrifice with the same passionate zeal and devotion to Allah with which the friend of Allah, Hadrat Ibrahim [A.S.] had placed the knife on the neck of his dear son Hadrat Ismail [A.S.]. Imbibe these feelings of sacrifices and let them be embedded in your mind and heart so that you may be willing to offer sacrifice in every field of life and your practical life reflects an image of: "Verily my prayer, and my sacrifice, and my living and my dying are for Allah, Lord of the worlds." (Al-Anam)

17. Occupy yourself continuously in the remembrance of Allah in the days of Hajj and never let, the memory of

Allah fade from your heart. Remembrance of Allah is the essence of all worship. Allah affirms: "Remember Allah during appointed days. (2: 203) Further Allah observes: "And when you have completed your devotion then remember Allah as ye remember your fathers or with more lively remembrance."

The main purpose of the articles of Hajj is that during the days of Hajj, you should keep yourself completely absorbed in the commemoration of Allah and then memory of Allah should so permeate through your soul that the mundane activities and struggles of life may not succeed in turning your thoughts away from the memory of Allah. In the days of paganism, people used to laud the memory of their ancestors and made loud boasts about them after performing the articles of Hajj. Allah ordained that these days should be spent in the remembrance of Allah and in acknowledging His grandeur alone Who is truly Great.

18. Perform circumambulation of Allah's House with feelings of great love and devotion. Allah ordains: "And you should circumambulate the House of Allah."

    The Holy Prophet [S.A.W.] has said: "Each day Allah confers a hundred and twenty favours on His pilgrims. Sixty blessings are showered upon those who circumambulate the House of Allah; forty blessings are bestowed upon those who offer prayers in the House of Allah; and twenty blessings are conferred upon such as only keep gazing at the Kaaba (Baihaqi). Furthermore, the Holy Prophet [S.A.W.] observed: "He who has performed fifty circumambulations of the Baitullah (House of Allah) is purged of all his sins and is transformed into that state of innocence in which he was on the day of his delivery from the womb of his mother." (Tirmidhi)

READING AND RECITING HOLY QURAN

- The best Muslims are those who learn and teach the Quran. Knowledge of the Quran and reciting it are two merits.

- The Quran should be held, taken or given with the right hand not the left.
- Women during child-bed or during the menstrual cycle and men and women who are seminally defiled, may neither touch nor read the Quran.
- All chapters of the Quran and all of its words are benevolent and beneficial.
- Gathering in a group to read and study the Quran is recommended.
- Listening carefully while the Quran is being recited or read is not only an act of politeness, but an obligatory duty upon every Muslim.
- Reading the Quran with proper contemplation, thinking and concentration is necessary to understand the meaning fully.
- The Quran is a book of guidance. It is not a book of history, science, geography, etc., in spite of the fact that it contains historical, scientific, geographical and various other facts.
- The Quran is a book of guidance for mankind in every respect of life. It is not meant to be recited only at ceremonial openings and such occasions.
- When buying or selling the Quran and no fixed price is attached, using terms and tones of language usually used when bargaining should be avoided.
- A Muslim's knowledge of the Quran should be refreshed by re-reading it frequently; this applies especially to those who memorize it, for it is difficult to remember it when it is abandoned for a while.
- When reading or reciting the Quran, the established rules of pronunciation and intonation included in an independent science called al-tajwid should be followed; these rules have been passed down from the time of the Prophet and the Companions.
- When reciting the Quran, it should be beautified with a good voice and the verses chanted, not sung, for a

beautiful voice increases the beauty of the Quran. This however should not be done in a way contradicting the rules of al-tajwid. The inclination of some, to recite the Quran with a melodious voice approaching singing, thus contradicting the rules of al-tajwid, is forbidden. The listener should take the first opportunity to correct such a recitation and politely draw attention to its incorrectness.

- When reciting one of the fourteen special verses of the Quran requiring prostration upon completion of the verse, the Quran should be laid aside, and a sajdah (a prostration) made.
- A Muslim should not be hasty to judge others' reciting of the Quran.
- Disputing, arguing or engaging in controversy about the Quran must not be indulged in, for it is the Book of God.

BEHAVIOUR ON FRIDAYS

- Though Friday, according to Islam, is the best day on which the sun has ever risen, and the lord of days, it is not the Islamic sabbath, because sabbath does not exist in Islam.
- A Muslim should bathe or purify himself with 'wudu' as perfectly as possible before going to prayer. Though bathing is not obligatory, it has a more cleansing effect; though 'wudu' is good, bathing is more excellent.
- Best clothes should be worn and perfume applied, if this is available, or pleasant-smelling oil should be put on the hair.
- A tooth stick or toothbrush should be used to ensure that the mouth is clean and has a pleasant odour. This is more important on Fridays before leaving for prayer than on other days.
- Before leaving for prayer, nails should be cut and cleaned, and one should ensure that clothes are clean and beard and moustache tidy.

- The Friday prayer in congregation is a necessary duty for every Muslim, with certain exceptions, e.g. children, women, invalids and those too ill to perform prayer.
- If there is more than one mosque available, it is yet better to say the Friday prayer together at one mosque.
- Going as early as possible to the mosque on Friday is recommended. Walking to the mosque, if this is possible, and not riding is also more worthy.
- On entering the mosque, the rules of behaviour in the mosque must be observed.
- Care should be taken to avoid annoying others in the mosque; for example, squeezing between two men or stepping on others.
- Most mosques on Fridays become full of worshippers. No individual has the right to make another get up and then move into his place. He should politely ask those present to make room for him.
- While in the mosque, the worshipper must avoid any sitting position which could cause him to drowse, to sleep, or which would invalidate his 'wudu'.
- If a worshipper should find himself dozing, he should try to change his place. In this case, he should change places with his neighbour.
- A worshipper should avoid taking any position that would uncover his body between the navel and the knees.
- The Prophet Muhammad forbade worshippers to sit together in a circle in the mosque before Friday prayer, because this hinders straight rows, and reduces the available space.
- Facing the imam while he is giving khutbah from the minbar (pulpit) is polite conduct.
- When the imam asks God's blessings, etc. for the Muslims, he should not raise his hands in an attitude of supplication.
- When the Friday prayer is finished worshippers should not rush to leave the mosque, or crowd the exits.

- As mentioned above, a sabbath does not exist in Islam, therefore, it is not required that a Muslim abandons working during the whole of Friday. What is required, is to stop working during prayer time.
- A worshipper should listen to the imam as soon as he starts his khutbah and keep silent until he finishes. To attend prayer with a frivolous attitude is against the aim of the Friday prayer.
- It is undesirable to fast on Friday alone; to fast on Friday, however, in conjunction with Thursday or Saturday is allowed.
- It is neither necessary nor required to abandon travel on Friday.
- Friday is a good occasion to remember the Prophet, peace be on him, and invoke a blessing on him by saying: Allahuma Salli ala Muhammad wa ala ali Muhammad (O God, bless Muhammad and Muhammad's family).
- Reading the Quranic chapter of Al-Kahf every Friday is recommended.

Khutbah at Friday Prayer

- The imam should avoid the custom of always wearing black clothes on Fridays.
- As soon as the imam ascends the minbar he salutes the worshippers, just before he sits or immediately after.
- The imam should face the worshippers while he is delivering the khutbah.
- Topics discussed in the khutbah should be related to current, relevant issues.
- The Friday khutbah is of two parts in each of which the imam must speak while standing; in the interval between he must sit for a short while on the minbar.
- The voice of the imam should be clear, but he should not shout in order to be heard. His language should be simple and understandable.

- The imam should not interrupt his khutbah in order to greet someone or to make an announcement of any kind.
- The imam should not make his khutbah or his prayer lengthy. Each must be of moderate length. In fact, the shortness of the khutbah is a sign of the imam's understanding and knowledge of Islam.
- The second part of the khutbah should not be devoid of information.
- The khutbah is a message and not a performance. The imam should avoid being conspicuously eloquent or poetic; he should also avoid speaking in a voice or in a manner which tends towards musicality.
- The imam's raising his hands in the khutbah while saying 'dua' for the Muslims is not recommended. It is enough that he points with his forefinger.
- The imam should prepare his khutbah beforehand; his 'dua' should preferably be spontaneous and not memorized.
- The imam should not begin the actual prayer until he has convinced himself that the rows of worshippers are straight.

THE MOSQUE

The mosque is where Muslims should pray five times every day, where they seek refuge from the troubles of this world, from its everlasting daily demands, its complications and its vanities.

Design

- A mosque should be built in every residential district.
- The design of the mosque should be characterized by simplicity, as must its furnishings.
- The mosque should be devoid of any lavish kind of ornamentation, representation of anything, pictures or images.
- Extravagance in spending large sums of money to build luxurious mosques should be avoided.

- Members of the Muslim society should neither vie with one another about the virtues or beauties of any particular mosque nor compete in building ostentatious mosques.
- Attaching pieces of gold of silver to any part of the mosque or its furnishings is forbidden.
- The carpets and walls of the mosque should be devoid of a multiplicity of colours for that distracts the concentration of the worshippers.
- Writing on the walls of the mosque, inside or outside, including Quranic verses or God's attributes, should be avoided. The names of the Prophet and the first four rightly-guided Caliphs likewise should not be written.
- The minbar should not be placed in the middle of the mosque. Its height should not exceed three steps.
- Every mosque should have two entrances, one for men and one for women.
- Lavatories should be sited as far from the mosque as practicable, and from the fountains or basins for ritual ablution.
- Raising flags inside the mosque is an innovation.

Cleanliness and Tidiness: The mosque deserves to be the cleanest place on earth. Therefore:

- Muslims must be sure before entering the mosque that their body and clothes are clean and do not smell bad.
- Filth must be removed from shoes and the shoes removed before entering the mosque.
- Although it is not forbidden to eat anything in the mosque, it is not a place for taking meals and drinks.
- Whoever brings in or causes dirt in the mosque has a duty to clean it up and remove it. It is not the duty solely of the mosque caretaker to keep the mosque clean and tidy; it is also the responsibility of every Muslim entering the mosque and seeing any uncleanliness, to remove this from the mosque.

2

Real Worshipping

The Holy Prophet [S.A.W.] observed that Allah has affirmed as follows:

"My creatures! Each one of you is misguided, save the one whom I guide. So seek guidance only from Me so that I may instruct you. My people! Each one of you is famished, save the one whom I feed. So apply to Me only for subsistence, so that I may grant you livelihood. My slaves! Each one of you is naked, save the one whom I dress with an apparel, so beseech clothing from Me so that I may dress you with garments. My bondmen! You commit sins day and night and I can forgive all sins. So seek forgiveness from Me so that I may forgive you your sins." *(Sahih Muslim)*

1. Never lose hope of acceptance by Allah of your repentance and petition for forgiveness. Whatever the magnitude of your sins, purify your soul by offering repentance and be hopeful of Allah's mercy, Despair is the characteristic of unbelievers, It is the distinctive trait of the believers that they repent the most and under no circumstances do they lose hope of Allah's clemency. It is disastrous to succumb to dismay and lose hope of Allah's Mercy and clemency considering the magnitude of sins. The most outstanding quality of the favourites of Allah is that they do not stick to the wrong and guilt but admit their fault clearly and unconditionally. They are never supposed to be above faults and omissions, but when they commit any fault and realise the wrong done, they

do all within their means to beg forgiveness from Allah and to purify themselves of that fault and misdeed.

"And those who when they do an evil thing or wrong them selves remember Allah and implore forgiveness for their sins. Who forgiveth sins save Allah only?-and will not knowingly repeat (the wrong) they did." (3: 135)

And Allah affirms in another verse:

"Lo! those who ward off (evil) when a glamour from the evil troubleth them they do but remember (Allah's guidance) and behold them seers." (7: 201)

And the Holy Prophet [S.A.W.] observed:

"All human beings without exception are sinful, but the best sinners are those who repent the most."

(Tirmidhi)

In the Holy Quran, Allah has mentioned it as a distinct virtue of the believers that they offer penances before Allah at dawn and repent and seek His Forgiveness and Allah has urged the believers that they should rest assured that Allah shall cover their sins with His Forgiveness and Clemency, for He is All Forgiving and the Most Affectionate towards His creatures.

"Ask pardon of your Lord and then turn unto Him (repentant). Lo! my Lord is Merciful, Loving."(11: 90)

2. Always be hopeful of Allah's Blessings and rest assured that however great your sins may be, Allah's Munificence is wider and all-encompassing. When a person who has committed a greater volume of sins than the surf of the sea feels ashamed and offers sincere penance before Allah, He listens to his entreaties and grants him refuge under His Mercy.

"O My slaves who have been prodigal to their own heart! Despair not of the Mercy of Allah who forgiveth all sins. Lo! He is the Forgiving the Merciful. Turn unto Him repentant; and surrender unto Him before there come unto you the doom, when ye cannot be helped."

(39: 53, 54)

3. Whenever you feel shame and remorse and at whatever stage of your life, consider this feeling and realisation a special favour of Allah and be sure that the doors are always open for repentance. Allah accepts repentance of His slaves as long as they are alive. However, when they are at the threshold of death and are about to pass over to the next world, the time for offering repentance expires. The Holy Prophet [S.A.W.] observed: "Allah accepts the repentance of His slaves, but only before the slave has breathed his last." (Tirmidhi)

The brothers of Hadrat Yusuf [A.S.] pushed him into a dark well and felt sure that he was dead. In other words, they stood guilty of the murder of a Prophet. They soaked Hadrat Yusuf's shirt in blood and presented it as a positive evidence of his death to their father Hadrat Yaqub [A.S.]. They assured him that a wolf had devoured Hadrat Yusuf [A.S.] Many years after the commission of this grave offence when the sense of guilt prevailed upon them, they went to their father remorsefully and requested him: "Dear father, pray to Allah on our behalf and intercede with Him to grant us forgiveness." The Messenger of Allah Hadrat Yaqub [A.S.] did not disappoint his sons by confronting them with the question: "Your offence is grave. Many years have elapsed since you committed this heinous crime, why ask for forgiveness now?" Instead he undertook to offer a prayer to Allah that He should grant them salvation and assured them that Allah would certainly forgive them for Allah is the Most Forbearing and Most Compassionate.

"They said. O our father! Ask forgiveness of our sins for us, for Lo! we are sinful." *(12: 97)*

"He said: I shall ask forgiveness for you of my Lord. Lo! He is the Forgiving, the Merciful." *(12: 98)*

The Holy Prophet [S.A.W.] told a strange tale to his Companions [R.A.A.] with a view to save them from falling a prey to dismay. The tale contains the moral that whenever at any stage of his life a believer feels ashamed of his misdeeds and he sincerely entreats Allah to forgive him, Allah shall bestow upon him salvation and He shall never refuse him His favour.

The Holy Prophet [S.A.W.] observed: "There was a man in ancient days who had committed ninety-nine murders. He enquired from people: "Who is the greatest scholar of the time?" The people gave him the name of a Allah-fearing monk. The man approached the monk and said. "Respected Sir, I am guilty of ninety-nine murders. Can my repentance and petition for forgiveness be accepted?" The monk replied: "No, you stand no chances for forgiveness." In utter dismay the man killed the monk too. Now he had completed a century of murders. He again went round asking the people as to who was the greatest religious scholar on the earth. The people gave him the name of another monk. The man approached the monk to offer repentance. He related his problem in detail and enquired from him: Sir, I have committed a hundred murders. Tell me, can my repentance be accepted?" The monk replied: Why not? Nothing stand in the way of acceptance of your repentance. Go to such and such country. You will find a few venerable slaves of Allah engaged in prayer and devotions to Him. Join them and devote yourself to the worship of Allah and never return to your homeland, as this place is no more virtually suitable for you (In other words, it is impossible for you to remain firm upon your vow of repentance and to strive to reform yourself while living in this place)." The man set out according to the directions of the monk. He had hardly covered half the distance when death overtook him. Now the angels of grace and the angels of torment fell into a dispute. The angels of grace argued, "This man repented of his sins and went a long way to offer submission to Allah." The angels of torment countered: "No, he has not yet performed a single act of virtue-thus the argumentation between the angels went on. In the meantime an angel appeared in the shape of a human being. The angels requested him to settle their dispute. He gave his verdict: "Measure the distance on both sides and determine which side is nearer; the place from where he set out or the place where was he going." When the angels measured the distance on both the sides, it came out that the destination was nearer as compared to the distance he had so far covered. Thus Allah had in fact forgiven him.

(Bukhari, Muslim)

4. Confess your sins only before Allah; beseech Him only for forgiveness; express your sense of humility, helplessness and guilt only before Him. Humility and prostration is a tribute which you should pay only to Allah. The unfortunate one, who pays this tribute of humility and prostration to other human beings who are as helpless and humble before Allah as he himself, becomes insolvent and is left with nothing to pay as tribute to Allah. Such a man is condemned to disgrace and ignominy. He goes to everybody in search of honour and respect but he gets none.

Allah affirms:

"Thy Lord is the Forgiver, Full of Mercy. If He took them to task now for what they earn, He would hasten on the doom for them; but there is an appointed term from which they will find no escape." *(18: 58)*

The Quran alarms:

"And He it is Who accepts the repentance from His bondmen, and pardoneth the evil deeds and knoweth what ye do." *(42: 25)*

In fact, one must himself be convinced that there is only one way to salvation and whoever is denied that approach, is condemned to ignominy and destitution for ever. The befitting attitude of mind in a believer is that whatever the degree of his offence he should only offer penitence to Allah and shed tears of shame only before Him. There is none except Allah Who only has the authority to grant pardon. So much so that even if someone tries to propitiate the Prophet excluding Allah, he will be deprived of favour before Allah, and will be discarded outright. The Prophet of Allah [S.A.W.] is also a slave of Allah soliciting His favour and mercy. The Prophet has been appointed to the exalted office by virtue of his surpassing humility among the creatures of Allah and he makes greater penances to Allah in comparison with others. The Holy Prophet [S.A.W.] observed:

> *"O People! Seek forgiveness of Allah for your sins and return to Him. Look at me. I offer prayers to Allah for salvation hundreds of times in a day."* *(Muslim)*

Concerning the hypocrites Allah affirms:

> *"They swear unto you, that ye may accept them, Though ye accept them. Allah verily accepteth not wrong doing folk"* *(9: 96)*

The terrible episode of Hadrat Kaab b. Malik [R.A.A.] as related in the Holy Quran gives us a lesson that man should suffer hardships and endure all trials, but he should never think of abandoning submission to Allah. The trials that come in the way of Islam and the maximum pain and suffering he has to bear in the way of Allah are means to purify and illumine the life of man and to elevate his rank. This humiliation is the sure means of securing eternal prestige and he who abandons submission to Allah and seeks dignity elsewhere shall find it nowhere. Such a man will meet with disgrace everywhere and no eye on earth or in the sky shall regard him with respect.

> *"And to the three also (did he turn in mercy) who were left behind, when the earth, vast as it is was straitened for them and their own souls were straitened for them till they bethought them that there is no refuge from Allah save towards Him. Then turned He unto them in mercy that they (too) might turn (repentant unto Him). Lo! Allah! He is the Relenting, the Merciful."* *(9: 118)*

The three referred to above are Hadrat Kaab bin Malik Hadrat Murarah ibn Rabi' and Hadrat Halala b. Umayyah [R.A.A.]. The example of their penitence serves as a beacon light for the believers as long as the world exists. Hadrat Kaab b. Malik [R.A.A.] who had lost his eyesight in old age and used to walk with the help of his son, had himself related the instructive episode of his exemplary penitence to his son which has been preserved in the Books of Tradition.

"When the preparations were being made for the battle of Tabuk and the Holy Prophet [S.A.W.] used to call upon the people to join the war I regularly attended all his meetings. Whenever I heard him speak, I made a resolve that I would join the war. However, on returning home I relapsed into laziness. I thought there was plenty of time yet and I had all the provisions of the journey. Moreover, I was in good health and could afford the best mount. There was nothing that could delay me in joining the battle. In this mood, I continued to postpone my departure until all holy warriors had reached the field of battle and I lingered on in Medina entrapped in indecision and lethargy.

"Soon the reports began to pour in that the Holy Prophet [S.A.W.] was returning and one day I heard that he had arrived in Medina and was staying as usual in the mosque. So I went to the mosque. On arrival I found that the hypocrites were trying to convince the Holy Prophet [S.A.W.] of the genuineness of their excuses on oaths. The Holy Prophet [S.A.W.] heard their insincere speeches and indicated his acceptance of their lame excuses by observing 'May Allah forgive you'.

"When my turn came, the Holy Prophet [S.A.W.] enquired: 'Say, what prevented you from coming'? I saw that his smile had a trace of annoyance, so I spoke the truth. "O Messenger of Allah [S.A.W.]! As it happened I had no excuse. I was healthy and prosperous and possessed the mount. It was my lethargy and negligence which deprived me of this privilege.

"On hearing me speak the truth, the Holy Prophet [S.A.W.] observed: "Well, then, go and wait the verdict from Allah." I got up and went among the people of my tribe. The people of my tribe railed at me and said: "Why did you not offer some plausible excuse. You have always been in the forefront in the service of Islam." However, when I found that two other friends of mine had also told the truth, I felt at ease and determined to hold firmly to the truth.

"Afterwards, the Holy Prophet [S.A.W.] issued a general proclamation that no one should speak to us. As soon as this proclamation was issued forth, the attitudes in Medina suddenly changed for me. I became a helpless stranger among my own kith and kin. No one in the society exchanged greetings or entered into a conversation with me. One day, I felt extremely depressed and went to a childhood friend and cousin Abu Qatada [R.A.A.]. I offered him salam, but he did not reciprocate. I, then, said: "Abu Qatada! I ask you in the name of Allah, tell me, am I wanting in love for Allah and His Messenger [S.A.W.]." Qatada [R.A.A.] remained silent. I repeated my question, but he made no answer. When I asked him in the name of Allah for the third time, he said: "Allah and His Messenger [S.A.W.] know better." My heart overflowed with a surge of emotion and I burst into tears and returned home with the burden of my grief enhanced. It was during those days that a Syrian trader in the bazar delivered to me a letter from the monarch of Ghassan. The Christian monarch had written: "It has come to our knowledge that your chief is subjecting you to extreme repression. You are not a lowly person. We know the worth of a man like you. Come to us. We shall treat you as befits your status and rank."

As soon as I read the letter, my tongue uttered: "Here is another calamity that has befallen me." And I threw the letter into the hearth.

"Forty days had passed in this state when a courier of the Holy Prophet [S.A.W.] delivered his command that I should separate from my wife also. I enquired: "Shall I divorce her?" The answer came: "No, just live separately from her." I despatched my wife to the home of her parents and told her: "Now, wait for the verdict from Allah."

"On the fiftieth day after dawn prayers, I was sitting on the roof of my house highly dejected, stricken with extreme grief and considering life as no longer bearable, when suddenly someone shouted to me: 'Kaab! Congratulations'. On hearing this, I understood that the hour of my deliverance had come and fell in prostration to my Allah. Later people rushed towards me. They came in crowds and congratulated me. I rose and went straight to the presence of the Holy Prophet [S.A.W.]. I saw his august face glowing with happiness. When I moved forward and greeted him, the Prophet [S.A.W.] observed: "Kaab! Congratulations! This is the happiest day of your life."I submitted: "Prophet of Allah [S.A.W.], is this clemency a favour from you or from Allah?" The Holy Prophet [S.A.W.] observed:

"This is a favour from Allah" and then recited the verses of *Surah Taubah* (9)."

5. Do not delay in offering repentance. Nobody knows when his life will end, and the next moment will bring death to him or his life shall continue. Always remember your fast approaching end and continue to cleanse the impurity of sins from your heart and soul and mind and speech.

The Holy Prophet [S.A.W.] observed:

"Allah extends His mercy during the night so that the person who committed a sin during the day should return to Him in the night. Allah extends His mercy during the day so that the person who has committed a sin during the night may return to his Lord in the day time and see His forgiveness until the sun rises from the east." *(Muslim)*

The expression 'Allah extends His mercy' means that Allah beckons His sinful slaves towards Himself and desires to cover their sins with His blessings. If the person has committed a sin under the pressure of a temporary impulse, he should immediately turn towards his kind and All-Forgiving Allah and should lose no time, for sin begets sin. The Satan constantly lies in ambush for the human being and never misses an opportunity to lead man astray.

6. Offer repentance with such true and deep sincerity of heart that the entire course of your life is altered and after repentance you may appear an entirely different man.

Allah decrees:

"O ye who believe! Turn unto Allah in sincere repentance! It may be that your Lord will remit from you your evil deeds and bring you into Gardens underneath which rivers flow on the day when Allah will not abase the Prophet and those who believe with him." *(66: 8)*

In other words, offer such sincere and true repentance that not a trace of any temptation to return to the sin remains in your heart or mind. Such a repentance has three or four ingredients. If the sin relates to a transgression of Allah's right, repentance should have three elements:

(i) Man should be sincerely ashamed of his sins.

(ii) Man should firmly resolve to avoid sin in future.

(iii) And man should put his heart and soul in the task of reforming and embellishing his life.

If a man has committed a sin which involves the violation of a human right, repentance should consist of a fourth element also:

(iv) Man should restore the right of another human being or seek forgiveness of the person whose right he has violated.

This is the repentance which really cleanses the man of all his sins. His soul is cleared of sins and adorned with pious deeds, is presented before Allah and is awarded a dwelling place in His Paradise.

The Holy Prophet [S.A.W.] observed: "When man commits a sin, his heart is stained with a dark spot. Now if he:

(i) renounces the sin;

(ii) is ashamed of his sin and seeks salvation;

(iii) and turns to Allah with a firm determination to avoid sin in future;

Allah illumines his heart. But if he again commits sin, the dark spot is enlarged until it covers the whole of his heart. This is the rust about which Allah affirms in His Book:

"Nay, but that which they have earned is rust upon their hearts." *(83: 14)*

7. Take a firm resolve to remain true to your repentance and be vigilant day and night that the commitments you have made before Allah are duly fulfilled. Test the firmness of your resolve by constant efforts to purify and reform yourself. If despite all your efforts to guard against evil, you slip and commit an offence, do not lose hope even then. On the contrary seek refuge in the Mercy of Allah and offer fervent prayers to him: "O Creator! I am weak and infirm. Do not banish me in

disgrace from Your threshold. For, I can seek asylum nowhere except in Your Mercy."

Repentance of a wrong-doer invites the pleasure of Allah. Taubah (Repentance) literally means 'return, to turn to'. When thoughts and emotions go astray and one gets entrapped in the quicksand of sin, his connection with Allah is severed and he is so far removed from Allah as if he is lost to Allah. And when such a man returns and turns to Allah in utter shame for his sins, it is as if a lost slave has come back to his master. This situation has been graphically described by the Holy Prophet [S.A.W.] in the following eloquent allegory:

"If one of you loses his camel in a waterless desert with all his provisions of food and water laden on the lost camel and having vainly searched for the camel in all directions of the desert he despairs of his life and lies down under a tree awaiting death and in this state he suddenly beholds his camel laden with all the provisions standing by his side, imagine then his happiness!-the happiness of your Lord and Creator far surpasses the happiness of this man when His lost slave returns and having gone astray resumes allegiance to Him."

(Tirmidhi)

On another occasion, the Holy Prophet [S.A.W.] elucidated Etiquette of Life in Islam the same fact by means of another impressive allegory:

Some prisoners of war were brought before the Holy Prophet. [S.A.W.] The group included a woman who had lost her infant. The maternal instinct so overpowered the woman that she found no peace or rest unless she picked up and breast-fed any baby she found near her. On seeing the woman in such state the Holy Prophet [S.A.W.] enquired from the Companions [R.A.A.]: "Can you imagine that this woman will fling her baby into fire with her own hands?" The Companions submitted: "O Messenger of Allah [S.A.W.]! Leaving apart the matter of throwing the child herself, she would stake her life to save the child if it were falling by itself." The Prophet [S.A.W.] thereupon observed:

"Allah is by far even more Compassionate and Kind to His slaves than this woman is considerate towards her child."

8. Offer repentance to and seek forgiveness of Allah continuously. There are countless offences which a man commits from morning till evening; sometimes man is not even conscious of these transgressions. Do not imagine that repentance is called for only when a capital sin has been committed; man needs to repent and pray for his salvation at all times, because he is liable to make a slip at every step. The Holy Prophet [S.A.W.] himself used to repent and pray for his salvation seventy or even hundred times in a day. (Bukhari, Muslim)
9. Do not look down upon a sinner who repents and reforms his life. Hadrat 'Imran b. al-Haseen [R.A.A.] has reported an incident of the time of the Holy Prophet [S.A.W.]: "A woman of the tribe of Juhainah presented herself before the Holy Prophet [S.A.W.]. She had become pregnant as a result of an unlawful relation. She submitted: "O Messenger of Allah [S.A.W.]'. I deserve punishment for adultery. Enforce the Shariah in my case and punish me." The Holy Prophet [S.A.W.] sent for the guardian of this woman and observed to him: "Treat this woman well and when she has delivered the child, bring her to me." When the woman returned after the delivery of her child, the Holy Prophet [S.A.W.] commanded that her garments should be tied fast around her body (so that the garments may not slip off during stoning and her physical veil may not be torn off) and when this had been done, the Holy Prophet [S.A.W.] ordered that she should be stoned to death. The order was carried out. The Holy Prophet [S.A.W.] later offered funeral prayers for her. Hadrat 'Umar [R.A.A.] submitted to the Holy Prophet [S.A.W.]: "O Messenger of Allah [S.A.W.]! This woman committed the offence of adultery and you are saying funeral prayers for her." The Holy Prophet [S.A.W.] thereupon observed: "She repented and offered repentance of such magnitude that if it were portioned

among seventy men of Medina, it would secure their salvation. Did you see any one better than the one who presented the gift of life to Allah?"

10. Say the 'finest prayer' to Allah. The Holy Prophet [S.A.W.] observed to Hadrat Shaddad ibn Aus [R.A.A.] 'This is the *Sayyed-ul-Istaghfar'* ('the finest prayer'). "Allah! Thou is my Creator! There is no deity except Thee. Thou created me and I am Thy slave. I shall remain faithful to the pledge of devotion which I have given to Thee to the best of my capability. I seek asylum with Thee against the fearful consequences of my sins. I acknowledge all the blessings Thou hast conferred on me and I confess that I am a sinner-Hence, O My Creator, Forgive my sins. Who else except Thee will forgive my sins?" (Bukhari, Muslim)

REAL PRAYERS

1. Pray to Allah only. Do not call upon any one else except Allah to fulfil your needs. Prayer is the essence of worship and worship should be rendered to Allah alone. The Holy Quran affirms: "Unto Him is the real prayer. Those unto whom they pray beside Allah respond to them not at all, save as (is the response to) one who stretches forth his hand, towards water (asking) that it may come to his mouth and it will never reach it. The prayer of disbeliever goeth (far) astray." (13: 14)

In other words all powers to fulfil prayers and to dispose of things lie in the hands of Allah. All powers vest in Him and no power lies with any one else. All are dependent upon Him. There is none except Him Who hears the petitions of human beings and fulfils their prayers.

"O mankind! Ye are the poor in your relation to Allah. And Allah! He is the Absolute, the Owner of Praise."
(35:15)

The Holy Prophet [S.A.W.] observed:

"Allah affirms, 'My creatures! I have declared tyranny unlawful for Me. So you should also consider acts of

oppression and excess on each other as forbidden. My slaves! Each of you is misguided, except the one whom I guide on the right path. So seek guidance from Me alone, so that I may guide you aright. My people! Each of you is hungry, except the one whom I feed. Hence call upon Me for sustenance, so that I may provide for your livelihood. My servants! Each of you is naked, except the one whom I have blessed with garments. So entreat Me to confer dress on you and I shall provide you clothing. My worshippers! You commit sins in the night as well as in the day and I shall forgive all sins"!

(Sahib Muslim)

The Holy Prophet [S.A.W.] also observed: "Man should call upon Allah alone to provide for all his needs, so much so that even if a shoelace is broken, man should pray to Allah to provide a shoelace, and if he needs salt, he should beseech Allah to send it to him." (Tirmidhi)

The Implication is that man ought to turn to Allah for the fulfilment of his most insignificant and ordinary needs. None except Allah can hear the prayers and none except Him can fulfil wants.

2. Ask Allah for only that which is lawful and good. To beseech Allah's help for the execution of unlawful purposes and sinful acts is the height of impertinence, immodesty and irreverence. To pray to Allah for the fulfilment of unlawful and forbidden desires and to make vows for such desires is to perpetrate the basest joke on religion. Similarly, do not offer prayers to Allah to change those realities which He has determined once for all and which are now unalterable. For example, a short man should not pray to Allah to make him tall, nor should a tall man pray to Allah to make him short; nor indeed should a man pray to Allah for eternal youth so that he may never experience old age etc.

The Holy Quran affirms:

"And set your faces upright (towards Him) at every place of worship, and call upon Him, making religion pure for Him (only)." *(7: 29)*

He, who would present his needs before Allah, should not take to the path of infidelity and pray for the fulfilment of unlawful desire, but should display good character and virtuous passions and beseech Allah for the fulfilment of lawful wants.

3. Say prayer with profound sincerity and a righteous disposition and with the conviction that Allah Whom you beseech is perfectly aware of your condition and is Most Considerate towards you; it is He alone who hears the petitions of His servants and fulfils their prayers. Always offer a pure prayer unmixed with all taint of exhibition, display, deception or polytheism.

The Holy Quran affirms:

"Call ye then Allah devoting your obedience wholly to Him." *(40: 14)*

And Surah Baqarah bears the command:

"And when My servants question thee concerning Me, then surely I am nigh. I answer the prayer of the supplicant when he crieth unto Me. So let them hear My call and let them trust in Me, in order that they may be led alright." *(2: 186)*

4. Offer prayer with perfect concentration and devotion of mind and heart and with a positive conviction of Allah's favour. Instead of gazing at the enormity of your sins, look towards the unlimited mercy, kindness and the countless bounties and blessings of Allah. The prayer of an inattentive man whose thoughts are not concentrated on Allah and who is only mumbling a few words halfheartedly at a whim without anticipating the favour of Allah is vain.

The Tradition relates:

"Offer prayer with the firm conviction of Allah's favour. Allah does not accept a prayer sent forth by an inattentive heart." *(Tirmidhi)*

5. Say prayer in utmost humility with awe and fear of Allah. Your heart should be astir with the awesome majesty, grandeur and power of Allah and fear of Allah

should be obvious from your physical posture. Your head should be bent and eyes downcast. Your voice should be muffled, limbs limp, eyes damp with tears and the whole demeanour should present a picture of helpless misery before Allah. The Holy Prophet [S.A.W.] on beholding a man stroking his beard during worship, observed: "Had he the fear of Allah in his heart, his body too would have been overcome by it."

In point of fact while praying a man should tremble with the realisation of his destitution and helpless misery and with the fear that if he were repulsed from the threshold of Allah, he would not find refuge anywhere. He should have deep awareness of the fact that he possesses nothing of his own; everything he has is a bounty from Allah; if Allah withholds, no other power in the world can bestow anything on him. Allah is the Master of everything; He alone holds the treasure of everything; man is only a miserable beggar.

The Holy Quran commands:

"Call your Lord with humility."

The dignity of worship consists in the servant calling upon his Creator in desperate humility and in a lowly manner so that his heart and intellect, emotions and feelings and all parts of his body should be bent in homage to Him and the servant's soul and body should bear evidence to his destitution and plea for help.

6. Say prayer in a muted, faint voice. Do present your petition before Allah in a desperate manner, but never display your desperation and misery openly. Man should display his humility, lowliness and the plea of misery only before Allah.

There is no doubt that sometimes you may say prayers in a loud voice, but only in privacy, or amid a congregation so that the others may say 'Amin'.

Generally, however, you should say prayer quietly in muffled tones and take full care that your expression of misery and destitution and your supplication is not just a show intended for other people.

"And do thou (O Muhammad) remember thy Lord within thyself humbly and with awe below thy breath at morning and evening. And be thou not of the neglectful."
(7: 205)

The Holy Quran praises the beauty of the worship offered by Hadrat Zakriya [A.S.] in these words:

"When he cried unto his Lord a cry in secret." (19: 3)

7. You should execute some pious deed before saying prayer. For instance, make some sacrifice, give alms, feed the hungry one or offer supererogatory worship or observe a fast. In case, Allah forbid, you land in some trouble, offer prayer to Allah reminding Him of all these pious deeds which you have performed with true sincerity of heart for His sake only.

The Holy Quran says:

"Pure utterances ascend towards Him only and pious deed propel them to higher altitudes." ***(35: 10)***

The Holy Prophet [S.A.W.] once related the incident of three men who were entrapped in a cave during a very dark night. They prayed to Allah reminding Him of their truly sincere deeds and Allah rescued them from the calamity.

It so happened that during a dark night a group of three men took refuge in a cave. As Allah willed, a rock slided down the hill and falling over the mouth of the cave closed the passage completely. It was a massive rock and was too heavy for them to push aside and clear the passage. On consultation among themselves, they resolved to pray to Allah reminding Him of their truly sincere deeds in anticipation of His Favour to rescue them from this calamity. In accordance with this resolution, one of them related his pious deed as follows:

I used to take goats for grazing in the forest and earned my living by means of this occupation. On returning from the forest I used to offer milk first to my old parents and then to my children. One day, I arrived late. My old parents had gone to sleep. The children were awake and hungry. But I could not bear to feed the children before my parents had taken the milk, nor

> *did I wish to put them to inconvenience by waking them up. So I stood all night at the head of their beds holding the cup of milk in my hand. The children clung to my feet and cried for milk all the night, but I remained unmoved and stood there until night gave way to morning.*

"O Allah! I performed this deed for Your sake only. Remove this rock from the mouth of the cave in recompense for my deed." And Allah caused the rock to move aside just so much as to let in a view of the sky.

The second man spoke thus: I put some labourers to work and paid wages to all of them except one man who went away without receiving payment for his labour. A short while later when the man returned to claim his wage I said to him: "All these cows, goats and servants are yours. Take them where you will." He said: "For Allah's sake, don't cut joke with me." I answered: "This is not a joke. All this is yours. I invested the money which you had left behind in business. By the Grace of Allah, the business thrived. All this which you see is the profit derived from that business. Take it with an easy mind. All this belongs to you." And that man went away taking everything with him. "Oh Allah! I acted in this way to earn Your Goodwill alone. Oh Allah! Remove this rock in recompense of my deed." By the gracious will of Allah the rock moved further away from the mouth of the cave.

The third one narrated the following account of his pious deed: I had a cousin sister for whom I conceived an extraordinary liking. She asked for some money which I supplied. But when I sat close to her to satisfy my need, she said: "Fear Allah and refrain from this act." I rose at once and I pronounced that sum as a gift to her. "Oh Allah! You know perfectly well that I did this to win your favour only. Oh Allah! Open the mouth of the cave as a reward for this pious deed." Allah removed the rock from the passage of the cave and liberated the three men from this calamity.

8. Along with offering prayers for the fulfilment of pious purposes, try to reform and adorn your life in conformity with the Ordinances of Allah. Avoid all sins and forbidden

things. Respect and observe the Commands of Allah in all matters and lead a pious life. It is the height of folly and insolence to eat and drink forbidden thing, clothe yourself out of unlawful gains and fatten your body on illicit earnings and then anticipate acceptance of your prayer. If you wish your prayer may be accepted, your words and action both should conform to the tenets of Islam.

The Holy Prophet [S.A.W.] observed:

"Allah is Pure and He accepts only pure goods. Allah has enjoined upon the pious the same deeds as He has upon the Messengers. Allah affirms:

"O Messengers! Partake of lawful provisions and perform good acts."

Addressing the pious, Allah enjoins:

"O ye who believe! Partake of those lawful and pure things which We have bestowed on you."

The Holy Prophet [S.A.W.] then referred to the case of a man who travels a long distance and arrives at a sacred spot to pay homage; he is covered all over with dust; he raises both hands towards the sky and says: 'My Lord', 'O My Lord', yet because he partakes of unlawful food and drinks and dresses out of forbidden gains and fattens his body on illicit earnings, how can the prayer of such a contumacious and disobedient person be accepted? (Sahib. Muslim)

9. Offer prayers regularly. The expression of one's humility, destitution and sense of loyalty to Allah is in itself a worship. Allah Himself has commanded His servants to offer prayer to Him. Allah has said: "Whenever the servant calls Me I listen to him."

Do not get tired of offering prayer. Do not be tied down by the doubt whether your prayer would change your destiny or not. The obstinacy or flexibility of fate or the acceptance or rejection of prayer depends on the Will of Allah Who is All-Knowing and All-Wise. All the same, it is the duty of the slave to offer prayer to Him like a beggar and destitute person and not to consider himself independent of Him for a single moment.

The Holy Prophet [S.A.W.] observed:

"The humblest person is the one who is humble in prayer." *(Tibrani)*

In addition to that the Holy Prophet [S.A.W.] affirmed: "Allah considers nothing as nobler and as more honourable than prayer." *(Tirmidhi)*

The most luminous trait of the believer is that in distress or ease, pain or pleasure, poverty or prosperity, adversity or luxury — under all souls of condition he turns to Allah only and presents his needs to Him alone and prays to Him regularly for grace.

The Holy Prophet [S.A.W.] observed:

"The person who does not pray to Allah invokes wrath of Allah." *(Tirmidhi)*

10. Put complete faith in Allah as to the acceptance of your prayer. Never commit the blunder of renouncing prayer in desperation if quick results of the acceptance of your prayer are not forthcoming. Concentrate on offering prayer instead of feeling anxious about the acceptance of your prayer.

Hadrat 'Umar [R.A.A.] observed:

"I am not concerned about the acceptance of my prayer. I am only anxious to pray. When the favour of offering a prayer has been granted to me, the acceptance will also be granted."

The Holy Prophet [S.A.W.] observed:

"When a Muslim turns towards Allah to ask for some favour, Allah inevitably supplies his want. Either his wish is granted or Allah adds the thing desired to the balance of reward which the Muslim will receive in the eternal world. On the Day of Judgement, Allah shall summon a pious man to His Presence and enquire from him face to face: "O My slave! I commanded you to pray and promised that I shall grant your prayer. Did you

then offer prayer?" The man will submit: "Yes, I offered prayer." Allah will then observe: "I granted whatever prayer you offered. Did you not pray to Me on that day for the alleviation of sorrow and pain which had seized you and I had succoured you." The slave will submit: "True, O Creator." Allah then will observe: "I granted that prayer and fulfilled that desire of yours in the mortal world. But on the other day you were struck by another calamity and you prayed to Me for succour, but you found none and, therefore, continued to labour under pain and sorrow." The slave will submit: "Yes, it is true beyond doubt, My Creator." Thereupon Allah will observe: "In Paradise many bounties have I reserved for you in reward for that prayer,"-and in the same manner Allah shall ascertain other needs and make a similar observation in regard to all of them."

Afterwards, the Holy Prophet [S.A.W.] observed:

"There shall not be a single prayer offered by a pious person concerning which Allah will not state. "I granted this prayer of yours in the world and I added that desire of yours to the balance of your reward in eternity." The pious person will ponder then: "Would that none of my prayers had been granted in the mortal world! Hence the servant should continue to pray under all conditions."
(Hakim)

11. Observe all external etiquettes, purity and cleanliness at the time of prayer. Keep your heart clear of all evil passions, illicit designs and absurd beliefs.

The Holy Quran affirms:

"Truly, they are the favourites of Allah who repent most and those others who keep themselves pure and clean."

In Surah Muddaththir, Allah enjoins:

"Thy Lord magnify and thy raiment purify."

12. Offer prayer for others also, but begin with yourself. Seek favour for yourself first and then for others too. The Holy Quran reproduces two prayers offered by

Hadrat Ibrahim and Hadrat Nuh [A.S.] which bear the above moral:

"My Lord! Make me to establish proper worship and sons of my posterity (also) our Lord! and accept the prayer. Our Lord! Forgive me and my parents and believers on the day when the account is cast."

(14: 40, 41)

"My Lord! Forgive me and my parents and him who entereth my house believing, and believing men and believing women." *(71: 28)*

Hadrat Ubay b. Kaab [R.A.A.) reports:

"Whenever the Holy Prophet [S.A.W.] happened to mention some person, he [S.A.W.] used to offer a prayer for that person and commenced the prayer by asking Allah's favour for himself first." *(Tirmidhi)*

13. If you are acting as leader in the prayer, you should always offer prayer on behalf of the whole congregation using plural parts of speech. The prayers which have been reproduced in the Holy Quran generally contain plural parts of speech. The leader in fact is the spokesman for the whole congregation. When he utters a prayer using plurals, the congregation should say 'Amin' at the end of each prayer offered by them.
14. Avoid prejudice and selfishness in prayer. Do not fall into the error of considering the vast and common blessing of Allah as limited and thus praying for the grant of His Grace and Bounty to you especially.

Hadrat Abu Hurrayrah [R.A.A.] relates: "A Beduin entered the mosque of the Prophet [S.A.W.] and said his prayer and then said: "O Allah: Grant your favour to me and to Muhammad [S.A.W.] and to none else besides us." On hearing this, the Holy Prophet [S.A.W.] observed:

"You have narrowed the vast limits of Allah's blessings."

(Bukhari)

15. Avoid formal and conscious rhyming in prayer. Utter your prayer in a simple manner with profound sincerity.

Abstain from singing or rhyming. However, it does not matter if by chance your tongue does utter a rhymed speech or an alliteration. A few such prayers as have an informal rhyme and perfect balance in stress are reported to have been uttered by the Holy Prophet [S.A.W.]. For instance, Hadrat Zaid b. Arqam has reported a very comprehensive prayer offered by the Holy Prophet [S.A.W.]:

"Allah I seek Thy refuge from the heart which is devoid of Thy fear, from the being that lacks contentment, from the knowledge that is unprofitable and from the prayer which is unacceptable." *(Tirmidhi)*

16. Offer praise and thanksgiving to the Lord before putting your needs and requirements before Him. Afterwards, say two Rakats of supplementary prayer and say (Darood) 'peace and blessings be on the Holy Prophet' at the beginning and end of your prayer.

The Holy Prophet [S.A.W.] has observed:

"At times when a person seeks the favour of Allah or the assistance of man in connection with some need or requirement, the needy person should perform ablution, say two Rakats of prayer, offer praise and thanksgiving to Allah and say (Darood) 'peace and blessings of Allah be on the Holy Prophet'. (Afterwards, he should put his need before Allah)." *(Tirmidhi)*

The Holy Prophet [S.A.W.] affirmed the fact that the prayer of a man which is accompanied by praise and thanksgiving to Allah and by the invocation of Allah's peace and blessings on the person of the Holy Prophet is granted the honour of fulfilment. Hadrat Fadala [R.A.A.] narrates: "The Holy Prophet [S.A.W.] was seated in the mosque when a man entered, performed the worship and at the end uttered. Allahummaghfirli (Allah grant me pardon). On hearing this, the Holy Prophet [S.A.W.] said to the man: "You were rather quick in offering the prayer. When the worship is over, you should first of all render praise and thanksgiving to the Allah, invoke peace and blessings upon the Prophet and finally say your prayers. As the Holy Prophet [S.A.W.] was speaking to the person, another man came in, offered worship and at the end, rendered praise to Allah and invoked His peace and blessings upon the Holy Prophet. The Holy Prophet, thereupon, observed to him: "Now say your prayer, it shall be granted." (Tirmidhi)

17. Offer prayer to Allah at all times and at every step, for He is never tired of hearing the prayers of His slaves. However, traditions reveal to us that there are certain special times and circumstances in which prayers are accepted very soon. Hence, do not miss the opportunity of offering prayer at these hours and circumstances:

   (i) In the stillness of the latter part of night when most people are enjoying sweet slumber, the man who gets up and engages in communion with Allah and places his needs before Allah in sincere humility shall be blessed with special favour of Allah.

"Allah holds court on the sky of the world every night. When the latter part of the night begins Allah observes, "Who calls Me? I will accept his prayer. Who begs ? I will fulfil his need. Who asks for salvation? I will grant him salvation." (Tirmidhi)

   (ii) Offer the maximum number of prayers in the night of *Shab qadr*, for in auspiciousness this night is better than a thousand months. Say the following prayer especially:

"Allah: Thou art All-Forgiving. Thou likest showing Mercy the best. Hence Forgive me."

   (iii) In the field of Arafat when the 'guests of Allah' assemble there on the 6th Dhul-Hajja. (Tirmidhi)

   (iv) At particular moment on Friday which falls between the commencement of the sermon and end of the worship or from the time when the 'Asr prayer is over till the hour of the Maghrib prayer.

   (v) At the hour of announcement of the Prayer-Call and at the time when the Holy warriors are being lined up for battle in the field.

The Holy Prophet [S.A.W.] has observed:

"Two things are never repulsed from the Court of Allah. One, the prayer offered at the hour of the announcement of Prayer-Call. Second, the prayer uttered at the time of lining up for battle in the field." *(Abu Daud)*

(vi) In the interval between the announcement of the Prayer Call and the Takbir.

"The Holy Prophet [S.A.W.] observed:

"The prayer offered in the interval between the Adaan (Prayer-Call) and the Iqamah is never rejected." The illustrious companions [R.A.A.] submitted: O, Prophet of Allah, what should we pray during this period. The Holy Prophet observed: Say this prayer.

"Allah! I implore of Thee forgiveness, kindness and protection in this world and in eternity."

(vii) During the auspicious days of Ramadan and specially at the time of breaking fast (Bazaz)

(viii) After the performance of obligatory prayers whether you offer prayer individually or in a congregation.

(ix) In the state of prostration.

The Holy Prophet [S.A.W.] has observed:

"In the state of prostration, the slave gains the nearest proximity to his Allah. Hence offer the optimum prayer while you are lying in prostration before Allah."

(x) When you are seized by a serious calamity or the deepest sorrow and pain. (Hakam)

(xi) When a religious assemblage takes place for the purpose of remembrance and worship of Allah. (Bukhari, Muslim)

(xii) When a reading of the Holy Quran is completed. (Tibrani)

18. Offer prayers at the following places, especially. On the eve of his departure from Mecca to Basra, Hadrat Hasan Basri [R.T.A.] wrote a letter to the residents of Mecca stating the importance of putting up in Mecca and the

favours thereof and also clearly mentioned that prayers offered at the following fifteen places in Mecca are especially accepted by Allah:

(i) Near the Multazim (ii) Below the Mizab (iii) Inside the Kaaba (iv) Near the fount of Zam Zam (v) At Safa and Marwa (vi) Near Safa and Marwa at the place where 'Sai' is performed (vii) At the rear of the 'Place of Ibrahim' (viii) In 'Arafat (ix) In Muzdalfa (x) In Mina (xi) Near the three Jamarat. *(Hisn Hassin)*

19. Make constant efforts to memorise the same words of prayer to Allah as are contained in the Holy Quran and the Traditions of the Holy Prophet [S.A.W.]. It is clear that no better words of prayer and no better manner of offering prayer can be found than that which Allah taught to His Prophet [S.A.W.] and to His pious slaves [R.A.A.]. Besides there is no speech which can possibly surpass the word taught by Allah and adopted by His Messengers in effect, sweetness, comprehensiveness, grace and acceptability! The repetition of the prayers taught by the Holy Quran and the Traditions and a thoughtful consideration of their meanings trains and educates one's mind as to what wishes and prayers should a pious person entertain. What deeds are worthy of his striving and what goals should he set for himself. There is no doubt that prayer transcends all barriers of language, style. It is, however, a supplementary Blessing of Allah that He has revealed to us what to ask for and in what manner by prescribing words of prayer. Moreover, Allah taught the pious what attitude to adopt for achieving grace in religion and in secular matters and what wishes and aspirations should a pious man entertain in his heart. There is no religious or secular need as well as there is no aspect of grace, for which a prayer has not been prescribed. It is more propitious, therefore, that you should pray to Allah in those words which are contained in the Holy Quran and the Traditions and you should repeat only those prayers which are incorporated in the Quran or those which

were uttered at various times by the Holy Prophet [S.A.W.] himself.

However, until such time as you take into memory the words of the prayers contained in the Holy Quran and the Traditions, you ought at least to reproduce their sense in your prayers.

We reproduce in the following pages some comprehensive prayers from the Holy Quran as well as from the Traditions of the Holy Prophet [S.A.W.]. You should learn these prayers by heart gradually and then repeat only these prayers afterwards.

SPECIAL PRAYERS

Prayer for Mercy and Forgiveness: Our Allah! We have wronged ourselves. If Thou forgive us not and have not mercy on us, surely we are of the lost. (7.23)

No doubt unless Allah absolves man of his sins and showers endless Mercy on him, man will go to ruin.

Prayer for Grace in Both the Worlds: Our Allah! Give unto us in the world that which is good and in the Hereafter that which is good and guard us from the doom of the Fire. (2: 201)

Prayer for Forbearance and Fortitude: Our Allah! Bestow on as endurance, make our foothold sure, and give us help against the disbelieving folk. (2: 250)

Prayer for Protection Against the Mischief of the Devil: My Allah! I seek refuge in Thee from suggestions of the evil ones and I seek refuge in Thee, my Lord! lest they be present with me.*(23: 97, 98)*

Prayer for Protection Against the Torment of Hell: Our Allah! Avert from us the doom of hell: Lo! the doom thereof is anguish. Lo! it is wretched as abode and station. (25: 65, 66)

Prayer for the Correction of Heart: Our Allah! Cause not our hearts to stray after Thou halt guided us, and bestow upon us mercy from Thy presence. Lo! Thou, only Thou art the Bestower.(3: 8)

Prayer for the Purification of Heart: Our Allah! Forgive us and our brethren who were before us in the faith, and place not in our hearts any rancour towards those who believe. Our Allah! Thou art full of pity, Merciful. *(59: 10)*

Prayer for Favourable Turn of Events: "Our Allah! Give mercy from Thy presence and shape for us right conduct in our plight." (18: 10)

Prayer for Salvation: Our Allah! We believe therefore forgive us and have mercy on us for Thou art best of all who show mercy. (23: 109)

Prayer for the Grant of Satisfaction and Peace in the Family: Our Allah! Vouchsafe us comfort of our wives and of our offspring, and make us patterns for (all) those who ward off (evil). (25: 74)

In other words, grant us such a pure and noble life that the pious should take us as a model and emulate our example.

Prayer for Parents: Our Allah! Forgive me and my parents and the believers on the day when the account is cast. (14: 41)

Prayer for Protection from Trials and Tribulations: Our Allah! Condemn us not if we forget or err: Our Allah! Lay not on us such a burden as Thou didst lay on those before us: Our Allah! Impose on us that which we have not the strength to bear: Pardon us, absolve us and have mercy on us. Thou art our Protector and give us victory over the disbelieving folk. (2: 286)

Prayer for Getting Rid of the Disbelievers' Domination: In Allah we put trust. Our Allah! Oh, make us not a lure for the wrongdoing folk. And of Thy mercy, save us from the folk that disbelieve. (10: 85)

Prayer for a Propitious End: Creator of the heavens and the earth Thou art my protecting Friend in the world and the Hereafter. Make me to die submissive (unto Thee), and join me to the righteous. (10: 101)

Our Allah! Lo! We have heard a crier calling unto Faith: Believe ye in your Lord! So we believed Our Lord! Therefore forgive us our sins, and remit from us our evil deeds and make us die the death of the righteous. Our Allah! And give us that which Thou hast promised to us by Thy messengers. Confound us not upon the Day of Resurrection. Lo! Thou breakest not the trust. (2: 193, 94)

Some Prayers of the Holy Prophet [S.A.W.]: The Muhaddithin (Reporters of Traditions) have worked hard and devoted whole of their lives in collecting and compiling the books of Traditions, the prayers which the Holy Prophet [S.A.W.] used to offer during journeys and in camp. Along with the prayers incorporated in the Holy Quran, you should also utter these prayers of the Holy Prophet [S.A.W.]. These prayers are not only comprehensive, impressive and propitious, but also teach the correct thinking to the believer as well as the desires and ambitions he should cherish. In fact, a man's real nature is reflected in his desires, especially moments when he is satisfied that no other human being is present and that his murmur can only be heard by his Creator. Each word of the prayers offered by the Holy Prophet [S.A.W.] in the darkness of the night, in privacy, in the midst and outside the company of the people, is characterised by profound sincerity, devotion and eagerness and one feels that the utterer of such prayers is the most exalted person who is perfectly aware of his status as the servant of Allah and he constantly begs from his Allah as a needy person. Moreover, his eagerness and devotion is constantly increasing in depth and intensity as he continues to offer prayers to Allah. The essence of all his prayers is as follows: "Allah! Draw me closer! Spare me from Thy wrath! Bestow upon me Thy favour! Give me success and grace in Eternity."

Prayers to be Offered in the Morning and Evening: Hadrat 'Uthman b. 'Affan [R.A.A.] narrates: "The Holy Prophet [S.A.W.] observed: No harm can come to a man from anything who utters the following prayer morning and evening":

> *In the name of Allah by virtue of Whose name naught in the heaven nor earth doth hurt and He is the Hearer the Knower.* *(Musnad Ahmad)*

Hadrat 'Abdullah b. 'Umar [R.A.A.] reports: "The Holy Prophet [S.A.W.] used to offer the following prayer in the morning and evening regularly without respite":

O Allah! Behold, I beg to Thee peace in this world and the Hereafter. O Allah! Behold, I beg of Thee forgiveness and safety in my faith, in my world, in mine household and in my wealth. O Allah! cover my defects and give me peace from my apprehension. O Allah! protect me from my front and from my rear, from my right and from my left also from above me; and I seek refuge in Thee lest I be surprised from beneath me! (Tirmidhi)

Prayer Against Lethargy and Cowardice: Hadrat Anas b. Malik [R.A.A.] states:

"I used to remain in attendance on the Holy Prophet [S.A.W.] and I used to hear him offer this prayer very often: "O Allah! Behold, I seek refuge in Thee from anxiety and grief, from inability and sloth, from faint heartedness and niggardliness, from the burden of indebtedness and the domination of men.

(Bukhari, Muslim)

Prayer for the Attainment of Piety and Purity: O Allah! Behold! I beg of Thee, guidance, piety, purity and contentment. This is the most comprehensive prayer. In these four words the Holy Prophet [S.A.W.] has asked for everything that a believer needs.

Prayer for Protection Against Degradation in this World and the Hereafter: "Allah! End all our activities in grace and protect us from the torment of degradation in this world and in the Hereafter." (Tibrani)

Prayer to be Offered after Worship: Hadrat Muadh [R.A.A.] states that one day the Holy Prophet [S.A.W.] took my hand and observed: "O Muadh! I love thee', and then proceeded to affirm: "O Muadh! I advise you that you should never miss uttering the following words after each prayer:

"O Allah! help me in remembering Thee, in expressing gratitude to Thee and in worshipping Thee in the best manner."

Will of the Holy Prophet [S.A.W.]: Hadrat Shaddad b. Aus [R.A.A.] states: "The Holy Prophet [S.A.W.] advised me: Shaddad! when you see the worldly people busy in amassing gold and silver, you should gather the blissful treasure by uttering the following words off and on":

> *"O Allah! Behold, I beg of Thee steadfastness in keeping (Thy) command and firmness of resolution in (pursuing) the right course. I beg of Thee (the feeling of) thankfulness for Thy grace and (ability for) adoring Thee best. I beg of Thee a sound heart and a truthful tongue. I beg of Thee the good of that which Thee knowest, and I seek refuge in Thee from the evil which Thee knowest. I seek Thy forgiveness for all of my wrongs thou knowest. No doubt Thou knowest all that is unknown to us.*
>
> *(Musnad Ahmad)*

Prayer for Forgiveness and the Favour of Allah: Hadrat Abu Hurrayrah [R.A.A.] states that the Holy Prophet [S.A.W.] while bequeathing a will to Hadrat Salman Farsi [R.A.A.], had observed: "I wish to bequeath a few words to you. Beseech the Most Kind in these words. Rush towards the Most Kind and offer prayer to Him in these words day and night:

> *"O Allah! Behold! I beg of Thee vigour and health in my faith and effect of faith in my dealings and behaviour and success leading to peace and mercy from Thee; and also security, forgiveness and Thy pleasure."*
>
> *(Tibrani, Hakam)*

Prayer for Purification from Sins: Hadrat Umm Salama [R.A.A.] narrates: "The Holy Prophet [S.A.W.] used to offer the following prayer:

> *"O Allah! clean my heart from sins, just as you clean white cloth of dirt. O Allah! cause as great a distance between me and my faults, as there is between East and West.* *(Muljam Kabir)*

Prayer for the Attainment of Respect Among the People: O Allah! make me patient and thankful to Thee, and make me small in my own eyes, but great in other people's eyes.

A Comprehensive Prayer: Hadrat 'Aishah [R.A.A.] states: "It so happened once that when the Holy Prophet [S.A.W.] came to see me I was engaged in offering worship. The Holy Prophet [S.A.W.] needed me immediately but I was delayed, whereupon the Holy Prophet [S.A.W.] observed: 'Aishah, you should utter brief and comprehensive prayers. When I came to the Holy Prophet [S.A.W.] I submitted: "O Messenger of Allah [S.A.W.]! Teach me a brief and comprehensive prayer." The Holy Prophet [S.A.W.] observed: "You should utter the following prayer:

> *O Allah! I ask of Thee all the good which is in the present or in the future, and I ask of Thee paradise, and the works and deeds, which would take me nearer to the same, and I seek refuge in Thee from Fire and the works and deeds which would take me nearer to the same. And I ask of Thee that which was sought by Muhammad, and I seek refuge in Thee from that regarding which Muhammad sought Thy Protection, and that the end of all Thy decrees above me should be good." (Hakam)*

Prayer for Holding firm to Islam: O Allah! maintain my faith in Islam, while I am standing or while I am sitting or while I am lying and let not the enemy, the envious pass sarcastic remarks about me.

Prayer of a new Convert to Islam: Hadrat Abu Malik Ashja [R.A.A.] reports: "My father narrated that whenever a person embraced the religion of Islam, the Holy Prophet [S.A.W.] used to teach him Salat and also the following prayer:

> *"O Allah! forgive me, have mercy on me, guide me, grant me peace and give me sustenance."*

Prayer for the Avoidance of Dissensions and Immorality: O Allah! I seek refuge in Thee from evil morals, deeds and desires. O Allah! Behold, I seek refuge in Thee from schism, hypocrisy and evil morals.

Invocation of Peace and Blessings on the Holy Prophet [S.A.W.]: Invoke peace and blessings of Allah upon your venerable benefactor Hadrat Muhammad [S.A.W.]. Truly, we can make no recompense for his countless favours and limitless love and affection. What we can do, however, is to invoke the peace and blessings of Allah on him with the deepest sense of reverence, love, devotion and loyalty to his person. We should pray to Allah, "Creator! Your Messenger [S.A.W.] had to suffer terrible torments in his task of communicating your message to us. He [S.A.W.] took great pains to guide us on the path of righteousness. Creator! We can make no return for this favour. We implore You, O Creator! to shower Your boundless benefactions upon the Prophet [S.A.W.], to exalt him in Your favour; to protect his religion from the onslaught of falsehood; to extend his religion and to bestow upon him a higher rank than all other favourite companions of Yours in the eternal world." The Holy Quran enjoins upon the Muslims:

"Lo! Allah and his angels, shower blessings on the Prophet. O ye who believe! Ask blessings on him and salute him with a worthy salutation." *(33: 56)*

The Holy Prophet [S.A.W.] observed to Hadrat Ubay bin Kaab [R.A.A.]:

"Ubay! If you devote all your time to invoking peace and blessings of Allah upon the Prophet, Allah shall take it upon Himself to provide for your sustenance in this world and in eternity." *(Musnad Ahmad)*

Hadrat Anas b. Malik [R.A.A.] narrates that the Holy Prophet [S.A.W.] observed:

"A person who invokes peace and blessings of Allah on me is recompensed by Allah in the following manner:

"Allah showers blessings on him ten times. Allah adds ten virtues and erases ten vices from his record of deeds. And Allah elevates his rank by ten grades." *(Nasai)*

In addition to this, the Holy Prophet [S.A.W.] affirmed:

"The angels continue to invoke the blessings of Allah upon a man as long as he devotes himself to invoking peace and blessing of Allah upon me."

(Ahmad and Ibn Majah)

The Holy Prophet [S.A.W.] observed:

"The man who hears my name mentioned yet fails to invoke the peace and blessings of Allah on me is a miser." *(Tirmidhi)*

The Holy Prophet [S.A.W.] declared the person most deserving of the honour of his companionship and attendance in the life Hereafter who invokes the peace and blessings of Allah on him the most. The Holy Prophet [S.A.W.] observed:

> *"The person who invokes peace and blessings of Allah on me the most, will be the best deserving my companionship and attendance on the Day of Judgement."* *(Tirmidhi)*

There is a slight variation in the wordings of the texts of the invocation of peace and blessings of Allah which the Holy Prophet [S.A.W.] taught to the illustrious companions [R.A.A.] on various occasions. You may use any of these texts. The text which is generally recited in worship and which has been declared as the most propitious one by Hadrat 'Abdullah b. 'Abbas [R.A.A.] is as follows:

> *"O Allah! Shower Thy mercy upon Muhammad and the followers of Muhammad, as thou didst shower Thy mercy upon Ibrahim and the followers of Ibrahim! Behold Thou art Praiseworthy, Glorious! O Allah! shower Thy blessing upon Muhammad and the followers of Muhammad, as Thou didst shower Thy blessings upon Ibrahim and the followers of Ibrahim. Behold, Thou art Praiseworthy, Glorious."*
>
> *(Sihah Sitta, Musnad Ahmad)*

Hadrat 'Abdullah b. Masud [R.A.A.] observed to the people: "You should invoke peace and blessings of Allah on the Holy Prophet in a proper manner. Who knows this invocation may be presented before the Holy Prophet [S.A.W.]?" The people requested him to teach the proper invocation to them. Thereupon he observed: "You should recite the invocation thus:"

> *"Allah! Shower Your favour, blessing and benefactions upon the lord of Prophets, leader of the pious and the seal of Prophets, Muhammad who is Your servant, Your Messenger of Blessings. Allah, elevate him to an exalted position which may be the envy of his predecessors. Allah! Show Your blessings to Muhammad and the progeny of Muhammad as you blessed Ibrahim and the progeny of Ibrahim. Truly, You possess the purest attributes and are Great. Allah! Show Your favour to*

Muhammad and the progeny of Muhammad as You showered favour on Ibrahim and the progeny of Ibrahim. Truly, you possess the purest attributes and are Great."
(Ibn Majah)

Hadrat Abu Masud Ansari [R.A.A.] narrates: "Once Bashir bin Saad [R.A.A.] submitted to the Holy Prophet [S.A.W.]: In what manner should we invoke peace and blessings of Allah on you? The Holy Prophet [S.A.W.] remained silent for a while and then observed: Say these words:

O Allah! shower Thy mercy upon Muhammad and the followers of Muhammad as Thou didst shower Thy mercy upon the followers of Ibrahim! Behold! Thou art Praiseworthy, Glorious. O Allah! shower Thy blessings upon Muhammad and the followers of Muhammad, as Thou didst shower Thy blessings upon Ibrahim in the worlds. Behold Thou art Praiseworthy, Glorious.

Supplication of Sacrifice: Lay down the animal parallel with the direction of the Qibla and utter the following prayer first:

Behold I have turned my face earnestly towards Him Who originated the heavens and the earth and I am not of polytheists. Behold, my salat, my offering, my living and my dying are all for Allah, Lord of the worlds. No partners hath He, concerning this I have been bidden and I am of the Muslims O Allah! (I offer this) to you and You gave it to me.

After reciting this prayer, Say *'Bismillahi Allahu Akbar'*. (In the name of Allah Who is Great) and cut the throat of the animal with a sharp-edged knife. Having performed the slaughter read this prayer:

"Allah' Accept this sacrifice offered by me as Thou accepted the sacrifice offered by Thy friend Ibrahim and that offered by Thy loved one Muhammad. May peace and blessings descend upon both."

Although it is permissible to let someone else perform the slaughter of your sacrificial animal, yet it is better if you perform this act with your own hands. While you perform the slaughter, try to think and feel in the same way as you express through the words you utter at the time of sacrificing the animal i.e., all that we have got belongs to Allah and it is all to be spent in His way only. The act of sacrificing the animal in His name is in submission to His will and if ever required we shall readily sacrifice even our own life in the way of Allah and shall be grateful to Him that He conferred upon us the honour of martyrdom by affording us an opportunity to shed our blood in His name.

Aqiqa Prayer: 'Aqiqa' refers to the goat or ram which is sacrificed on behalf of a newborn child on the seventh day after his birth.

The Holy Prophet [S.A.W.] observed; "On the seventh day a name should be prescribed for the child. Its hair and all filth should be removed and sacrifice should be performed on his behalf."

Before sacrificing the animal, first make it lie down parallel with the direction of the Qibla and recite the prayer which is uttered at the slaughter of a sacrificial animal i.e. from his wards say and cut the throat of the animal with a sharp-edged knife and then recite the following prayers:

> *"O Allah! This is the 'Aqiqah of........... Accept it as Thou accepted the 'Aqiqah offered by Thy loved one Muhammad [S.A.W.] and by Thy friend Ibrahim [A.S.]. The blood of this sacrifice is ransom for the blood of the child; its flesh is the ran some for the flesh of the child, its hair are a ransom for the child's hair and its bones are ransom for the child's bones. Allah! Accept it."*

The people who possess means must offer sacrifice on behalf of their children. 'Aqiqah is a desirable sacrifice. Two lambs or goats on behalf of the male child and a single goat or lamb on behalf of the female. It is permissible also to sacrifice a single goat on behalf of a boy. However for those who lack means, it is certainly improper to perform the sacrifice by begging loans.

Non-cooked 'Aqiqah meat may be distributed. It is preferable, however, to send cooked meat to the beggars, the poor and your neighbours. On the eve of the *'Aqiqah* of Hadrat

Hasan [R A.A.] the Holy Prophet [S.A.W.] instructed: "Send one chopped leg of the animal to the midwife and eat the rest yourself and feed others." (Abu Daud)

Taravih Prayer: The word 'Taravih' is the plural form of 'Tarviha'. 'Tarviha' denotes the period of rest and relaxation at the end of every four Rakats of prayer. It is in this context that this supplementary prayer of the month of Ramadan is called 'Taravih'. Tarviha, i. e. to pause and relax at the end of every four Rakats of prayer, is a Sunnah.

The following prayer should be recited during *'Tarviha'*:

"Pure is the Ruler and the Sovereign. Pure is the Exalted and the Supreme, the Awesome and the Powerful and the Great Wielder of Authority. Pure is the Immortal Sovereign Who neither sleeps, nor will ever die. Purest and free from all blemishes is our Sustainer Who is the Provider of angels and of Jibbrail.

Allah! Grant us asylum from the Fire of Hell. O Protector, O Protector, O Protector."

Offer the 'Taravih' prayer in congregation and if possible listen to the recitation of the full text of the Holy Quran during *'Namaz'*. Offer 'Taravih' behind a 'Hafiz' (the one who has memorised the full text of the Holy Quran) who recites the Quran with full reverence, devotion and eagerness in moderate pace and with proper pauses and correct accents so that the listeners do not get tired and the Quran may be recited so clearly as to make every word of it audible and distinct. It is a great injustice with the Holy Quran to read it rapidly without understanding as if you are trying to get rid of a burden. The Book of Allah deserves to be read with a will, devotion and concentration pondering over its meaning and implications and trying to grasp its real sense and spirit.

Similarly the 'Taravih' prayer must be offered with ease and concentration showing no haste and hurry. To perform Ruku and Sajda (Prostration) in rapid succession without knowing what is being uttered amounts to sheer disregard of the objectives of prayer and missing the relish of real taste and enjoyment of worship.

Qunut-i-Nazila: Whenever, Allah forbid, the Muslims are faced with a critical situation and the menace and terror of the enemy has overcome them, they should recite Qunut-i-Nazila during prayers, especially in the course of the dawn prayer (Fajr). In the second Rakat of the morning prayers, after performing the Ruku' recite the following prayer in the standing posture before performing the prostration. Traditions reveal that this prayer was recited during worship by the Holy Prophet [S.A.W.] and his illustrious Companions [R.A.A.] at critical times, they offered this prayer especially during morning worship:

> *O Allah! guide us amongst those whom Thou hast guided aright, and preserve us among those whom thou hast preserved. Include us amongst those whom Thou hast taken under Thy protection. Bless us in that which Thou hast bestowed upon us and protect us from the evil of that which Thou hast ordained, for it is Thou Who ordainest and none can ordain against Thee indeed! Never is he abased whom Thou takest as friend and none is respected whom Thou takest as a foe. Blessed art Thou Our Allah and exalted. We ask repentance from Thee and turn to Thee; O Allah! send torment upon the unbelievers, who prevent us from following Thy way and refute Thy messengers, and fight against Thy friends. Allah! grant forgiveness to us and to the Faithful males and females and Muslim men and women and bring reconciliation among them and foster affection (for one another) in their hearts and bless them with conviction and insight and make them firm and unwavering followers of the Holy Prophet [S.A.W.] and enable them to fulfil the pledge You have taken from them; help them against Thy enemies and against their enemies. O Real Deity! hear our prayers and deal us with these people!"*

Prayer for the Fulfilment of a Need: Whenever any need, big or small, arises, you should stand before Allah and offer two Rakahs of supererogatory prayer, (Salat al Hajat). Afterwards, offer thanksgiving and praise to Allah and invoke peace and blessings upon the Holy Prophet [S.A.W.]. Then utter the following prayer. There is every hope that Allah will not reject your prayer. The Holy Prophet [S.A.W.] observed:

> *"When someone seeks fulfilment of a need from Allah or man, he should first carefully perform ablution, say two Rakats of supererogatory prayer and then offer thanksgiving and praise to the Lord; afterwards, he should invoke peace and blessings of Allah on the Holy Prophet; [S.A.W.] and finally utter this prayer to Allah:*
>
> *"There is no deity save Allah the Clement the Bountiful. Glory be to Allah, Lord of the Magnificent Throne! Praise be to Allah, Lord of the Worlds! I beg of Thee the means of (obtaining) Thy mercy and securing Thy pardon; participation in every righteousness and protection from every sin. Leave no sin of mine unforgiven no anxiety unrelieved and let no need of mine unfulfilled wherewith Thou art pleased. O Thou the Most Merciful of Those who show mercy! (Tirmidhi, Ibn Majah)*

Prayer for Memorising the Quran: To learn the Holy Quran by heart and to memorise its text for ever you should offer the prayer which was taught to Hadrat 'Ali [R.A.A.] by the Holy Prophet [S.A.W.].

Hadrat 'Abdullah b. 'Abbas [R.A.A.] reports: "Once we were sitting in the company of the Holy Prophet [S.A.W.] when 'Ali [R.A.A.] arrived and complained about his memory: O Messenger of Allah [S.A.W.]! My mind does not retain the verses of the Quran. I cannot remember what I have learnt previously." The Holy Prophet [S.A.W.] observed:

> *"O Abul Hassan! Let me teach you a prayer which will be of benefit to you and to those whom you will teach this prayer and having learnt this prayer whatever you commit to memory shall be retained and you shall always remember it." Hadrat 'Ali [R.A.A.] submitted: "O Messenger of Allah [S.A.W.]! Do teach me this prayer" Whereupon the Holy Prophet [S.A.W.] observed concerning this prayer: "Say this prayer on Friday night and offer it on three, five or seven Thursday nights in*

succession. By the Will of Allah, this prayer will prove efficacious, I swear by His Name Who has entrusted me with the Religion of Truth, this prayer by the believers never goes unanswered."

Continuing his narration, Hadrat 'Abdullah b. 'Abbas [R.A.A.] says: "Five or seven Thursday nights had passed when Hadrat 'Ali [R.A.A.] came to the company of the Holy Prophet [S.A.W.] and submitted: "O Messenger of Allah [S.A.W.] Before this whenever I memorised four verses, my memory failed me when I tried to I reproduce them. Now, however, the position is that I memorise forty verses and when I wish to reproduce them, it appears as if the Book of Allah is lying open before me. Similarly, I used to hear a tradition and later failed to reproduce it, but now I hear several traditions and retain them so well that I hardly miss a single word while reproducing those traditions."

On hearing this, the Holy Prophet Muhammad [S.A.W.] observed: "I swear by the Lord of Ka'ba that Abul Hassan is a true believer."

Giving detailed instructions about this prayer, the Holy Prophet [S.A.W.] observed: "Say this prayer on Friday night. When the sons of my brother Yaqub requested him to pray for their redemption, Ya'qub replied: "Yes, I shall offer a prayer for your redemption shortly." Ya'qub meant that he would pray for their redemption on the next Friday night. So 'Ali! Rise at the hour of 'Tahajjud' on Friday night, for this is the most propitious time for the fulfilment of prayer; one's soul is eager at this time and the heart is fully devoted to Allah. If perchance you are unable to rise in the later part of the night, get up at midnight. If you can't wake up at midnight, then offer four Rakahs of supererogatory prayer in the first part of the night in the following order: In the first Rakat, recite Surah Fatiha and after this Surah Yaseen; in the second Rakat, recite Surah Fatiha and Surah Ad-Dukhan, in the third Rakat, read Surah Fatiha with Surah Alif Lam Mim Sajdah; and in the fourth Rakat, recite Surah Mulk, after Surah Fatiha. Afterwards, having recited 'Attahiyyat and offered Salam on both sides, offer thanks to Allah and praise Him. Invoke Allah's peace and blessings upon the Holy Prophet and all other Messengers in a proper manner. Implore Him to grant redemption to all the believing men and believing women and offer prayer for the salvation of those brethren who preceded you in faith. And finally say this prayer:

> *"O Allah! Be thou gracious unto me by enabling me to eschew sins altogether as long as Thou sufferest me to live; and have mercy upon me lest I concern myself with ought which is of no consequence to me. And vouchsafe me the aesthetic sight which will cause Thee to be well pleased with me."*

"O Allah! Originator of the heavens and the earth Lord of Majesty and Glory and of Might is comprehensible! I beseech Thee O Allah' O Beneficent Allah in the name of Thy Majesty and of the Light of Thy countenance to cause mine beau to retain Thy explaint as Thou hast taught to me. And grant that I may recite it in such manner as will cause Thee to be well pleased with me. O Allah, Originator of the heavens and the earth, Lord of Majesty and Bounty and of Might Who is unchallengeable. I beseech Thee O Allah, O Beneficent Allah! in the name of Thy Majesty and of the Light of Thy countenance, to illuminate my sight with Thy scripture, make my tongue fluent with its words to comfort mine heart therewith, to make me fully receptive to it and to wash my body clean with its blessings. For indeed, none aideth me in (attaining) the truth besides Thee and now giveth it unto me besides 'Thee. There is no strength nor power save in Allah, the Exalted, the Magnificent."

Prayer for Gaining Understanding of the Quran: The favourite worship of the pious is to recite the Holy Quran and to meditate and reflect upon its meaning. Love of Quran is proof of attachment to Allah as it is also a means to establish communion with Allah. The believer obtains spiritual bliss by contemplating and meditating on the meanings of the Quran and it is through this process only that he secures access to the founts of wisdom contained in the Quran.

The Holy Quran is undoubtedly an easily comprehensible Book. As regards obtaining guidance from it and carrying out its injunction, the teachings of the Holy Quran are very simple, clear and free of all ambiguity or complexity of meaning. However, to grasp its inner meanings and significance and to derive wisdom from it, it is imperative that you should study the Quran after having fulfilled all the conditions and obligations for gaining comprehension of it; reflect upon its contents with sincere application and never adopt a careless and listless attitude towards the Book, but study it constantly for the rest of your life.

It is quite natural that at certain points during study, you will come across a text upon which you will deliberate long and hard without arriving at any one interpretation which your mind will accept. You will then feel at a loss. But if you are a devoted student of the Quran, don't ever feel dejected or lose heart, nor should you entertain any impudent notion of levelling criticism upon the Holy Book. And feeling hopeless, don't abandon the practice of deliberating and meditating upon the meanings of the Quran. On the contrary, you should turn towards Allah with full concentration and reposing complete trust in Him you should seek His aid in the unravelling of this problem. Do not make an impudent bid to make a whimsical exposition of the Quran or to give it an interpretation which conforms to your ideas. Like a true seeker of Truth, stick to the meaning which the text of the Quran makes plain and pray to Allah in extreme humility and with a sense of helplessness: 'O Allah! Eliminate my confusion; make the true meaning manifest to me and let my heart be content with that interpretation and meaning which is really true'. For this purpose, recite the Holy Quran rather loudly but distinctly with pauses in the course of supererogatory prayers at night. Offer the prayer reproduced below. It is hoped from Allah that the prayer will prove efficacious.

The Holy Prophet [S.A.W.] observed: "Any person who offers this prayer while in a state of sorrow and distress, Allah shall alleviate his suffering and bestow upon him felicity and rejoicings."

"Allah! I am Thy slave. I am the son of Thy bondman and the son of Thy bondmaid. My brow is in Thy grip. I am under

Thy command. Thy judgement in regard to me is just and fair. In the Name of all Attributes applicable to Thee and all Attributes which Thou hast reserved for Thyself, or those which Thou bast revealed in Thy Book, or have transmitted to one of Thy creatures or have kept them hidden in the treasury of the unseen with Thee in the Name of all these Attributes I implore Thee to make the Holy Quran the joy of my heart, the light of my bosom, a panacea for my distress and a cure of my sorrows and perplexity."

The narrator of this Tradition Hadrat 'Abdullah ibn Masud [R.A.A.] states that the people submitted to the Holy Prophet [S.A.W.]: "Shall we learn this prayer?" Whereupon the Holy Prophet [S.A.W.] observed: "Any one who hears this prayer, must learn it and memorise it."

WEEKLY SERMON

The Friday sermon is an extremely effective and disciplined means of arousing Islamic sentiments, keeping the Faith alive and carrying out the duty of remembering Allah constantly and in an orderly manner. It is a unique religious institution designed to remind the Muslims of their obligations each week in a perfectly natural way and to inculcate in them a sense of the requirements of religion and an impassioned spirit to serve Islam. But you can make an effective use of this institution only when you address the congregation in their vernacular.

As regards the second sermon, it must be delivered in Arabic; however, the first sermon ought to be delivered in a speech which the audience can understand. It is proper for you to prepare a brief but comprehensive address on the requirements of religion in the context of current affairs and try to develop the mind of the people and rouse them to live each week regularly and in a disciplined manner. If for some reason it is not possible for you to prepare an address yourself, you should at least read the Arabic text and deliver its meaningful translation in the vernacular of your audience. Among the Arabic texts, your best choice is a sermon delivered by the Holy Prophet [S.A.W.] or the illustrious companions [R.A.A.]. Below are reproduced quotations from the authentic speech of the Holy Prophet [S.A.W.]. One of these is the historic sermon which he [S.A.W.] delivered on the first Friday after his migration to Medina. The second address contains an eloquent call to the Muslims to acquire a deep sense of the Holy Quran and to deliberate and ponder over its meanings constantly for it is impossible to hold on to religion without a firm attachment to the Holy Quran.

The First Sermon of the Holy Prophet [S.A.W.] in Medina:

"Thanksgiving and Praise be to Allah. I pay Him gratitude. I invoke His aid. I beseech His Forgiveness and seek Guidance from Him; and I put my faith in Him; and I disbelieve Him not and I consider him as my enemy who disbelieve Him. And I bear witness that there is no deity except Allah; He is Alone and has no partner; and I bear testimony that Muhammad [S.A.W.] is the servant of Allah and His Apostle. Allah sent him with guidance, light and exhortation and instituted him as His Messenger at a time when the office of Prophethood had long remained dormant; the light of true knowledge had faded; evil was dominant; society was in a state of upheaval; doom was hanging overhead; and death was hovering over the head of each man. Hence he who believed in the Messenger and obeyed Allah and His Messenger was righteous. And he who defied the both went astray, transgressed limits and fell into shortsightedness and having lost the path of righteousness advanced far into wrong. I instruct you to fear Allah. The best counsel that a Muslim can offer to another Muslim is that a Muslim should persuade the other to make provision for the life Hereafter and urge him to fear Allah. Fear Allah as hath He ordained you to fear Him. Hence no exhortation is better than this, nor can there be a better reminder. The fact is that awe and fear of Allah is the real aid to secure a propitious destiny in the eternal world for the man who passes his life in constant fear of Mighty and the Exalted. Allah affirms: "My word suffers no change and I never do the least injustice to any of My people." Hence fear Allah

in all the public and private affairs relating to this world or the life Hereafter. Verily Allah redeems the sins of a person who fears His wrath and He enhances the reward of such a person to the maximum degree. And he who constantly fears Him achieves the highest success; and behold, the fear of Allah saves man from His punishment, protects him from His wrath and behold! the fear of Allah makes your faces radiant and lively; it pleases Allah and elevates the man before Allah Almighty.

So, gather virtues of your share and never fail, or lack in submission to His Commands, especially when He has taught you what is right and what is wrong through His Book and has guided you to the right path. This is to differentiate the truthful from those who are liars. Behave well with the people, as Allah has treated you with kindness. Consider His enemies as your own, and strive hard in the way of Allah. He has chosen you and has designated you as 'Muslim' so that one who is to perish should meet his doom with manifest reason and logic and one who is to live, should live with manifest reason and all power and authority rests in Allah and Allah one.

So, ever remember and mention Allah and mind your deeds and actions keeping in view the day to come; for the man who sets the matters between him and the Almighty, Allah suffices him in all the matters between Him and the mankind because Allah decides the fate of the mankind and the mankind wields no authority over Him. Allah is the Master of every thing that men possess; men exercise no power on anything that men possess; men exercise no power on anything divine; He is Paramount and there rests no power but with Allah." (Al-Tibri, Vol. 12, p. 255)

Advice to Develop Interest in the Quran: "Verily, thanksgiving and praise are due to Allah alone. I offer Him gratitude and praise and beg His aid; and we seek asylum with Him against our misdeeds and wrongs committed by us. Whomsoever He guideth (and he guideth only those who really look for His guidance) no one can lead him astray. Whomsoever He deflects from the right path (and He deflects only those who yearn not the guidance) no one can guide him aright." I bear witness that there is no deity save Allah. He is Alone. He has no partner.

> *Verily, the best word is the Book of Allah. Indeed, successful is he who adorns his heart with the word of Allah and whom Allah has favoured with Islam and turned him away from paganism and who preferred the word of Allah over all the human thinking and theories. Verily the word of Allah is the truth, most impressive and most effective. Love him who loves the word of Allah. Develop real love and attachment with Allah with your heart and soul. Let not the recitation of the word of Allah and remembering Him bore you and let not your hearts be indifferent and adamant to the word of Allah. Worship Allah alone; and attribute none as His partner or associate, fear Him ever to the extent He should be feared. Confirm your pious deeds by your words also i.e. say what is proper and becoming of you; and love each other for the cause of Allah and in total submission to Him. May Peace and Mercy of Allah be upon you!"* *(Ijaz-ul Quran)*

The Second Sermon: "The praise is due to Allah, the abundant praise, and benediction and peace be upon His Messenger whom Allah has sent as a witness, a warner and an inviter towards Allah with His mandate and as a radiant light and may peace and abundant peace be on his progeny, followers and companions.

Thereafter, O mankind, I exhort you to fear Allah, for verily fear of Allah is supermost virtue and incumbent upon you is the obedience. And verily he, who obeys Allah and His Messenger, achieves great success, Allah, the Exalted, has declared in His Dignified Book (the Quran): Verily, Allah and His angels invoke Sense of Devotion benediction on the Apostle. So, O ye who believe, invoke blessings on him and seek abundant peace for him.

Allah! Bestow on our Master and our Guide Muhammad and on his progeny, followers and his companions who obeyed him in adversity. Allah! Shower Thy perfect pleasure on those who excelled (to affirm faith) amongst the emigrants and the helpers, particularly on the unanimously admitted the most excellent of mankind, next to the Prophets the Amir of the believers, our master, Abu Bakr the most truthful [R.A.A.] and on the Amir of the believers, our master Umar Al Farooq [R.A.A.] and on the Amir of the believers, our master, Uthman b. Affan [R.A.A.] and on the Amir of the believers, our master, Ali [K.A.W.] and on his two noble sons, the masters of the youth of the inmates of Paradise Hasan and Hussain [R.A.A.] and on their mother, the leader of the ladies of the paradise, Fatima-Zohra [R.A.A.] and on all companions of the Holy Prophet and their successors [R.A.A.].

Allah! Grant success to those who uphold the way of life taught by the Deen of Muhammad [S.A.W.] and make us amongst them; and humiliate those who humiliate the teachings of Muhammad [S.A.W.] and make us not amongst them. O servants of Allah! May Allah show mercy on you. Verily, Allah enjoins justice and kindness, and giving to kinsfolk, and forbids indecency, abomination and transgression. He exhorts you so that you always remember. Remember Allah, He will remember you (in adversity) Pray unto Him, He will respond to you. And remember Allah the most High, most Excellent, most Dignified most Superior, most Grand and the Greatest."

SERMON ON BIRTH

It is propitious to read a sermon at a wedding ceremony in order to explain the significance of 'Nikah' (marriage contact) in Divine law, and to bring home to the parties the requirements and heavy responsibilities imposed by this contact. With a view to derive the maximum benefit from the sermon, it is advisable for the preacher to translate the sermon and offer a brief exegesis of the text in the vernacular so that the assembly may fully appreciate the sermon. To this end, we reproduce below the text of the Nuptial Sermon along with its translation:

"Thanksgiving and praise are due to Allah alone, we seek aid from Him alone; and we beseech forgiveness of our sins from Him only; and we consign ourselves to the protection of Allah against the evils of our souls and

against all offences: Truly, whomsoever Allah guides on the straight path (and He puts him only on the straight path who sincerely desires to walk along that way), no one can lead him astray. And whomsoever Allah deflects (and He deflects only him who yearn to be deflected), no one can put him on the straight path. And I bear witness that there is no deity except Allah and I testify that Muhammad [S.A.W.] is the bondman of Allah and His Messenger."

O Believer! Fear Allah, as He should be duly feared; and die not save you be Muslims.

O mankind! Fear the wrath of your Allah Who created you from a single soul and from it created his spouse; and from then twain bath spread (all over the world) a multitude of men and women. Fear Allah, in Whom you claim your lights from one another and (be careful in observing your duty to) the wombs (that bore you). So! Allah is Watchful over you.

O Believer! Fear Allah constantly and utter what is fair and sound. Allah, then, will rectify your deeds and cover up your sins with forgiveness; and whosoever obeys Allah and His Messenger, he indeed shall secure a glorious success. *(Mishkat)*

The Holy Prophet [S.A.W.] says:

"By Allah! I fear Allah more than all of you; I save myself from the wrath of Allah more than do all of you; but I observe fast and sometimes I do not keep fast. I say prayers at night and I sleep also; and I also take women in marriage. Hence whosoever turns away from my way, he bears no relation with me." *(Bukhari)*

GUIDELINE FOR DECISIONS

Do have 'Istikhara' on the eve of such important events of life as journey, Nikah (marriage contract), employment and in commercial matters. 'Istikhara' means 'to beseech goodness and welfare'. When your mind is in doubt as to which aspect of an important and lawful problem is propitious for you, you must perform an 'Istikhara' and, then, adopt the course suggested by your heart, taking it was the will of Allah. Whenever you are confronted with an issue of extraordinary importance, and find it difficult to reach the correct decision and adopt the right course, perform two Rakats of supererogatory prayer at any hour outside the unpropitious and forbidden timings. Afterwards, offer the 'Istikhara' prayer. Hadrat Sad b. Abi Waqqas [R.A.A.] reports that the Holy Prophet [S.A.W.] observed:

> *"It is propitious for the progeny of Adam to beseech goodness and welfare from Allah; and it is also propitious for the progeny of Adam to submit to the Will of Allah; and it is most unfortunate for the progeny of Adam if they do not beseech goodness and welfare from Allah and are not happy in the Will of Allah."*
>
> *(Musnad Ahmad)*

The Holy Prophet [S.A.W.] also observed:

> *"One who observes 'Istikhara' is never disappointed; and the one who takes counsel is never put to shame; and the one who observes economy does not have to depend on others."* *(Tibrani)*

> *Hadrat Jabir [R.A.A.] states: "As the Holy Prophet [S.A.W.] taught us the Quran, so also he [S.A.W.] instructed us to observe 'Istikhara' in every matter. The Holy Prophet [S.A.W.] used to observe: When anyone among you is perplexed over an important matter, he should perform two Rakats of supererogatory prayer and then offer this prayer:* *(Bukhari)*

O Allah! I ask of Thee the good through Thy knowledge, and ability through Thy power and beg (Thy favours), Thine infinite bounty. For, behold, Thou hast power; I have none. Thou knowest, I know not; and Thou art the great knower of things hidden.

O Allah! If in Thy knowledge this matter be good for my faith, for my livelihood, and for the issue of my affairs, then ordain it for me, and make it easy for me and bless me therewith. But if in Thy knowledge, this matter be bad for my faith, for my livelihood, and for the issue of my affairs, then turn it away from me, and turn me away therefrom and ordain for me the good wherever it be, and cause me to be pleased there with.

THE SUBMISSION

The Holy Prophet (S.A.W.) has said:

"O believers, adorn your lives with the virtues of service. Cover yourselves with the sheet of the fear of Hereafter, make Hereafter the goal of your life; and be ever prepared to make your abode there. Bear in mind, you have to depart from this world and to present yourselves before Allah."

Only two things will save you there; firstly your good deeds done during your lifetime in this world, and secondly that source of charity which you might leave behind, after your death.

DEVOTED PRAYERS

Ablution and Cleanliness are Prerequisites of prayers, while performing wuzu, clean your teeth with a miswak also. The Holy Prophet (S.A.W.) has said: "The distinguishing sign of my followers on the Doomsday shall be that their foreheads and the limbs washed in ablution shall glow with radiance. Thus, whosoever wishes to enhance his radiance may do so."

Offer Prayers in clean and proper dress. The Holy Quran lays down "O the offsprings of Adam! Go to pray adorned with proper apparel for each prayer. (7: 31)

Prayers should be Offered Punctually.

(Innas salata Kanat, alal-mominina kitaban mauqoota)

"Worship has been made obligatory upon the Muslims with fixed hours." (4: 103)

Hadrat Abdullah bin Masud (R.A.A.) once asked the Prophet (S.A.W.) "O Prophet of Allah! Which action pleases Allah the most?" The Holy Prophet (S.A.W.) said: "The act most liked by Allah is to offer prayer at its proper time."

The Holy Prophet (S.A.W.) has also said: "Allah has made five prayers obligatory. One who offers them with

> *submission and humility having performed the ablution at the prescibed time, becomes entitled for salvation by Allah. But one who fails to do so, may get salvation or may not."* *(Malik)*

Importance of Congregational Prayers: Prayers should always be offered in congregation even if the congregation is missed, the obligatory (farz) (prayers should be offered in the mosque. Sunnah prayers may, however, be offered at home.

> *The Holy Prophet (S.A.W.) has said: "He who offers prayers with the first takbir (i.e. immediately on hearing the call) for forty days consecutively in a congregation, is made safe from both Hell and hypocrisy."*
>
> *(Tirmidhi)*

> *And further: "If people come to know the recompense and reward for collective prayers, they would flock to the mosque despite a thousand impediments. The first line of the congregation is like the row of the angels. A two-man party of worshippers is better than one man's and the greater the congregation, the more it is liked by Allah."* *(Abu Daud)*

Prayers should be offered with composure and peace of mind. Perform all the forms (postures) of prayer with an undisturbed mind and peacefulness. There should be a resonable pause between the two prostrations (Sajda) and the following prayer is to be recited during this interval.

"Allah forgive me and bless me with The Mercy, guide me on the straight path, relieve me of my distress, grant me peace, and arrange for my livelihood."

The Holy Prophet (S.A.W.) has said: "He who offers his prayers properly, is in return blessed by Salat in these words, "May Allah protect thee as thou hast protected me."

He has also said: "The worst kind of theft is the pilferage of prayer." When asked by the companions. "Prophet of Allah, how can one steel prayers?" The Holy Prophet (S.A.W.) said. "By performing imperfect postures in prayers."

How to Pray: Offer prayers with concentration, humility, and submissiveness which may inspire you with the majesty and sublimity of Allah. Unnecessarily moving one's hand or feet, scratching the body, combing beard with fingers, putting finger in the nose, and setting clothes right are acts of extreme insolence and should be avoided.

Prayers are a Means of Achieving Nearness to Allah: Offer prayers as if you are before Him; or at least imagine that Allah is watching you. The Holy Prophet (S.A.W.) has said:

> *"The servant of Allah is closest to Him when he prostrates himself before Him. Therefore, when you prostrate yourself, pray fervently."* *(Muslim)*

You should act upon the teachings learnt in the prayers in your daily life and let its sublimity reflect in your worldly affairs. The Holy Prophet (S.A.W.) has pointed to this aspect through a beautiful metaphor. He shook a dry twig with some force. All the leaves dropped off. The Holy Prophet (S.A.W.) said: "The sins of persons offering prayers drop off like the leaves of this dry twig." He then recited the following ayat (verse) of the Holy Quran:

> *"And establish prayers on the two points of the day (i.e. morning and sunset) and after some time when night has set in. Verily, good deeds erase misdeeds. This is an admonition for those who wish to acquire it. (11:114)*
> *(Nasai)*

While offering prayers, the Holy Quran should be recited slowly and clearly. This applies to other utterances during the prayer, which should be recited with appropriate pauses and with concentration, ardour, and alertness of mind. If prayers are offered with understanding and care, they become real prayers.

Prayers are to be offered regularly and with punctuality. It is a basic distinguishing feature of the Muslims that they offer their prayers regularly and in time. The Holy Quran says:

> *"(And the believers are those) who guard their prayers,"*

Optional Prayers: Together with obligatory prayers, the worshippers should also offer nafl or optional prayers. These prayers should be offered as much as possible. The Holy Prophet

(S.A.W.) has said: "For the person who offers twelve rakats of nafl or optional prayers in addition to the five compulsory prayers, has his house built in the Paradise." (Muslim)

Offer Some Prayers at Home Also: Sunnat and Nafl prayers (other than compulsory) should occasionally be offered at home. The Holy Prophet (S.A.W.) has commanded this by saying. "After having offered prayers in the mosque, do offer some prayers at home. Allah will bless your homes on account of such prayers."

The Holy Prophet (S.A.W.) himself used to offer such prayers very often at home.

When leaving your home, for the morning prayers, recite the following supplication:

> *"Allah enlighten my heart, my vision, my hearing; creat light on my right, on my left, on my rear and light in front of me. Enlighten me from above and below. O Allah, bestow upon me light, and make it light for me, fill my muscles, flesh, blood, hair, skin, tongue and my breath with light and make light within myself. Give me; Allah! the great light, and make me all light."*

Supplication to be Recited after Prayers: Hadrat Sauban (R.A.A.) says that the Holy Prophet (S.A.W.) after completing the prayer with the Salam used to say Astaghfirullah (Allah forgive me) thrice and then recited the following supplication:

> *Allah! Thou art peace, and the fountain-head of peace is from Thee. Thou art Blessed, Thou art Great, and Munificent.*

RECITATION OF HOLY QURAN

The Quran should be recited with full ardour and keen interest, believing that love for the Quran is love for Allah. The Holy Prophet (S.A.W.) has said:

> *" The best form of prayer for my Ummah is the recital of the Quran."*

Reward for reciting the Holy Quran: A Muslim should recite the Quran very often and he should never feel tired or bored by its recitation. According to the Holy Prophet (S.A.W.):

"Allah has said that a servant of His who is so engrossed in reciting the Quran that he will not have an opportunity to pray to Him for his needs, shall be granted more than that which He shall grant to those who ask."

(Tirmidhi)

The Holy Prophet (S.A.W.) said:

"Allah's servant gains the maximum proximity to Him through the reading of the Quran." *(Tirmidhi)*

In a beautiful simile, the Holy Prophet (S.A.W.) has compared the individual who reads the Quran daily is like a bottle of musk, perfume of which spreads in all the four directions, while he, who has read the Quran but does not recite it, is like a bottle full of musk which has beensealed." (Tirmidhi)

The Quran should be recited for guidance and inspiration only. It should not be chanted for any other purpose, e.g., for endearing oneself to others or impressing people, or for trying to create an impression of piety. These traits should be eschewed. The are impure motives and anyone who recites the Quran for such a purpose shall not get guidance from the Quran.

Before Recital, Ensure Absolute Cleanliness: Avoid touching the Holy Quran without first having performed ablution and recite it in clean place.

Manner of Recitation: While reciting the Holy Quran, read it with full concentration, ardour and utmost devotion. Allah has said:

"The Book we have revealed upon you, is full of blessings; so that (people) may ponder upon it and the wise men may receive instructions and inspiration from the same."

(38: 30)

Recite the Holy Quran Distinctly in a Melodious Tone: Read the Quran in a measured and deliberate tone, pronouncing each word correctly and distinctly in an easy tone making sentences quite intelligible. The Holy Prophet (S.A.W.) has directed that the reciter should recite the Quran in a pleasing manner, making it charming with his voice and melody. (Abu Daud)

The Holy Prophet (S.A.W.) recited the Quran pronouncing each word clearly and each ayat (verse) separately. The Holy Prophet (S.A.W.) has said:

> *"The reciter of the Quran shall be commanded on the Day of Judgement to recite the Quran melodiously with the same measured tone and sustained pitch, with which he used to recite the Book in the world, and get elevated a step higher as a reward for each ayat. His real abode lies near the last* ayat *he had recited."* *(Tirmidhi)*

Tone of Recitation: The pitch to be adopted in recitation should neither be too high nor too low. It should be intermediate as Allah has set down:

"And offer your prayers neither too loudly nor slowly, instead follow the middle way." (17: 110)

Best Time for Recitation: Although it is always good to recite the Holy Quran, yet the best time to do so is during late midnight with Tahajjud prayers and at dawn, before or after Fajr prayer. Recitation of the Holy Quran at these hours is very gracious and rewarding. The wish of every Muslim should be to achieve this privilege.

Don't Rush Through the Quran: The recitation of the Quran should never he completed within less than three days. The Holy Prophet (S.A.W.) has said: "One who has recited the whole Quran within less than three days, has not comprehended it."

The Holy Quran is not to be Recited Rapidly. It should be read with understanding and meditation. Hadrat Abdullah Bin Abbas (R.A.A.) used to say that it is much better to read short surahs like Al Quraish and Al-Qadr with understanding and comprehension, than rapidly going through long *surahs* like *Al-e-imran* and Al-Baqarah without following them. The Holy Prophet (S.A.W.) once continued to recite only one ayat for the whole night:

> *"(O Allah) if Thou submitest them to Thy wrath, they are Thy servants. If Thou forgivest them, Thou art Most Powerful and All Wise."*

Have Due Rregard for the Majesty and divinity of the Holy Quran. And as you care for the visible cleanliness of your person, while reading the Holy Quran, in the same way cleanse your heart of evil thoughts, foul ideas and base motives: A heart that is polluted by evil thoughts and impure motives will neither admit the sublimity of the Holy Quran nor its significance. Hadrat 'Ikramah (R.A.A.), on opening the Holy Quran for recitation, frequently fainted and on regaining consciousness, would say; "This is the word of my Majestic and Dignified Sustainer."

Study Holy Quran in Order to Correct and Remould your Life: The Quran should be studied with the view and the goal that one's life is to be reshaped and remoulded according to the commands contained therein: One should try to wash off wrongs in ones life in the light of the teachings of the Holy Quran. The Holy Quran would show our wrongs to us like a mirror; and now it is for us to cleanse ourselves.

Inspiration from the Holy Quran: While reciting the Holy Quran, one should try to imbibe the effect conveyed by each ayat. When one recites the ayats concerning Allah's compassion, forgiveness, and the eternal gifts of the Paradise, one should feel elated with beer. While reciting ayats pertaining to Allah's wrath and the torture of the Hell, your body should tremble with awe and fear and tears should spill out of your eyes; even your heart should be moved with the emotions of repentance and shame. On reading the accounts of success of the pious Muslims, your face should glow with happiness; and while reading the stories of destruction of nations having gone astray, you should feel sorrow and unhappy. Verses containing warnings and threats of punishments should send a wave of sensation through your body; and verses which bring joyful tidings should make your soul overflow with the spirit of thanksgiving.

Supplication after Recital: After reciting the Holy Quran supplicate to Allah, Hadrat Umar (R.A.A.) has recommended the following prayer after recital:

"O Allah, make me familiar with the wilderness in my grave. O Allah, have mercy upon me for the sake of the great

Quran, and make it my leader, light, guide and mercy. O Allah, let me remember what I have forgotten of it, and teach me what I do not follow, and give me capacity to recite it in the parts of night and day and O Lord of the worlds, make it my argument on the Final Day."

RESPECT FOR THE MOSQUE

Love for the Mosque: For Allah, the best part of the earth is that piece of land on which a mosque is built. People who love Allah are identified by their love for the mosque. On the dreadful Day of Resurrection, when there will not be any shade (to escape from scorching heat) such people shall be afforded protection by Allah under the cover of His Throne.

The Holy Prophet (S.A.W.) has said:

"And the man dedicated to the mosque shall be under the cover of the Throne." *(Bukhari).*

Serve the cause of mosque by keeping it congregated. This is a symbol of Faith. Allah has said:

"Only those persons who believe in Allah and the Day of Judgement, tend the mosques." *(9: 18)*

Mosque Nucleus of your Life: Farz (Obligatory) prayers should invariably be offered with a congregation in the mosque. Congregation and calls for prayers *(Adaan)* should be properly organized, and your daily life be drilled in harmony with the system of the mosque. A mosque is a nucleus round which the life of a Muslim rotates. Go to the mosque with a passionate desire for prayers. The Holy Prophet (S.A.W.) has said:

"Visit to the mosques every morning and evening is like going for Jihad (i.e., struggle or fight for the sake of Allah)."

He (S.A.W.) has further said: "Those who go to the mosque at the break of dawn, shall have full light around them on the Day of Judgement."

And further "Each step of the worshipper who goes for the congregational prayers in the mosque, earns a virtue and erases a sin." *(Ibn Habban)*

The Mosque is to be Kept Clean and Tidy: Incense should be burn inside the mosque, particularly on Fridays. The Holy Prophet (S.A.W.) says:

> *"It is the job of the people destined for the Paradise to sweep the mosque, keep it clean, to throw out all the dust and litter outside and to burn incense especially on Fridays"* *(Ibn Majah)*

> *He (S.A.W.) further said: "Clearing the litter of the mosque is like the meter (payment of dowry) of a Houri with beautiful eyes."* *(Tibrani)*

Sancity of the Mosque: One must not enter the mosque nor should one pass through it unless one is neat and clean. If unavoidable, one should perform Tayammum and then enter or pass through the mosque.

While Entering the Mosque: You should wear a sober and dignified department. As soon as you enter the mosque, call the greeting "As-salamo Alaikum" (Peace be upon you), take your seat and start praying in such a way which may inspire you with the greatness and sublimity of Allah.

Entering the mosque unconsciously, talking and laughing loosely is a characteristic of careless and insolent persons whose hearts do not harbour any fear or respect for Allah. Some peoplerun to the mosque in order to join the Imam in the prayer from the very start and not to miss any part. This is against the etiquette of respect due to the mosque. Whether you miss any part of the prayer or not, you should go to the mosque with dignity, poise and humility and refrain from running.

The Mosque is not a Place for Irreligious Business: Be seated in the mosque peacefully and with poise. Making noise in the mosque, cutting jokes, discussing daily life affairs, or asking and telling market prices, etc., amounts to desecration of the mosque. The mosque is the House of Allah; one should pray there.

Small children who do not know about the respect to be given to the mosque and who are likely to urinate, defecate and spit there should not accompany the worshippers to the mosque.

Grown up Children should be Taken to the Mosque: Mothers should encourage their children to go there; this would create love for the mosque in them. Children should be treated very tenderly and affectionately in the mosque. If they do something wrong or commit some mischief, they should be gently advised rather than chided. They should be taught the advantages of good behaviour.

Do not Make the Mosque a Thoroughfare: Once an individual has entered the mosque, it is incumbent upon him to offer prayers there or recite the Quran.

If a Worshipper has Lost Something Outside: Its loss should not be announced within the mosque. If such an announcement was ever made in the mosque of the Holy Prophet (S.A.W.) he would feel displeased, and used to say: "May Allah not give thee the thing thou hast lost."

How to Eenter and Leave the Mosque: While entering the mosque, the right foot is to he put in first, and recite the following prayer:

O Allah! open the doors of Your favours for me.

Two rakats nafl (voluntary) prayer should be offered on entering the mosque. These two nawafil are known as "Tahiyyat al-masjid" (Greetings for the mosque), On returning from a journey, one should go to the mosque first and offer two rakats of nafl prayers, and then go home. This is based upon the Sunnah (practice) of the Holy Prophet (S.A.W.).

When leaving the mosque, the left foot should he put out first and the following prayer be recited.

Allah! I ask Thee for Thy favours and munificence.
(Muslim)

Proper arrangements should be made for calls for prayers and congregation in the mosque. Appoint such persons as callers for prayers (Muazzins) and Imams to lead in prayers, who are the best as regards their piety and morality. As far as possible, the callers and the Imams should perform their tasks without any return for the sake of reward in the Hereafter.

Deviors of Imamat: If you happen to be an Imam to lead in prayers, lead the prayers, keeping in view all the requirements of the office of the Imam. Keep in view the convenience of the congregation. The Holy Prophet (S.A.W.) has said:

> *"Imams who lead the assembly in prayers well and believe that they are responsible for the prayers of the congregations, are rewarded with the recompense of the prayers of the assembly, and the Imam becomes entitled for as much recompense as that of the persons praying under his leadership. The recompense of the latter is, however, not reduced.* *(Tibrani)*

The Call for Prayer: Start preparations for prayers immediately after hearing the call, perform ablution and reach the mosque early; sit quietly in the line and wait for the congregation to be formed. It is an action reminiscent of the munafiqs (hypocrites) to show lethargy after the call, mark time and to go to the mosque unwillingly. Sound the call for prayer with ardour and zeal. A person asked the Holy Prophet (S.A.W.) "O Prophet of Allah! Tell me something that may help me to go to the heaven." The Holy Prophet (S.A.W.) said:

> *"Give call for the prayer." And further: "As far as the voice of the* Muazzin *can reach, people hearing his call will testify in favour of the* Muazzin *on the Day of Reckoning. If a shepherd announces a prayercall in the jungle, all the things which have heard him, on the Day of Judgement shall stand witness for him."(Bukhari)*

Prayer to be Recited after the Adaan: The Holy Prophet (S.A.W.) has said that anyone who offers the following prayer after having heard the Adaan, shall invariably have the intercession of the Holy Prophet (S.A.W.) on the Day of Judgement:

> *"Allah the Master of this perfect call and this assembly of prayer! Bestow upon Muhammad 'al Waseelah' and grant him that high position which Thou hadst promised him."*

Adaan and your Response Thereto: When the caller (Muazzin) is calling for the prayer, the listeners should repeat the call and when he says "Hayya 'alass Salah" and "Hayya 'ala al-Falah ", the listeners should respond with, (La hawla wala quwwata illa bil lahil-Azim). "There is no power nor strength except that of Allah the Great." When the Muazzin during the early morning call says "As-Salatu Khairum Min An-Naum". Prayer is better than sleep," the listener should say: "Sadaqta wa bararta" "You have uttered the truth and good thing."

When Lining up for Prayer: When the reciter of the "Takbir" says: "Qad Qamatis salah" (verily, the prayer has stood), the listener should say: *"Aqamaha-Allaho wa Adamaha"* (May Allah always keep it established)

Line up in Congregational Prayers: Be careful about the alignment while offering prayers in congregation and to stand shoulder-to-shoulder in such a way that there may not be a gap in between. A new row should not be formed until the first has been completed.

Performance of Hajj: When your means permit, proceed to the Holy Land for the performance of Hajj, and the same should not be delayed unnecessarily and should be performed, for nobody knows how long he is going to live. The holy Quran has ordained:

> *"And Allah has the right upon people that those who have the means to reach the House of Allah (in Mecca) should go on pilgrimage. And he who refuses to carry out this command, ought to know that Allah is independent of all in the world,"* *(3: 97)*

What greater misfortune can there be for a person than that Allah may forsake him: The Hadith has it:

> *"He who intends to perform Hajj, should do it expeditiously, for it is quite possible that he may fall sick, lose his she-camel (means of transport) or some other contingency may crop up hampering (his journey for) Hajj "* *(Ibn Majah)*

And further:

> *"If a person who has no sickness or some (other) genuine excuse and is not, prevented by a cruel and oppressive*

ruler and still he does not perform Hajj, it is immaterial whether he dies as a Jew or as Christian."

(Sunan Kubra, Vol. IV)

And Hadrat Umar (R.A.A.) was once heard saying: "I sometimes feel like imposing Jizya on those who avoid going to Hajj despite having the means for the same; they are not Muslims, they are not Muslims."

Hajj to be Performed for the Pleasure of Allah Only: The House of Allah is to be visited and Hajj performed only in order to please Him, and',this pious intention should not be polluted with any worldly motive. In the Quran we are told:

"And do not obstruct those persons who are going to the venerable house in search of Allah's mercy and pleasure."

(5: 2)

At another place Allah has commanded:

"Perform Hajj and Umrah for the pleasure of Allah alone." *(2: 196)*

The Holy Prophet (S.A.W.) said: "The recompense for Hajj Mabrur is not less than that of Paradise."

(Muslim, Kitab al-Hajj)

Hajj Mabrur is that pilgrimage which is undertaken only to please Allah and performed with all the rules and rituals observing faithfully.

Proceed on the pilgrimage of Hajj without any fanfare or publicity. You should leave quietly and return quietly, desisting from all acts that would show publicity and self-advertisement. Although the criterion for a pious act, is the fact that it is done only for the sake of Allah and nothing else, yet, this factor is more pronounced in the case of *Hajj* which is considered as an act of self-purgation, purification of mind and soul, and spiritual refreshing. It is all the more important as it is the last chance for the spiritual treatment for those who are in search of salvation and, if one is not spiritually cured by it, there is little hope for his cure by any other method.

Yearning to visit Holy Land Even if, it is beyond your means to proceed on pilgrimage, you should still keep your heart inspired with the burning desire of visiting the mosque of the Holy Prophet (S.A.W.) and having the honour of, preforming Hajj, and keel your soul alive with the spirit of sacrifice established by Hadrat Ibrahim (A.S.) The Holy Prophet (S.A.W.) in this context, has said: "Those proceeding on Umrah and Hajj are the special guests of Allah. Allah accepts their prayers and grants them redemption, if prayed for." (Tibrani)

The best travelling provision one takes with him on Hajj is that of piety. In this holy journey one who fears Allah and tries hard to win His pleasure and avoids His disobedience, shall benefit from the blessings of Huy. The Holy Quran says:

"And for (Hajj) take travelling provisions, and the best (provision) is piety." (2: 197)

Once you have made up your mind to perform Hajj, you should start making preparations for the same with all the mental devotion and earnestness. You should recall acid enact the history and traditions of Hajj fonder over every rite and details of the Hajj and try to understand what the religion of Allah want; to create and the heart of a true believer Through these rituals And then a true and conscious Muslim try to imbibe the spirit of Hajj and with full awareness remould your life accordingly.

Allah says:

"And remember Allah as He has guided you to remember Him. And it is a fact that in the past you I had gone astray." (2: 198)

To achieve this objective a deeper study of those parts of the Quran wherein are described the spirit and importance of Hajj is useful. A study of the traditions and of literature describing the history and rituals of Hajj is also necessary.

The prayers offered during Hajj contained in the literature on Hadis should be memorized and recited. Supplicate to Allah in the words of the Holy Prophet (S.A.W.)

Do not impair your Hajj by any sinful act. Be careful that your Hajj does not become like a show piece of the people hankering after the world, and who have no regard or interest far the hereafter. Allah has said about these people:

> *"Our Lord ! Give unto us in this world"; Such (world loving) people have no share in the Hereafter.(2: 200)*

Hajj is the means through which you should solicit Allah's blessings and munificence in the world and the Hereafter and pray in these words:

> *Our Lord ! Give Unto us what is good in this world and also what is good in the Hereafter; and guard us from the agony of Fire (Hell). (2: 201)*

Be very particular to avoid the slightest disobedience of the commands of Allah during Hajj. This pilgrimage is a journey to the House of Allah, and you are His guest. You have gone there to affirm your oath of allegiance and servitude. By touching the Black Stone (*Hajar-i-Aswad*), you are holding the hand of Allah pledging your fidelity, and your kissing the stone is like kissing the Threshold of Allah. By repeatedly chanting Takbir (Allah-o-Akbar) and Tahlil (La ilahail-lal-lah) you are proclaiming your fidelity flow disgusting even the idea of sinfulness in such circumstances. Allah has cautioned those who approach His House in these words:

> *"There is (to be) no lewdness nor abuse nor angry conversations on the pilgrimage. (2: 197)*

You should abstain from quarrels bickerings during Hajj. When during the pilgrimage there is large gathering of pilgrims causing troubles at various places, conflicts, annoyance and irritation, you as the guest of Allah, should display broad-mindedness, self-sacrifice, restraint, kindness and magnanimity towards everybody. You should not even rebuke your personal servant.

You should scrupulously avoid all talks and thoughts relating to sexual matters. You should be particularly careful during your journey when there will be chance of getting excited and the eyes becoming freer and covetous. If your mate accompanies you, not only sexual contact but oven things that are likely to whip up sexual sentiments are to be avoided. Allah has cautioned in these words:

"The months of pilgrimage are known to everybody. And therefore, whoever intends to perform Hajj should remember that there is (to be) no lewdness nor abuse nor quarrel during the Hajj." *(2: 197)*

And the Holy Prophet (S.A.W.) has said:

"He who has come to perform pilgrimage to the house of Allah, and has saved himself from immoral or sexual acts and also from lewdness, returns home purified like a newly born baby." (Bukhari-Muslim)

Obey all commands and carry out all rituals that have been ordained by Allah in order to have the awareness and knowledge of some spiritual reality. This thing is known as the Shariah of which the plural is Shaair. Allah has said in the Quran:

"O ye who believe! Profane not Allah's monuments (the symbols of Allah's worship) nor the sacred months, nor lay your hands upon animals ear-marked for sacrifice, nor those animals which have been dedicated to Allah and have bands in their necks as distinguishing mark, nor obstruct persons repairing the sacred House seeking the grace and pleasure of Allah. (5:2)

And in Surah Al-Hajj it has been said:

"And one who honours the symbols of Allah's worship, which have been prescribed by Allah, then this is matter of piety of the hearts." (22: 32)

Utmost humility, want and submissivness should be expressed in the performance of the rituals of Hajj. Allah likes the expression of the virtues of humility and submission by his servants. On being asked as to who is Haji (Pilgrim), the Holy Prophet (S.A.W.) said, "a pilgrim is one whose hair is dishevelled and bears a dust-ridden appearance."

Recitation of Talbiyah Having put on the Ahram, loudly recite Talbiyah after every prayer, while climbing every ascent or descending a slope or meeting another carvan, and when waking up each morning. The Talbiyah is as follows:

"Here I am! O Allah here I am! Thou hast no partner, here I am. Verily, all praises are only for Thee. All the

gifts are Thine: All sovereignty is Thine. Thou hast no partner."

Prayers and Supplications in Arafat Most Important Ritual of Hajj: On reaching the plain of Arafat, you should supplicate and solicit Allah's mercies and forgiveness for sins to the maximum extent.

The Holy Prophet (S.A.W.) has said:

"The day of Arafat is the best before Allah. He especially directs His attention to the world on that day and takes pride (Pleasure) on the humility and submissiveness of the pilgrims and says to the angels: 'O angels! See how my bewildered servants are standing in the sun in my presence. From afar have they come here, in the hope of my munificence although they have not witnessed My wrath." Having expressed His pride in His servants, He orders their redemption from Hell. On no day are so many persons redeemed as on the Day of Arafat."

(Ibn Habban)

***Sacrifice at Mina*:** On return to Mina, you should offer sacrifice with the same sentiments that governed Prophet Ibrahim (A.S.), the friend of Allah, when he placed his knife upon the neck of his beloved sun Prophet Ismail (A.S.) and this spirit of sacrifice should henceforth govern all your activities in life, you should be prepared to offer sacrifices in all fields of your life, and your actual way of living may reflect this picture:

Verily, my prayers, my sacrifice, my life and my death are for only One Allah, who is the Sustainer of the worlds, and Who has no partner." *(7: 163-164)*

You should remember Allah throughout the Hajj period and do not let his remembrance go out of your mind. Remembrance of Allah is the substance of all prayers and supplications, as Allah says in the Quran:

"Keep busy in remembering Allah during the appointed days." *(2: 203)*

And further in Surah *Al-Baqarah:*

"And when you have completed your rituals of Hajj, then remember Allah as you remembered your forefathers, or even more than them." *(2: 200)*

It is the aim of the Arkan (rituals) of Hajj that you should be continuously absorbed in the remembrance and so deep into your thoughts that no other worldly activities and attractions may distract you from this remembrance. During the pre-Islamic days, the Arabs, having performed Hajj used to engage themselves in talking tall and boasting about their ancestors. Allah has commanded that (instead of this) He should be remembered in these days, and His Greatness alone is worthy of being narrated, for He is really the Great.

The *tawaf* (circumambulation) of the House of Allah should be performed with great love and devotion. Allah has ordained, "And you ought to circumambulate the old house (of Allah)." (22: 29)

The Holy Prophet (S.A.W.) has said:

"Allah showers one hundred and twenty blessings each day for the Hajj pilgrims. Out of these sixty blessing are for those who circumambulate it, forty for those who offer prayers (at the Kaaba) and twenty for those who merely gaze at it."

And the Holy Prophet (S.A.W.) has also said:

"One who has circumambulated the House of Allah fifty times, has been washed all of his sins as if he is born only today." *(Tirmidhi)*

3

Natural Faith

Like other divine religions, Islam also keeps the reform of man's self as the first item in its programme of reforms. It makes the human self as the first target of its efforts and sows the seeds of the Islamic teachings in its depths, so that self and training become inseparable. The teachings of the Prophets lasted till the Doomsday and around them gathered the group of faithful people. Its secret was this that the self of man was the objective of all its work and it was the axis of all its activities. Their teachings were not like something externally pasted that they could be separated from men in the movements of their daily life. These were not like the paint or varnish that could be worn out by the passage of time. They had imbibed their principles and teachings into the depths of man's hearts, which had turned into a very strong power that could keep it safe from the wickedness of men's nature and could rule over their decisions.

Many times some divine religions raised objections against the society and its culture and governments and its nature, and also presented remedies for the ills which had appeared in these quarters. In spite of this, the nature of all the divine religions has been this that they kept righteous self as the basis of all their programmes of reform, and considered firm and strong moral character as a permanent guarantee for the establishment and upkeep of every civilization.

But this does not mean that the importance of those who are striving for the construction of a better government and society is being reduced, or that their efforts are considered to be less important. No. Not at all. Here an attempt is being made to make the people realize the value of the reform of man's self for the safety of life and for the security of healthy and virtuous living.

The self that has become wicked can only spread disruption and disorder in the system of government, and can make use of the enforcement of the laws of that system for meeting its mean and wicked objectives. But a purified and noble self will perform the responsible task of stitching the tears in the garment of the environment and repairing it. It will try to enhance society's greatness and decency. It will consider it its responsibility to bring in regularity in the use of power, and to remove all kinds of defects from the government.

It is like a judge. If he is well trained and decent, he can reform the defects of the law by his selfless decisions and just orders. But a cruel and unkind judge can show indifference to the correct commands and authorities. Same is the condition of the self, when it is confronted with my ideas and views about world, and personal likes and interests.

That is why the reform of the self is the first foundation pillar of the supremacy of virtue in this life.

If no attention is paid to the reform of the individuals (selves), this world becomes the dominion of the dark forces, men's present and future will be ruled by corruption. That is why Allah says:

> *"Verily, Allah will never change the condition of a people until they change it themselves. But when Allah wills a people's punishment, there can be no turning it back, nor will they find, beside Him any to protect."*
>
> *(Raad: 11)*

Stating the cause of the corrupt communities, Allah says:

> *"Like (the deeds of) the people of Pharaoh and of those before them ; they rejected the signs of Allah and Allah punished them for their crimes ; for Allah is Strong and Strict in punishment; because Allah will never change the Grace which He has bestowed on a people until they change what is in their (own) souls."—(Anfal: 52-53)*

From the viewpoint of reform and training, Islam considers this matter in its two aspects:

The first aspect is this: Every self has a decent and pure nature in itself which rushes towards righteousness and good, and feels happy on getting it. It hates wickedness and evil. It becomes sad and sorry on committing it. It sees the extension and development of its existence and the health of its life in truth and justice.

With this there is its second aspect also. Every self is in its exciting emotions and Satanic inclinations, which turn away from the right path. The present harm is in a glamorous way and throw it into the pit of meanness and lowliness. We are not interested in talking a survey of the principles and elementaries of these harmu inclination from a historical point of view so that it may be ascertained whether these emotions or desires enter the human nature from outside or whether they are ingrained in the nature itself. We are concerned with the fact that both these conditions are found in men, which are locked in mutual struggle for attaining leadership for guiding man's life. And whatever kind of leadership man accepts decides his final destination. Allah says:

'By the soul, and the proportion and the order given to it; and its enlightenment as to its wrong and its right; truly he succeeds who purges it, and he fails who corrupts it."

—*(Shams: 7-10)*

The achievement of Islam is this that it helps man fully, so that he may be able to make his nature strong and firm, he may make its rays more bright and more illuminating, and in its guidance and leadership may successfully complete his long journey of life. Similarly it also prepares man to be free from the ways of wickedness and the inciting of the devil, because these try to mislead him and turn him away from the right path, and finally cause him to fall from his high rank.

GOD'S RELIGION

Islam has called itself a 'Natural Religion' which is free from all these impurities

"So (O Prophet !) set your face steadily and truly to the faith. (Establish) Allah's nature on which He has framed mankind. There is no change in what Allah has created; that is the standard religion ; but most among mankind do not understand." *—(Rum: 30)*

The function of the eye is to see until there is some disturbance in it. The ear hears the sound till it becomes deaf. The function of the nature is to follow the right path, and to rush towards it with such alacrity as the water rushes down from a height, unless it is overcome by corruption and wickedness, which may take its reins in hands and turn it away from the path of righteousness and blessings.

The disturbing things which corrupt nature are sometimes the result of the past centuries or sometimes they are the creation of the lowly environment and habits and customs, or both these things together are responsible for the disturbances. These things are a great danger for the nature of man. They cause a variety of diseases in it.

The real Jihad of a reformer is to fight these inhibitions and customs and to weaken their strength. He tries to relieve Nature of these dangers in order that its original purity may be regained and it may be able to fulfil its real responsibility. Islam has given a full clarification of this method.

After explaining the natural religion in the above quoted verses, the holy Quran says immediately thereafter:

"Turn back in repentance to Him, and fear Him ; Establish regular prayers, and be not you among those who join gods with Allah, those who split up and become sects, each party rejoicing in that which is with itself." *—(Rum: 31-32)*

To encourage faith in place of disbelief, righteousness in place of wickedness, to adopt the policy of fearing God, in place of disturbed thoughts in respect of Allah the righteous people's unity of thought and action-these are the manifestations that show that man has remained on the righteous nature.

This has been clarified in the following verse of the Quran:

"We indeed created man in the best of moulds, then we have abased him to be the lowest of the low, except such as believe and do righteous deeds." —*(At-Teen: 4-6)*

What is the best mould or form of man? The understanding of Truth and adopting it, fulfilment of its requirements and meeting of its demands.

This is called the attachment to virtuousness and decency, and consideration of these two good qualities in man's individual and collective life is the real achievement. And attempts to make them operative in all the departments of life is the real mould and form.

But there is a very large number of people who do not reach this high level. They remain attached to the earth only. They follow their own desires, and express disobedience of God's commands. In this way they fall to the lowest level. Quran has called this "Asfala safileen (lowest of the low), to which Allah has thrown such people.

To throw the men of such nature to the lowest level is according to the divine law regarding guidance and transgression. And these laws are true and based on justice. The holy Quran mentions them as under:

"And Allah will not mislead a people after He has guided them, to order that He may make clear to them what to fear (and avoid) for Allah has knowledge of all things." *(Tauba: 115)*

In Surah Araf this law of guidance and transgression has been mentioned thus

"Those who behave arrogantly on the earth in deterrence of right-them I will turn away from My signs; even if they see all the signs, they will not believe in them ; And If they see the way of right conduct, they will not adopt it as the way of error is the way they will adopt ; for they rejected Our signs, and 'failed to take warning from them." *(Aaraf: 146)*

Who is it then that remains on the 'best mould' and keeps himself away from the indignities of the world ? In the verses of the Surah At-Teen occurring immediately after those quoted above the answer is given

"Except such as believe and do the righteous deeds." *(At-Teen)*

In the foregoing pages we have seen that the outcome of Faith and the Righteous Deeds is the excellence of moral character.

ANSWER TO EVILS

Islam's stand vis-a-vis man's pure nature and its strength and firmness has been discussed. As regards its dealings with the devil-like natures, that has also been made clear. Islam warns mischievous-natured people. It entrusts its reins in the hands of the healthy intellect ; it encourages it to bow down to the pure nature and to surrender itself to Allah.

The prophet has hinted at some of these kinds of natures:

"The son of Adam reaches the old age and two of his habits do not leave him. One is greed and the second is the unending succession of hopes." —*(Muslim)*

"The worst evil found in man is the frightening cowardice and the undignifying miserliness." —*(Abu Daud)*

"If the son of Adam is given a valley of gold, he will desire to have another one. And if the other is also given, he will be greedy to have the third one. The hunger of Adam's son will not be satisfied except when his remains are mixed with the dust. And the one who turns to Allah, Allah accepts his repentance." *(Bukhari)*

The holy Quran has mentioned some of the habits in the Surah Ale Imran:

"Fair in the eyes of men is the love of things they covet, women and sons ; heaped up hoards of gold and silver ; horses branded (for blood and excellence) ; and (wealth of) cattle and well-tilled land. Such are the possessions of this world's life ; but in the nearness to Allah is the best of the goals (to return to)." —*(Al-e-Imran: 14)*

The first thing Islam wants man to pay attention to is this that to run after the carnal desires of the self and to follow its unending demands will never satisfy self and make it contented. Truth and right path will not be acceptable to it.

The condition of the self is that when its one desire is satisfied, it immediately demands to have some other desire satisfied. It is always busy in eating, drinking, and having a good time, and greedy with desire to have more and more of everything. It has no hesitation in committing sin and acts of aggression and cruelty. Therefore, Quran has forbidden men to follow the desires that have been considered Haram

> *"Nor follow you the lusts (of your heart), for they will mislead you from the path of Allah; for those who wander astray from the path of Allah, is a penalty grievous, for that they forget the Day of Account."* —*(Saad: 26)*

The policy of the infidels and the necessity of opposing it and its importance have been mentioned in these words:

> *"If the Truth had been in accord with their desires, truly the heavens and the earth and all beings therein would have been in confusion and corruption! Nay, We have sent them their admonition, but they turn away from their admonition."* *(Minimum: 71)*

It is necessary that a distinction be made between the forbidden desires of myself and the lawful desires, because some so-called religious people have mixed up these two very dangerously.

If man wants to enjoy the goods of the world, then there is nothing wrong in it, but it is a very serious error that this kind of lawful demands and desires have also been included in the list of forbidden, wicked acts.

Its consequence is this that man satisfies his lawful and respectable desires, but his conscience becomes like the conscience of those people who accept crimes as lawful and adopt them willingly. In this way their conscience becomes a victim of a great error.

When he realises that he has committed a mistake, and that sin is an inevitable part of his life, then he commits more serious sins and indulges in the strictly forbidden acts. In other words this time he becomes a criminal and a sinner in the real sense of the word.

The holy Quran has paid special attention to this aspect and has very clearly declared the pure desires of the self and the lawful wishes as proper and lawful, and provided it with a chance to use halal and clean things. It declared any interference of narrowness and inhibition in this respectable and lawful sphere by way of any checks on the self as bad and obscene, because it opens the gate for obscene acts and sinning.

> *"O you people I Eat on earth what is lawful (halal) and clean (tayyib) and do not follow the footsteps of Satan. Indeed, he is an open enemy for yours. He will command you (to do) what is evil and indecent and induce you to say about Allah that which you do not know."*
>
> *—(Al-Baqarh: 168-169)*

It is a fact that to put restrictions on the consumptions of what is lawful (halal) and clean (tayyib) is nothing but levelling false charges against Allah, and this thing amounts to evil and indecency which Satan commands men to do.

Islam does not like to repress such natures and inclinations with force and punishment, nor does it want to placate or flatter them, but Islam follows a balanced method which is free of any kind of excess.

Morality Holds the Reins: As the rules and regulations of the healthy nature are secure in faith and reform and they have no connection with heresy and agnosticism, similar is the case of the rebellious natures and habits.

In both the cases only a strong and firm moral character can control it. Where the holy Quran has mentioned man's weakness, his anxiety, his richness and indifference, there it has also made it clear that the remedy of these indignities lies in following the path of religion.

> *"Truly man was created very impatient ; fretful when evil touches him ; and niggardly when good reaches him; not so those devoted to prayer, those who remain steadfast to their prayer ; and those in whose wealth is recognised right for (the needy) who asks him and who*

is prevented (for some reason from asking) ; and those who hold to the Truth of the Day of Judgement ; and those who fear the displeasure of their Lord, for the Lord's displeasure is the opposite of peace and tranquillity ; and those who guard their chastity.

—(Al-Maarij: 19-19)

It is common knowledge that good moral character does not develop suddenly. Nor does it become strong and firm in the beginning. It requires consistency and gradualness. And in strengthening it there come many stages. That is the reason why in its nourishment and growth it is required to perform such acts that have to be repeated. The quality that is developed should have consistency, e.g. prayer, fasting, Hajj, Zakat, and the performance of other forms of worship, confirmation of the Day of the Judgement, and to be fearful of its punishment, etc.

When the rebellious natures insist on their acts and are steadfast on their wrong stance, and continue to attempt to traverse the wrong path from time to time, then to check and prevent it no fixed and temporary remedy can be found.

Their transgression and intensity can be brought to the normal level only by such an activist who is more strong and powerful than they and who may be able to bring them to a balanced level.

The long and short of the discussion is that Islam respects the human nature and considers its teachings as the voice of that nature. It warns the rebellious natures and reforms their point of view. Those forms of worship which have been made compulsory in Islam are such as strengthen the human nature and turn the wind of desires to the right direction. And these forms of worship do not perform their duties satisfactorily and the desired objective cannot be obtained from them unless they generate the excellent moral character and the tendency to exemplary treatment of others.

THE SANCTIONS

To generate goodness in someone by coercion and to call him a man of good moral character is not possible. Similarly no faith can be developed in any person by means of force or terrorism. Only personal and intellectual freedom is the sole basis of responsibility and accountability.

Islam understands this reality and respects it. It builds up its edifice on the foundation of the excellent moral character.

Where is the need for Islam to use force and coercion to bring man to the right path and to make him run towards righteousness, when it has full confidence in the human nature and is certain that if the obstructions before man are removed then the best generation can be developed ?

Goodness is ingrained in the human nature. It does not mean that it cannot do anything except good, but it means that only good can coordinate with his original nature and offer resistance. The nature wants to attach itself to good only and wants to function in its light, like the bird that after getting free from the cage flies round and round in the sky in ecstasy in accordance with its foremost wish.

According to Islam the right method is to break nature's checks and chains. After this when man falls down to the ground, and has no strength to rise and walk, then he should be considered as sick and efforts should be made to treat him.

Islam does not order such kind of sick persons to be thrown out of society, provided his existence is not harmful and damaging to others.

Within the limits of this sphere, Islam fights against moral crimes. At first it imagines that every man wants to lead a decent life and wants to live by the sweat of his brow and enjoy luxuries on what he earns from his own labours, that is he does not depend on thefts and looting.

Then what thing compels him to take to thieving? In order to provide him for the necessities of life, therefore, Islam says that the necessities and the means should be in such abundant quantities that they may make him indifferent and above taking wrong steps.

This is the responsibility of the society. If it is deficient and compels the individual to steal, then the responsibility for this crime falls on the deficient society, and not on the head of the wrong-committing individual.

But if the society provides his requirements, and after this the individual advances in the wrong direction, then the actual condition of the individual should be ascertained before inflicting any penalty (Hudd) on him. Probably there may be such extenuating circumstances that may save him from the punishment. As it is, Islam desires delay in inflicting punishment. The Messenger of Allah his reported to have said: "It is better if the Imam pardons somebody by error than he penalises him by error."

Fixation of Penalties: When after examining the conditions and problems it is ascertained that the individual's nature is bent on rebellion, and that the society which has brought him up and had provided for him is being subjected to his depredations and he wants to repay its kindness with disturbance of peace, then if that society inflicts some penalty on this kind of an individual and wants to cut away that harmful limb, it cannot be criticised or blamed.

The holy Quran has termed a theft deserving the penalty of cutting the hand as the theft of tyranny and corruption, and about such a thief it has stated as under

> *"But if the thief repent after his crime, and amend his conduct, Allah turns to him in forgiveness ; for Allah is Oft-Forgiving, Most Merciful."* —*(Maids: 42)*

The penalty which Islam inflicts is in reality for saving the reformist, welfare, and just society from the damage that a harmful member may cause it. A criminal who repays justice with cruelty and reform with corruption — who would like to consider him deserving of mercy ?

Appeals to the Hearts: I have mentioned this example merely to show that the penalties for moral crimes have not been fixed with a view to generating forcefully goodness in society, nor does it amount to coerce people to follow the right path.

For Islam the better way is to appeal to the hearts of men, to awaken their sleeping nature, to stir their repressed inclination and desire towards progress and perfection, to return them to the presence of God, and to adopt such a method that would have convincing arguments and the sweetness of love and brotherhood. The moral values should be explained and clarified in such a way that the heart may be convinced that it is necessary to adopt them for attaining the good and the righteous qualities.

In such an environment the rule of that law is necessary which helps in nourishing the human capabilities and in developing excellent habits and good moral character.

There is nothing wrong if this useless and profitless limb is cut and thrown away, because in the society we are undertaking farming of various kinds of produce. The purpose is growth and nourishment, whether it may involve the clearance of the wild plants or the thorn bearing shrubs.

The security of the interests of common man and their safety is not a thing of less importance, Therefore, there is no reason for being critical of these penalties which are inflicted by Islam. This thing has been mentioned in the Torah, and all the divine religions have placed emphasis on this.

Responsibility of the Society: According to Islam the society itself plays a very important role in the spread of good or evil that spreads in that society. It (Islam) wants to attain power because it wants, with other things, to form a society in such a way that it may be helpful in encouraging chastity, righteousness, aversion from wickedness, proliferation of good acts, indifference to love for world, steadfastness for the right path and consistency.

The Prophet has told the story of a murderer who wanted to repent for his crimes. He inquired of the address of the greatest learned man of the land. His name was given to him, whom he saw and said

> *"I have committed hundred murders. Is there any chance of repentance for me?" He was told: "What thing can come between you and repentance. Go to a particular place, where some good slaves of Allah reside and are always found worshipping Him. You also join them in*

worshipping, and do not return to your village, because it is a bad place." —*(Bukhari)*

In another version, it is narrated that he went to a monk and related his whole story and placed his difficulty before him. The monk told him

"You have committed a big mistake. How am I concerned with this ? However, there are two villages. One of them is named 'Nasrah' that is supporter of Allah and the other one is named 'Kaffarah' that is rejector of God. The people of Nasrah perform the deeds of the people of the paradise. Any person who follows other methods cannot stay there. The citizens of Kaffarah perform the deeds of the people of the hell. If you stayed there and worked like those people, then there would be no doubt about the acceptance of your repentance." —*(Tibrani)*

For this reason Islam says that for the safety of the healthy nature and for the training and reform of the rebellious tendencies the care and vigilance of the environment is necessary, and in the formation of the good moral character it plays a very important role.

We are sure that if all these aspects are taken care of, then a clean and tidy society can be brought into existence, in which pure qualities and chaste character may be nourished.

Treatment of the Minorities: Every religion has its characteristic symbols, which make it distinct from every other religion.

Undoubtedly there are certain fixed forms of worship in Islam which have been made compulsory for its followers. Besides there are certain values prevalent among the followers which have no relation with the Non-Muslims.

But the moral teachings do not come under this category or within the sphere of this principle. Every Muslim has been made responsible to employ good manners in dealing with all the citizens of the land unhesitatingly. For every Muslim it is necessary that he should be truthful in dealing with the Non-Muslims. Similarly good qualities like charity, keeping one's promise, tolerance, decency, generosity, cooperation, etc. are to be brought into play while dealing with Muslims and Non-Muslims alike.

The holy Quran has commanded us not to indulge in such debates with the Jews and the Christians that may encourage mutual enmity, clashes and quarrels. It says:

> *"And do not indulge in disputation with the people of the Book except in a refined way, unless it be with those of them who inflict wrong, and say: 'We believe in the Revelation which came down to us and in that which came down to you: Our Allah and your Allah is one; and it is to Him we bow'.* *(Ankabut: 46)*

> *And the followers of Moosa and Isa (Moses and Jesus) were asked, expressing wonder, whether they were indulging in this kind of argumentation and polemics? "Say: `Do you argue with us about Allah when He is our Lord as well as your Lord ? We are accountable for our deeds and you for yours ; so we are sincerely (dedicated) to Him'."* *(Baqarah: 139)*

It is a famous incident of the biography of the Prophet that he owed something to a Jew. The Jew demanded repayment and in a very harsh tone said: "O Son of Abdul Muttalib ! You people unnecessarily delay the repayment of your loans." At that place Hadrat Umar bin Al-Khattab was also present. He decided to teach the Jew, who insulted the Prophet, good manners, and drew his sword from the scabbard. But the Messenger of Allah silenced Umar saying: "I and he deserve better treatment. Teach him to demand his money in a better way and advise me to repay it in a refined manner."

Islam has commanded to deal justly and fairly even if the opponent may be a wrong-doer or an infidel.,Allah's Messenger has said:

> *"The prayer of the oppressed is answered. If he is wicked and wrong-doer, his ill effects will go against him."* *(Ahmad)*

In another Hadith it is stated: "Even if the oppressed person is an infidel, there is no obstruction between his prayer and its answer. Give up doubtful things and adopt those matters in which there may be no doubt." In the light of these authorities and the commands, Islam has advised its followers not to maltreat their ideological and religious opponents.

In connection with the insistence on treating the followers of the other religion kindly, there is one more *Hadith:*

> *Hadrat Ibn Umar says that a goat was slaughtered in his house. When he came home he inquired whether the gift was sent to the neighbouring Jew or not? He further says: "I have heard the Messenger of Allah as saying 'Jibbrail' had been regularly insisting on me to treat kindly my neighbours, so much so that I surmised that the neighbour would be made a recipient of the inheritance."* *(Bukhari)*

Similarly Islam has ordered that its followers should be kind to their relatives, even though they may have rejected this religion which they have made their own. Therefore, following the Truth does not mean that the rights of the relatives may be usurped:

> *"And bear them company in this life with justice (and consideration), and follow the way of those who turn to Me (in love); in the end the return of I meaning) of all that you did."* *(Luqman: 15)*

Need of Morality for the Nation and the Country: This discussion was on the importance of morality at the level of individuals. As regards the importance and need of morality at the public and collective level, Islam says that the progress and the survival of the nations, the nourishment and the development of their civilization and culture, and the consolidation of their power and strength depend on morality. If the people have good and excellent moral character, then all these good qualities will be found in them, but if their moral character is a lower level, then kingdom and rule will soon end.

"Nations live till their morality lives. When their moral character declines, they also decline." This reality is fully explained in a Hadith in which the Prophet says to the people of his nation that although they have control over the whole of Arabia, and are in a position to decide the fate of the people of the country, as they hold an important position, their power can be maintained on the pillar of morality only.

Anas bin Malik says: "We were sitting in a house where some members of the Ansar and Muhajir were present. The Messenger of Allah came into the room and everybody tried to make room for him near his own seat. Then he proceeded towards the door and stood taking support of the door and said:

> *"The leaders will be from the Quraish, and I have great right on you and they have also a right on you as they would do. When they would be requested to show mercy, they would show mercy. When they would give a judgment, it would be based on justice. And when they would make a covenant, they would honour it. He who does not do like this, there would be on him the curse of Allah, of the angels and of all the people."*
>
> —*(Tibrani)*

This *Hadith* unambiguously shows that any person, community, nation or government would be deserving of as much honour and respect as they would be the representatives of the best qualities in this world and would be striving to achieve high objectives.

If a government flaunts the label of Islam and Quran but the people are not satisfied with it, if it does not decide their matters justly, if it is not kind to the needy and does not honour its covenants, then it should be understood that in this government Islam and Quran are merely names, and this government is bereft of Islam's basic values and it deserves to be cursed from every corner of the earth and the skies.

Hadrat Hussain narrates that the Messenger of Allah has said:

> *"When Allah wants to deal kindly with a nation, He entrusts its reins in the hands of the wise men, gives wealth to its generous people ; and when He wants to deal with a nation harshly, he entrusts its wealth to its miserly men."* —*(Abu Daud)*

It is a famous saying of Imam Ibn Taimiyah: "Allah guards the justice-loving government, even if it is the government of the infidels, and destroys the tyrant government, even if it is the government of Muslims."

In the light of the holy Book and the Sunnah, morality is the perfect religion and also the perfect world. If any nation loses its honour in the eyes of Allah or commands no respect among the people, it so happens because of its losing good moral character and becoming deprived of decent and honourable traits.

CELEBRATING THE FEASTS

Feasts in Islam are confined to two occasions: Eid-ul-Fitr (Feast at end of Fast) which immediately follows the month of Ramadan, and Eid-ul-Adha (Feast of Sacrifice) which falls on the tenth day of the month of pilgrimage (Dhul-Hijja). Both are occasions to thank God for having allowed individual and community to fulfil their religious duty.

Observing the Feasts

- Taking a bath on the occasion of the two Feasts is recommended. This can be done any time after midnight preceding the Feast day.
- A Muslim should dress well and wear a pleasant perfume before leaving for the Feast prayers.
- Before going to pray in the morning on the day of Eid-ul-Fitr, eating some dates, or sweets, is recommended.
- It is preferable not to eat anything on the day of Eid-ul-Adha until performing the Feast prayer in the morning; then one should return home, slaughter an animal, and prepare the Feast meal.
- Walking to the place of the Feast prayer is recommended unless it is too far away to do so.
- The Feast congregational prayer is usually not performed in the mosque, unless it is raining. To perform it in an open square is recommended.
- It is recommended that the whole Muslim community, with the exception of invalids and the disabled, should gather in the open square for the Feast prayer. This

includes menstruating women, who may be present at the occasion but who may not participate in the prayer.

- It is strongly recommended to wait and listen to the Feast khutbah given by the imam.
- When going back to his home after the prayer a Muslim should return by a different road from the one he took when going to the prayer. This will provide him with an opportunity to meet a larger number of Muslims than would otherwise be the case.
- One should take the initiative and congratulate Muslims on this occasion by saying: Taqabbal Allah minna wa minkum (May God accept the work we have done for His sake).
- The rules of conduct and behaviour in the mosque, must be followed here as well.
- Fasting on the day of Eid-ul-Fitr or during the three days following the day of Eid-ul-Adha is forbidden.
- A Muslim should dress his children beautifully, buy them sweets, and help them to celebrate and experience the occasion. This is necessary to help them identify with their Islamic culture.
- A Muslim must avoid doing anything that would annoy his family or dampen their good spirits and spoil their good humour on this occasion.
- Fathers and responsible persons should ensure on such occasions that Islamic law is adhered to, as these Feasts are to thank God and not to indulge in disobedience to Him. Thus, such things as mixing of the sexes, etc. should not occur, although such happy occasions could easily give rise to the wish to do so.

Behaviour on Eid-ul-Adha: Eid-ul-Adha lasts two days after the day of sacrifice, which falls on the tenth day of the lunar Islamic month of Dhul-Hijja.

- It is recommended, whether one is a pilgrim or not, that every family offer a sacrifice on this occasion. By sacrifice is meant the slaughtering of certain kinds of animals.

- The sacrificial animal should be chosen from healthy stock. An animal whose ear or tongue has been clipped, whose horns have been broken, or who is crippled, should not be selected; the animal should be more than one year old; if sheep, goat, cow or ox, more than two years; and if camel or she-camel, more than five years.
- The sacrificial animal is replaceable by alms equal to the cost of the animal.
- The sacrifice may be a sheep, a goat, a cow, or a camel. A cow or a camel serves for seven people, who share with one another the sacrifice.
- The correct time for slaughtering is upon return from the Feast prayer. Therefore, slaughtering should be avoided before that time, since that will not be considered a sacrifice. If one sacrifice is made before the prayer, another sacrifice may be made after the prayer.
- If a person can slaughter well, then it is recommended that he performs the slaughtering himself, otherwise he should entrust someone to slaughter on his behalf.
- When slaughtering the sacrifice the knife must be sharp, the animal must face towards the Kaaba and God's name must be mentioned, saying: Bismillah, Allah Akbar (In the name of Allah, Allah is most Great).
- A sacrifice may be slaughtered at home, though it is preferable, if possible, to perform the slaughtering in the open square where the prayer was performed.
- Parts of the animal may be eaten or kept by the person making the sacrifice. A large part of it, however, should be given to the poor. Something may also be given to the relatives of the person making the sacrifice.
- The time of slaughtering sacrifices lasts three days including the first day of the feast.
- Selling any part of the sacrificial animal or giving any part of it, including the hide, to the butcher or person who slaughtered it, in payment, is forbidden.

Special Instructions for Eid-ul-Fitr

- Zakat or Sadaqah al-Fitr must be given by every financially able Muslim on the occasion of breaking the fast of the month of Ramadan.
- Zakat al-Fitr should also be given for those who are supported by a Muslim, such as his wife and children.
- Giving the above-mentioned alms to the poor must be done before the Muslims go out to pray the Feast prayer. This will enable the poor to participate in the festival. However, if one forgets to pay Zakat al-Fitr before the prayer, it must be paid as soon as possible afterwards.

ATTITUDE TOWARDS ANIMALS

Mercy and Kindness

- Mercy and kindness should characterize all aspects of the treatment of animals.
- Animals should carry loads according to their strength and capability.
- Slaughtering animals should be carried out skilfully and perfectly, so that an animal is not tortured in the process.
- As mentioned in the rules of travelling, when passing with a beast through an area where there is grass and water, a traveller should proceed slowly. When, on the other hand, he is passing through a barren, or desert area, he should proceed quickly.
- Killing non-useful but nevertheless unharmful animals or insects, such as moths or small birds, should be avoided.
- Slaughtering animals who produce milk, eggs, etc. should be postponed for as long as possible.
- Castrating (emasculating) animals or spaying the female is forbidden in Islam.
- Killing some types of creatures should be avoided, unless they become harmful, such as bees, ants, hoopoes and frogs.

- One should not hesitate to kill the following four types of creatures: scorpions, mice, snakes and geckos.
- To refrain from killing snakes out of superstition indicates a weak faith.
- To cross a horse and a donkey in order to produce a mule should be avoided.
- To use gold or silver in an animal's saddle or bridle, or in a dog's line, or to bedeck an animal with silk, is forbidden, for it is a waste of money and betrays arrogance and pride.
- To brand an animal on the face is forbidden. Branding an animal on any other part of its body is allowed, provided no harm is done to it, and branding is confined to necessary limits.
- When beating an animal, striking its face must be avoided.
- To set animals against each other, such as cocks, oxen or sheep, for the sake of fun or for any other reason, is completely forbidden in Islam and considered an act of cruelty.
- It is not allowed to sell or buy an animal which is still in need of its mother. If such a transaction has already been carried out, it must be annulled.
- When hunting birds or animals, hunting young animals still in need of their mothers should be avoided; likewise killing a mother who has young ones should be avoided, as the young ones would then die.
- Hunting animals during hajj or Umrah is forbidden. If it should happen that a Muslim does hunt or kill an animal or bird while performing hajj or Umrah, then it is his duty to make special atonement.
- Animals which feed on filth should be avoided for meat and for riding. Neither should their milk be used until the animals have been confined to clean fodder for a sufficient period.
- If a Muslim owns livestock, birds or animals, then it is his responsibility before God to feed them and to take care of them.

- Using an animal as a target for shooting practise with a gun or bow is forbidden.
- To seek refuge in God from the devil whenever one hears a donkey braying is a recommended act.
- A Muslim should ask God to bless him whenever he hears a rooster crow.
- Every animal is created for a certain purpose such as milking, riding, etc. Therefore, animals should be used according to their purpose.
- Dismembering a dead animal is forbidden.
- One should never curse an animal.
- Animals are of two kinds, clean and unclean. Unclean animals are dogs and pigs. When a dog drinks out of a vessel, it must be washed seven times, using earth once.
- A dog may not be owned by a Muslim except for two reasons: (a) as a watch-dog; (b) as a hunting dog. The place for such dogs, however, is outside the house, not inside.

4

Spreading the Message

And who is better in speech than him who calleth towards Allah, And Doeth Right and sayeth. Lo! I am of those who surrender (unto Him). (41: 33)

CONVERGING IDEOLOGY

1. Develop full appreciation of the position conferred upon you. You are the successor to the mission of the Holy Prophet [S.A.W.] and you have to discharge the same duty of communicating the message of Allah, testifying the truth through your practical life and propagating the teachings of Islam which the Holy Prophet [S.A.W.] performed all through his holy life. Try to develop the same degree of zeal and fervour for the propagation of Islam which was the unique and distinctive characteristic of the Holy Prophet [S.A.W.].

The Holy Quran affirms: "He hath chosen you and hath not put you in any hardship in the matter of faith; follow the faith of your father Ibrahim. He hath given you the nomenclature of Muslim long ago and in this (Scripture) too, that the Prophet of Allah [S.A.W.] may testify the truth before you and that you may stand witness to the whole of Mankind."

In other words, the Muslims are the successors to the mission of the Holy Prophet of Allah [S.A.W.] and required, therefore, to discharge the same duty which the Apostle of Allah performed during his auspicious life. In the same manner as the final Prophet of Allah [S.A.W.] struggled day and night by his words and action and made the way of total submission to Allah clear to the people, the adherents to Islam have also to preach Islam, the religion of Allah, to all the people of the world and what is more, they have to practise it in their every day life and testify.

Call to Religion and prove it the religion of truth with the same high sense of duty and missionary zeal.

2. Always keep in view your real position in this world and constantly endeavour to order your life accordingly. You are not like the other people of the world. Allah has conferred on you a distinction and a privilege. You have been vested with the honour of leading the affairs of the world. You don't believe in extremes and are expected to keep yourself firm on the straight path of Allah with moderation.

   The Holy Quran affirms: "Thus we have appointed you a middle nation that ye may be witnesses against mankind and that the Messenger may be a witness against you." (2: 143)

3. Seek knowledge of the real purpose and aim of your life and try to achieve it with confidence and conviction. The real mission and task before the Muslims is to establish and enforce the religion as a whole which the Holy Prophet Muhammad [S.A.W.] communicated to the mankind-a religion which contains divine guidance and injunctions in each and every aspect of life such as beliefs and worship, morality, and social, economic and political spheres etc. The Holy Prophet [S.A.W.] during his auspicious days enforced Islam with all its details. The Holy Prophet [S.A.W.] taught beliefs, principles of morality and the modes of worship; he [S.A.W.] established and organised a society on the principles of Islam and brought about countless favours and blessings to the people.

Allah has affirmed:

"He hath ordained for you that religion which He commended unto Nuh, and that which We inspire in Thee (Muhammad), and that which We commended

unto Ibrahim and Moses and Jesus saying: Establish the religion and be not divided therein." *(42: 13)*

4. Always remain determined to eliminate evil and establish good. This is an obligation you owe to your faith to justify your existence as upholders of the truth. Live to achieve this aim and idea serving this mission. Allah has named you as the best people on earth only because you live to uphold the truth and sacrifice even your life for this noble cause.

"Ye are the best Community that hath been raised up for mankind. Ye enjoin right conduct and forbid indecency and ye believe in Allah." *(3: 110)*

The Holy Prophet [S.A.W.] has affirmed:

"I swear by Him Who has power over my life you must enforce virtue and curb evil, otherwise Allah shall send very soon such calamity over you that you will cry and seek mercy from Allah but you will get no response." *(Tirmidhi)*

5. Develop, missionary zeal and exemplary fervour and enthusiasm for the propagation of the message of Allah and to save the people of Allah from the fearful torment of Hell. The Holy Quran has acknowledged the unique fervour and abounding zeal of the Holy Prophet [S.A.W.] in the following words:

"Yet it may be, if they believer not in this statement, that thou wilt torment thy soul with grief for them." (18: 6)

The Holy Prophet [S.A.W.] has himself described his feeling in these words:

"I am like a person who lit a fire and when the surrounding area became bright with light, the moths and insects began to drop in fire. The person is now trying with all the force at his command to stop these moths and insects from dropping in the fire, but the moths and insects are rushing towards the fire rendering all his efforts ineffective. Likewise, I am trying my level best to draw you back and keep you away from the fire, yet you are bent upon falling in it." *(Mishkat)*

One day Hadrat 'Aishah [R.A.A.] submitted to the Holy Prophet [S.A.W.]: "O Prophet of Allah [S.A.W.]! Have you passed a harder day than the day of Uhud in your life?" The Holy Prophet [S.A.W.] observed: "Yes, 'Aishah! The day of *'Aqabah* was the hardest in my life." This was the day when, dismayed with the people of Mecca, the Holy Prophet [S.A.W.] had visited Taif to convey the message of Allah to the people there. Their chief 'Abd Yalil set ruffians after the Prophet [S.A.W.] who hurled stones at him in response to his message of blessing and salvation. The Prophet of Allah [S.A.W.] sustained serious injuries. His whole body was stained with blood and he fainted. Deeply grieved and frustrated, the Holy Prophet. [S.A.W.] returned to Mecca. When the Prophet [S.A.W.] arrived at Qarn Aththaalib, he had overcome his grief. Allah sent the angel of calamity to the Prophet [S.A.W.]. The angel of torture submitted: "O Prophet of Allah [S.A.W.]! If you wish I shall collide Abu Qubais with Jabal Ahmar and crush all the wicked between the two mountains. The benefactor of the world [S.A.W.] observed:

> *"No, no, let me warn my people of the torments of Allah. May Allah open their hearts to accept the truth and concede to the Divine Guidance or else their succeeding generation may submit to the truth." (Bukhari, Muslim)*

The Meccans were constantly busy conspiring against the Holy Prophet [S.A.W.]. Some said that the Prophet [S.A.W.] should be exiled from the city while others counselled that he should be assassinated. In the mean time a famine struck Mecca. It was such a terrible calamity that the Quraish were constrained to eat leaves and bark of the trees. The children suffered from the terrible agony of hunger and the elder felt restless but helpless over the affliction of their children.

The benefactor of the mankind [S.A.W.] was deeply moved by the heart rending distress of the people. His devoted companions [R.A.A.] could not bear the grief and uneasiness of the Holy Prophet [S.A.W.]. The Holy Prophet [S.A.W.] conveyed his heartfelt sympathy to his deadly foes who had always been after him to harm and tease him and its unhappy memories were still fresh in his mind. The Holy Prophet [S.A.W.]

sent a sum of five hundred dinars to Abu Sufyan and an equal amount to Safwan with the instruction that the money should be distributed among the famine-stricken people.

Truly speaking, to be sorry for the misguided, to feel disturbed over their wickedness and distress, to be anxious to save them from the wrath of Allah, to be distressed at their affliction and to have an extraordinary craving for their right guidance-such are the attributes of a missionary of truth which create irresistible attraction in his life and an impression uncommon in history.

6. Serve your people with selfless devotion and do not ask for any recompense for your devotion from anybody. Do whatever good you can only to win the favour of Allah and expect reward and blessings from Him only. The desire to earn the favour of Allah and to demand reward and blessings from Him alone lends weight to a man's word and makes him dynamic. Allah has always been-and will remain for ever. He neither sleeps, nor dozes off. No move or activity of man is hidden from Him. He never lets the reward of any of His devotees go waste. He pays more than ones labour and never deprives any one of His blessings. The Prophets (peace be upon them) repeatedly observed to their people:

"I demand not any reward or recompense from you. My reward lies with the Lord of the worlds."

Do acquire a deep understanding of Islam and be sure that Islam is the only true religion in the eyes of Allah. No mode of worship, except the one enjoined by this true religion has any worth before Allah. Allah holds only that religion as true and valid which He has revealed in the Holy Quran and which the Holy Prophet [S.A.W.] translated into practice during his auspicious life. The Holy Quran enjoins upon the Prophet of Allah [S.A.W.] to make it clear to the people that he had adopted his path with careful deliberation and full awareness.

"Say, this is my way. I call on Allah with sure knowledge, I and whosoever followeth me-Glory be to Allah! and I am not of the idolators." *(12: 108)*

Allah makes clear affirmation:

"And whosoever seeketh as religion other than the surrender (to Allan) it will not be accepted from him and he will be a loser in the Hereafter." (3: 85)

"The only religion unto Allah is the surrender (unto Him)." (3:19)

And beware it is for the performance of this grand task that Allah had sent Prophets (peace be upon them) one after another—and be convinced in your own heart that this wealth of religion which the Almighty has vouchsafed to you is the key to attain excellence and honour in the world and Hereafter. The worldly pomp and show which is transitory and short-lived can not be compared with the eternal and inestimable wealth of religion! The holy Quran affirms:

"And We have bestowed upon you seven oft-repented verses and a great book, the Quran. Hence care not for this mundane wealth Allah, have conferred on others." Addressing the believers of other Revealed Books before Quran, the Holy Quran says:

"Say: O People of the scripture! I guidance till ye observe the Torah and the Gospel and that which was revealed unto you from your Allah." (5: 68)

9. Make constant efforts to grasp the real spirit of religion and the wisdom it contains. The Holy Prophet [S.A.W.] has observed.

"Allah endows, whomsoever He wishes to bless with good the real understanding and deep insight into religion." (Bukhari, Muslim)

As a matter of fact, it is tire real knowledge of religion and insight into the spirit of religion which is the fountain-head of all goodness and the man who is deprived of this goodness is deprived of the blessings of this world as well as of the world Hereafter. Such a man can never achieve balance and consistency in life, nor can he truly represent religion in any walk of life.

10. Whatever you wish to proclaim to the world, address it to your self first. Tell yourself first what you wish to tell

others and perform in your won life what you preach to others. The distinction of a missionary of true religion is that he tries to project in himself the true model of his preachings. His deeds and character stand testimony to his words. He himself yearns for the truths he propagates to other as a source of goodness. Whenever the Prophets (peace be upon them) rose to call the people to surrender themselves before Allah they proclaimed Ana awwalul muslimin (I am the first to surrender before Allah).

Testify by spoken as well as written word that truth is what you represent. Make it evident through your individual life, family relations, social dealings and through your national and political activities that piety can only be developed by adopting the way of life as enunciated by Islam. This system guarantees stability of homes, emergence of a morally oriented society and a culture and civilisation based on justice and equity. Those who ignore the duty of reforming and training their own character and ruminate over the reformation and training of others are completely devoid of common-sense. Their own house is on fire, yet they are carrying about buckets of water looking for a blaze anywhere else to extinguish. Such people are losers not only in this world but in the Hereafter also. Their inaction in this world will render all their preachings ineffective and weightless and in the next world they shall undergo the most deterrent punishment. It is most hateful in the sight of Allah that they do not practise what they preach and tell others to do what they themselves do not do. The Holy Prophet [S.A.W.] has warned such missionaries of Islam who do not do what they preach, of the most fearful punishment. The Holy Prophet [S.A.W.] observed:

> *"A man shall be brought on the Day of Judgement and will be thrown into the Fire. His intestines will spill out due to the Fire. He will then carry around his intestines as a donkey goes round the mill. On seeing him the denizens of hell will gather around him and enquire: "O man, what has become of you! Are you not the one who preached to us in the world to perform virtuous*

deeds? Are you not the one who dissuaded us from the performance of evil acts? How did you come into this place despite having performed such pious deeds?" The man will answer: "I did teach you piety, but never cared for it myself. I forbade you to do evil, but performed evil deeds myself." *(Muslim, Bukhari)*

The portentous account of the night of Ascension which the Holy Prophet [S.A.W.] related to the people contains a warning for the misguided to reform themselves. The Holy Prophet [S.A.W.] observed:

"I beheld some people in the night of Ascension whose lips were being clipped with scissors of fire. I enquired from Jibbrail [A.S.]: "Who are these people?" Jibbrail [A.S.] replied: "They are the orators of your Ummah. They preached piety and fear of Allah to people, but forgot to follow these teachings in their personal lives." *(Mishkat)*

The illustrious companions [R.A.A.] also used to issue stern warnings to such misguided and hypocritical people who did not follow what they preached. On one occasion, a person said to Hadrat 'Abdullah b. 'Abbas [R.A.A.]: "Hadrat I desire to instruct people in piety and forbid them to commit evil deeds. I wish to propagate religion among the people." Hadrat 'Abdullah enquired: "Have you acquired the proper qualifications for becoming a preacher?" The person submitted: "Yes, I believe I am capable of performing the task of a missionary." Hadrat ibn 'Abbas [R.A.A.] observed: "If you do not apprehend any condemnation in the light of three verses of the Holy Quran, do preach Islam." The person enquired: "Which three verses do you mean?" Hadrat ibn 'Abbas [R.A.A.] answered: The first verse is:

'Enjoin ye righteousness upon mankind while ye yourselves forget to practise it.?" *(2: 44)*

Ibn 'Abbas [R.A.A.] then enquired: Do you follow this verse in your practical life fully?" The man replied: "No." Ibn Abbas [R.A.A.] then recited the second verse:

"O ye who believe! Why say ye that which ye do not do? *(61:2)*

Hadrat ibn 'Abbas [R.A.A.] then asked: "Are you sure you are following this verse" The man replied: "No." Hadrat ibn 'Abbas [R.A.A.] observed: The third verse is:

"I desire not to do behind your backs that which I ask you not to do." *(11. 88)*

"Tell me now, have you fully carried out the instruction contained in this verse. The man submitted: "No." Whereupon Hadrat Abdullah observed: "Go then and instruct yourself in piety first and forbid your own self from evil."

11. Perform your prayers with full devotion keeping in view its rules, regulations and conditions. In addition to them also offer supererogatory prayers.

No one can propagate religion without establishing a close communion with Allah. Prayer is the sure means-a means prescribed by Allah Himself-of establishing a deep connection with Allah. Allah affirmed through a revelation to the Holy Prophet [S.A.W.].

"O thou wrapped up in the raiment! Keep vigil the night long, save a little-a half thereof, or abate a little thereof, or add (a little) thereto and chant the Quran in measure, for We shall charge thee with a word of weight."
(74: 1-5)

'Charge thee with a word of weight' implies 'Propagation of the Religion of Truth' and truly this responsibility is the most burdensome and heavy of all duties in the world. In order to be able to discharge this duty, it is important for you to derive strength from prayer and establish a firm connection with Allah.

12. Develop a fondness for and interest in the study of the Holy Quran and recite the Book regularly. Recite the Quran slowly and with deep concentration during the prayers as well as during the period other than prayers. When the Quran is recited with a interest and concentration, it becomes easy to understand and reflect upon the meanings of the Holy Quran. As soon as one starts appreciating the charms of the word of Allah, his interest and inquisitiveness increases and he goes deeper

and deeper in the Book of Allah. The Holy Quran is the only source of guidance and warning. It has been revealed to make the people ponder over its contents and derive benefit from its guidance and warnings, so ponder over the meanings of the Holy Quran and learn wisdom from it. Recite the Quran with a firm determination to mould your own self as well as your society as a whole according to the injunctions of the Holy Quran. Only those can establish the rule of Allah who mould their own thought and action according to the teachings of Quran. He, who forsakes Quran, can no longer maintain his allegiance to the faith, nor can he contribute any way in the struggle to establish Islamic system of life. Readers of the Quran have been advised:

"(This is) a Scripture that We have revealed unto thee, full of blessing-that they may ponder its revelations and that men of understanding may reflect." (38: 30)

Moreover, the readers have been instructed: "Read the Quran slowly with pauses." (73: 4)

The Holy Prophet [S.A.W.] affirmed: "These hearts get rusted as the iron rusts when water is poured over it." The people submitted: "O Holy Prophet [S.A.W.]! Tell us then what cleanses the rust of the hearts?" The Holy Prophet [S.A.W.] observed: "The rust of the hearts is cleansed when one remembers death frequently and secondly studies the Quran often." (Mishkat)

13. Be grateful to Allah under all circumstances. Look towards those who are below you in terms of material prosperity and social status. It will help you develop a sense of gratitude to Allah.

The Holy Prophet [S.A.W.] observed:

"Look at those who are below you in terms of material prosperity and social status. (You will then feel grateful to Allah). Do not look at those who surpass you in material riches, lest you depreciate the bounties and blessings that Allah has conferred upon you (as it may foster ingratitude to Allah)."

14. Abstain from pleasure-seeking and luxurious living. Be a watchdog of truth who is always on guard and never drops vigil.

The Holy Prophet [S.A.W.] observed:

"How can I live at ease or seek pleasure in life when I know that Israfil stands ready with the trumpet close to his mouth, to sound the call for Doomsday to descend as soon as he receives the Command of Allah." Addressing the Believers, Allah affirms in the Holy Quran:

"Make ready for them all thou canst of (armed) force and of horses tethered that thereby ye may dismay the enemy of Allah and your enemy, and others beside them whom ye know not. Allah knoweth them whatsoever ye spend in the way of Allah. It will be repaid to you in full and ye will not be wronged." *(8: 60)*

15. Be prepared to sacrifice everything for the sake of religion and if needed, be prepared even to migrate from your homeland. Check up yourself off and on as to what extent you have developed this devotion. Giving an account of the emigration of Hadrat Ibrahim [A.S.], the Holy Quran has urged believers to be prepared to emigrate and offer sacrifices in the following verses:

"And make mention (O Muhammad) in the scripture of Ibrahim, Lo! he was a saint, a Prophet. When he said unto his father: O my father! Why worshippest thou that which heareth not nor seeth, nor can in aught avail thee? O my father! Lo! there hath come unto me the knowledge that which came not unto thee. So follow me, and I will lead thee on a right path. O my father! Serve not the devil. Lo, the devil is a rebel unto the Beneficent. O my father! Lo! I fear lest a punishment from the Beneficent overtake thee so that thou become a comrade of the devil. He said: Rejectest thou my gods, O Ibrahim! if thou cease not I shall surely stone thee. Depart from me a long while! He said: Peace be unto thee! I shall ask forgiveness of my Allah for thee. Lo! He was ever

gracious unto me, I shall withdraw from you and that unto which ye pray beside Allah and I shall pray unto my Allah. It may be that, in prayer unto my Lord, I shall not be unblest." (19: 41-48)

16. Develop a burning zeal striving in the way of Allah, a spirit of fighting with all your means and soul and a pious desire to attain martyrdom in the cause of Allah. Truly speaking, 'Jihad' is the test of faith and the heart which is devoid of the spirit of Jihad is devoid of faith and right guidance and may be compared to a desolate ruin in the wilderness. It is really a great privilege to be able to reach the field of Jihad and to gain an opportunity of sacrificing one's life and property in the way of Allah. In case, the circumstances prevent you from availing of the opportunity to participate in the Jihad; if you lack means or wherewithal to prove your conviction in the field of Jihad, even then you may be counted among those soldiers in the eyes of Allah, who either attained martyrdom while fighting for His cause or returned from the field as the winners provided your heart is filled with the zeal of setting out in the way of Allah, you always take into account the feelings and sentiments which stir a man to perform heroic deeds in the way of Allah. On his return from the battle of Tabuk, the Holy Prophet [S.A.W.] addressed his illustrious companions [R.A.A.] on the way and observed:

"There are some people left behind in Medina who did set out with you and traversed the valley and remained with you throughout the battle." The companions [R.A.A.] were astonished end submitted: "Did they do all this while staying behind in Medina all the time!" The Holy Prophet [S.A.W.] observed: "Yes, they did all this even while staying behind in Medina all the time, for circumstances forced them to stay back, otherwise they would not have held themselves back of their own accord."

In the Holy Quran, Allah has also praised those people who could not take part in Jihad, despite their burning zeal and were ever afterwards smitten with sorrow over this deprivation.

"Nor unto those whom, when they came to thee (asking that thou shouldst mount them thou didst tell) I cannot find whereupon to mount you. They turned back with eyes flowing with tears, for sorrow that they could not find means to spend." *(9: 92)*

The Holy Prophet [S.A.W.] observed: "The man who died without waging a struggle in the way of Allah or had no yearning in his heart to wage such a struggle, has died in a state of hypocrisy." *(Muslim)*

In fact anybody whose heart is devoid of the spirit of fighting in the way of Allah and of sacrificing his life and resources for the cause of the Almighty is not a true believer.

PREACHING THE FAITH

1. Observe prefect decorum and propriety while preaching and propagating Islam. Adopt such an appropriate, dignified, and calculated technique to communicate your message as to generate fervour and zeal in the listener.

The Holy Quran affirms:

"Call to the way of thy Lord with wisdom and fair exhortation and reason with them in the better way." (16: 125)

This comprehensive verse of the Holy Quran contains instructions regarding three principles:

(i) The call must be made in the most appropriate manner.

(ii) The instruction and guidance must be provided in the best possible way.

(iii) Discussion and reasoning should be fair and courteous.

Calling in a wise manner means to communicate your message according to the situation and circumstances aptitude of the people, their intellect and understanding and their social environments and status. Do not waste this precious treasure of knowledge and wisdom in a haphazard way. Address each class, group or individual according to their ability, capacity, and their mental level. Always start your discussion from such universal truths as are mutually conceded to and pave the way for mutual understanding and agreement.

Arouse one's best sentiments with sincerity and devotion. Create and develop in him an urge and desire to know the truth. Thus he will not only achieve peace of mind but adopt and accept the faith as his own inner urge. It will serve as a source of nourishment for his soul and a tranquiliser for his passions and sentiments.

To be courteous in criticism, and discussion means that you should offer constructive criticism. Your criticism should reflect your earnestness and sincerity. Your style should be so convincing and simple that the intransigence, hate, obstinacy, prejudice or pride may get no inlet. Your approach should be so rational and impressive and your discussion so charming and thought provoking as to make the listener think over your arguments and to feel an irresistible attraction towards the truth. Whenever you feel intransigence in attitude and reasoning, stop discussion and take leave. Propagate religion as a whole and do not add to or expunge anything from its teachings or principles of your own accord. The preacher of Islam has no discretion to project what he thinks fit and to withhold what he does not think fit to project. Allah affirms:

> *"And when Our clear revelations are recited unto them they who look not for the meeting with us say: Bring a lecture other than this, or change it. Say (O Muhammad): It is not for me to change it of my own accord. I only follow that which is inspired in me: Lo' if I disobey my Lord I fair the retribution of an awful day. Say: If Allah had so willed I should not have recited it to you nor would He have made it known to you. I dwelt among you a whole lifetime before it (came to me). Have ye then no sense? Who doeth greater wrong than he who inventeth a lie concerning Allah and denieth His revelations? Lo! the guilty never are successful. (10: 15-17)*

However unfavourable the circumstances may be, the preacher must propagate religion in its true and whole form. It is a hideous crime to introduce innovations into or to make alterations in the principles and teachings ordained by Allah to suit the prevailing trends. The people who are guilty of such alterations are the losers in this world as well as in the world Hereafter. Islam is a religion ordained by Allah who is All Knowing and Omnipotent. His knowledge is eternal and there is nothing beyond His knowledge of whole of this universe right from beginning to the end.

Whatever be the human conquests in the field of science and technology, discoveries and explanations, all are subject to the supreme Will of Allah. Nobody has got any right to make any addition or alteration in the Code of life ordained by Him. So much so that the Holy Prophet [S.A.W.], through whom this code of life has been conveyed to us, has been introduced to us as the most ideal servant of Allah who follows what is ordained to him in letter and spirit and dares not overrule His mandate.

3. Convey the message of Islam in a natural way, so that it may not be taken as an unnatural burden. The people may take it as a remedy for all their ills and sufferings instead of feeling scared and developing hatred against it. You should be so polite and rational in conveying the message of Islam to the people that they may feel an irresistible attraction towards Islam. Hadrat Muawiyyah ibn Hakam [R.A.A.] states: "Once I was saying prayers behind the Holy Prophet [S.A.W.] when a man sneezed. I responded to the sneeze by saying in the course of the prayer. The people began to star at me. I said: "May Allah bless you! Why are you staring at me? The People indicated to me by gestures to keep quiet. I kept quiet. When the prayer was over, the Holy Prophet (peace and blessings of Allah be upon him) and may my father and mother be sacrificed for him, never did I see a better guide and teacher before or after him) neither reproached me, nor beat me, nor blamed me. He only said to me "Look. This is prayer and it is not admissible to talk during the prayer. Prayer is meant to acknowledge the purity, supremacy and exaltedness of Allah to recite the Holy Quran."

4. Be moderate in your writing, speech and conversation while conveying the message and call of Islam so that the listeners may feel hopeful as well as seized with awe. Neither overstress the terrifying aspects of the punishment for sins, lest the people should lose all hopes of mercy from Allah and consider salvation not only difficult but impossible; nor should you present such a rosy and one-sided picture of the kindness and forgiveness of Allah that people become fearless and irresponsible in their actions and feel free to transgress the divine commands trusting upon the Munificence and Forgiving Nature of Allah.

Hadrat 'Ali [R.A.A.] observed:

"The best scholar is he who invites the people to obey and submit before Allah in such a manner that people do not lose hope in Allah; he neither gives them allowances to commit transgressions against the Law of Allah nor makes them fearless of Divine punishment."

5. Observe perseverance and constancy in missionary activities. Continue implementing your programme with fortitude and a high sense of responsibility. Avoid the habit of abandoning your programmes half way and chalking out new schemes. Do little, but do it steadily.

The Holy Prophet [S.A.W.] has observed:

"The best deed is the one which, however little it may be, is done constantly and regularly."

6. Meet all hardships and trials that confront you while preaching and propagating Islam cheerfully and with patience and fortitude:

The Holy Quran affirms:

"And enjoin kindness and forbid iniquity and persevere whatever may befall thee." *(31:17)*

Hardships and difficulties do come in the way of truth and submission to Allah. These trials and hardships strengthen faith in Allah and season one's character and morals. This is why Allah puts those to trial who claim to be His servants and the trial gets harder and harder for those who are better seasoned in faith and devotion.

Allah affirms:

"And most certainly shall We try you by means of same fear, and hunger and loss of worldly goods, lives and fruits, and glad tidings to the patient who, when adversity overtakes them, say: Surely Allah's we are, and unto Him we are to return. It is they, upon whom there are blessings of their Lord and (His) mercy and it is they alone who are guided aright" (2: 155-57)

'Hadrat Saad [R.A.A.] submitted to the Holy Prophet [S.A.W.]: "O Prophet of Allah [S.A.W.]! Which person is put to the severest trial?" The Holy Prophet [S.A.W.] observed:

"The persons who are put to the severest trials are firstly the Prophets of Allah [A.S.], then those who are nearest to the prophets in conviction and devotion, and then those who are next to them in their faith and submission. In fact one is tried according to his conviction and devotion. Whoever is firm in his conviction and devotion is put to a hard test and whoever is weak in faith and submission is confronted with a mild trial and these trials continue till a man is purged of all traces of sin."

(Mishkat)

Recounting his own experience, the Holy Prophet [S.A.W.] observed:

"Never was a man more persecuted in the way of Allah than I was and never was a man more threatened in the way of Allah as I was. We spent thirty days and thirty nights in such state that Bilal [R.A.A.] and I had nothing that a living being could eat, save some little provisions in the small pack which Bilal [R.A.A.] kept under his arm." (Tirmidhi)

The Holy Prophet [S.A.W.] also affirmed:

"And person who will make an effort to be patient shall be granted patience by Allah. And there is no blessing which encompasses more good than patience."

(Bukhari, Muslim)

In fact, trials are essential for strengthening and carrying forward the movement. No movement can achieve success without passing through periods of trial, especially a movement which calls for a universal revolution in human society and plans to raise the social structure of human life on entirely new foundations. Reminiscing about the days when the stone-hearted Meccans were perpetrating endless tortures on the Holy Prophet [S.A.W.] and his illustrious Companions [R.A.A.], Hadrat Khabbab ibn al-Arat [R.A.A.] related:

> *"The Holy Prophet [S.A.W.] was resting with a sheet placed under his sacred head in the shade of Bait-Allah (House of Allah) when we reached his presence with the complaint: "O Prophet of Allah [S.A.W.]! Don't you seek aid for us from Allah! Don't you pray for an end to this oppression! (How long will this period of trial continue and when will it come to an end!) The Holy Prophet [S.A.W.] heard our complaint and observed: There had been people before you who faced unprecedented trials and oppressions. Often one of them was made to stand in a pit, half buried in the ground, and his body was sliced into two parts with a saw like a log of wood, yet the man refused to renounce his faith. Their flesh was pierced through with steel combs till the iron nails reached the bones and the fibres, yet the devotees of Allah did not resign from truth. By Allah, Islam shall prevail and you will see (such a state of peace and security) that a man riding from Sanaa (the Capital of Yemen) to Hadramut will have nothing to fear on the way except Allah. The shepherds will only fear the wolves lest they should carry off their goats. But, alas, you show impatience."* *(Bukhari)*

> *Hadrat Muawiyyah [R.A.A.] relates: "I have heard the Holy Prophet [S.A.W.] observing, "There shall always remain a group among my Ummah who will defend Islam and their faith. Those who do not support them or oppose them shall never be able to destroy or eliminate them till the final word from Allah. These defenders of Faith shall remain firm in their conviction.*
>
> *(Bukhari, Muslim)*

7. Do not show undue toleration, or shower undeserved praise on any one, nor sacrifice principles under any circumstances. In affirmation of a virtue of the believers, the Holy Quran says:

"They deal strictly with the non-believers."

In other words, the believers are extremely strict about matters of religion and principle and under no circumstances do they compromise their principles or tolerate wrongdoing. They can bear anything, but cannot sacrifice their religion or principles. Allah has transmitted through the Holy Prophet [S.A.W.] the following to the Muslims:

"Unto this then summon (O Muhammad). And be thou upright as thou art commanded, and follow not their lusts."

Accommodation for wrongdoing, undue toleration and compromise with falsehood are the weaknesses that destroy one's faith and religion.

The Holy Prophet [S.A.W.] has observed:

"When the tribe of Israel began to transgress the commands of Allah, their learned men checked them, but they did not refrain from their wicked deeds. Their learned men instead of boycotting their society, continued to attend their company and ate and drank with them. Consequently Allah equated these pious Ulamas with the transgressors and cursed them through His Prophets, Hadrat Daud and Hadrat 'Isa [A.S.]. Allah cursed the Israelites because they followed the path of disobedience to Allah and went too far on this way." The reporter of this Tradition 'Abdullah b. Masud [R.A.A.] relates: "The Holy Prophet [S.A.W.] changed his reclining posture and sat erect and observed: No, I swear by Him Who hath power over my life, you will certainly continue to enforce virtue and curb evil and you will hold the hand of the oppressor and bend the tyrant before truth. If you do not act as you must, you too shall assimilate with them and Allah shall withhold all His blessings and

guidance from you and forsake you completely, just as He deprived the Israelites of His clemency.

8. To train and reform your children and to prepare them for the duty of establishing religion is not only your foremost obligation, but a logical sphere of your activity. On the other hand, it is unwise and unnatural to ignore your children and get yourself busy in missionary activities outside. It is a gross negligence and an escape from duty. It is as if you leave your own family writhing in agony of hunger and thirst during famine and go out in search of the needy to distribute grain among them to display your munificence. It shows that you are quite incapable of perceiving the suffering of hunger and thirst and are devoid of the sense of kinship and love; nor can you appreciate the wisdom that lies behind the act of distributing grain. The Holy Quran enjoins upon the believers:

"O Believers! Save yourselves and your families from the fire of Hell."

The Holy Prophet [S.A.W.] has elucidated the same verse as follows:

"Each one of you is a guardian and is charged with a respon-sibility, and each one of you shall be held accountable for those who have been placed under your care. The ruler is a guardian and he shall be held to account for the affairs of his subjects. The husband is the guardian of his family; the woman is the guardian of her husband's home and children. So each one of you is a guardian and charged with a responsibility and each one of you shall be called to account for the affairs of those who have been placed under your care." (Bukhari, Muslim)

9. Expend some care upon reforming and cultivating your neighbours and the people living around you and consider this task as a part of your duty.

The Holy Prophet [S.A.W.] delivered a sermon one day and in the course of his sermon praised some Muslims and then observed: "Why is it so that some people do not impart religious knowledge to their neighbours and do not season them in religion, neither do they warn them of the fearful consequences of their ignorance of religion, nor restrain them from committing evil deeds? And why is it so that some of you do not care to learn religion from their neighbours and do not acquire an understanding of its purpose and spirit, nor do they try to ascertain the fearful consequences of remaining ignorant of religion. By Allah! The people must teach religion to their neighbours and inculcate an understanding of religion in them. The people should guide their neighbours, give them good counsel and restrain them from wrong and evil. Besides, it is the duty of people to learn religion and accept their counsels or else I shall punch them soon." The Holy Prophet [S.A.W.] then descended from the pulpit concluding his sermon.

Those who were present there enquired from each other: Against whom the Holy Prophet [S.A.W.] delivered this warning?" The others said, "The Holy Prophet [S.A.W.] was alluding in his speech to the people of the tribe of Ashar. These people are well-versed in religion, but their neighbours, who live in the Oasis, are ignorant yokels." When the people of the tribe of Ashar came to know of the sermon delivered by the Holy Prophet [S.A.W.] they presented themselves before the Holy Prophet [S.A.W.] and submitted: "O Prophet of Allah [S.A.W.]! You were pleased to shower praise on some people and expressed your displeasure towards us. Kindly let us know what is wrong with us?" The Holy Prophet [S.A.W.] observed: "It is the duty of the people to teach religion to their neighbours; they ought to preach to them, educate them and restrain them from wrong and evil. Likewise it is the duty of the people to learn religion from their neighbours and to accept their counsels. They should also cultivate an understanding of religion, otherwise I shall punish them soon in this world." The people of the tribe of Ashar again submitted: "O Prophet of Allah [S.A.W.]! Should we inculcate the spirit of religion among others?" The Holy Prophet [S.A.W.] observed: "Yes, indeed, it is your duty." Thereupon the people submitted: "O Holy Prophet [S.A.W.]! Allow us a grace period of one year." The Holy Prophet

[S.A.W.] granted them a grace period of one year within which they were to teach religion to their neighbours and inculcate an understanding of religion in them. The Holy Prophet [S.A.W.] then recited the following verses:

> *"Those of the children of Israel who went astray were cursed by the tongue of David, and of Jesus son of Mary. That was because they rebelled and used to transgress. They restrained not one another from the wickedness they did. Verily evil was they used to do." (5: 78,79)*

10. Respect and give due regard to the religious beliefs and sentiments of the people among whom you are performing your pleasant duty of preaching and propagating religion. Do not desecrate the names of their forbears or leaders; neither attack their beliefs, nor denounce their religious doctrines. You should preach your religion in a positive manner with sense and wisdom. Your criticism, instead of provoking the listeners, shall be earnestly aimed at driving home your preachings to them. Impassioned criticism and disparaging speech never succeeds in bringing about the desired change in the addressee. On the other land, there is an ever present danger in this case that feelings of pride in ignorance and prejudice may be ignited in the listener and under their influence he may pass impudent remarks upon Allah and religion and instead of drawing near to religion may go farther astray.

The Holy Quran affirms:

"(O Believers!) Do not revile those whom they call besides Allah lest they should unknowingly take to reviling Allah out of enmity."

11. When you become a missionary for spreading the message of Allah, you should confine your activities to calling people towards Allah and nothing else. Do not call the people of Allah towards anything other than Allah; do not issue your call in the name of a country, people, race, or language; nor call them on behalf of a party. The objective of the believer is to obey the Will

of Allah. Call people towards total submission to Allah and cultivate an assurance among them that the slave's duty is to worship his Creator and Master, be it in the sphere of his individual or family life or in social and political affairs. The slave should obey in all spheres of his life the order of his Lord and Creator and submit to His Law with sincerity and devotion. A Muslim can have no objective before him other than this. He should, therefore call others also to achieve this objective. Whenever a believer should dare turn his back upon the Commands of Allah and set up anything else than obedience to the Will of Allah as his objective, he shall be condemned and rejected in both the worlds.

"Who is better in speech than he who calls people towards Allah, acts righteously and says 'I am surely of those who submit."

THE SETUP

1. Form a strong organisation for propagating religion and make a concentrated and collective struggle to establish Islamic order.

And there must exist at least a group among you which should call people towards goodness enjoining good and prohibit the evils.

"*Al-Khair*" denotes all that is naturally good and which has always been regarded as good by human nature and which has been attested as good by the revealed Books. A comprehensive and systematic form of all that is good and virtuous is the religion of Allah which the Apostles (peace be upon them) have been transmitting to the world in every successive epoch and whose final, complete, authentic and fully preserved form is the Quran and Sunnah which the Holy Prophet Muhammad [S.A.W.] bequeathed to the Ummah. To call people towards this good and to enrich the world with virtue it is imperative that Muslims should form a party and perform this duty in an organised manner. They should forge strong and well-knit front and launch a well-organised and concentrated struggle to eliminate the wrong and evil from every sphere of life. Allah describes this unity and strength of the Muslims with appreciation and praise and lauds their collective and concentrated struggle.

"Verily Allah loves those who fight in His cause arrayed in ranks as though they were a structure cemented with molten lead."

Stressing the importance of collective struggle and advising Muslims to live as an organised body, the Holy Prophet [S.A.W.] observed:

> *"Three men who live in a jungle are forbidden to live together save they choose one from among themselves as their Amir (Chief)."* *(Muntaqa)*

Further the Holy Prophet [S.A.W.] observed:

> *"The person who wishes to secure a dwelling place in the centre of Paradise ought to remain firmly attached to the "Aljamaat" for the devil haunts a single person, but if two persons join together, the devil runs away as far as possible."*

"Al-Jamaat" implies a well-organised society of Muslims which is governed by the rule of Shariah under a Muslim Caliph and the Muslims as a whole agree and concede to his authority and leadership. In such a situation there is no justification, whatsoever, for any Muslim to keep himself away and aloof from such a society. In case such a society and such an organisation does not exist make an all-out concentrated and collective effort to bring about such a society which is called Al-Jamaat in Islamic terminology.

2. Make Islam the foundation of your unity and organisation as the distinguishing feature of an Islamic organisation is nothing but total submission to Allah. Any organisation, unity or alliance based on any thing other than total submission to Allah shall not be termed as Islamic, as it is not based on the foundation of Islam. The real base of brotherhood and bond of unity is Islam and Islam only. Anything other than Islam cannot cement relations of brotherhood and unison. It will rather disperse and disintegrate the people and instead of forming a powerful and well-knit unit and organisation

with singularity of purpose and procedure, they will be divided into several sects and factions.

Call to Religion if you form a party, the only objective before you should be to establish the rule of Allah and all your struggle and efforts should be devoted to achieve this goal only.

The Holy Quran affirms:

"And hold fast all of you together to this rope of Allah and do not separate. And remember Allah's favour unto you how ye were enemies and He made friendship between your hearts so that ye became as brothers by His grace." *(3: 103)*

"The rope of Allah' means Islam, the 'Religion of Allah'. According to the Holy Quran, it is Islam which forms the basis of the unity and organisation for Muslims. Anything else will only divide them into a number of factions instead of uniting and unifying them.

3. Love those working for the cause of Islam from the core of your heart and consider this connection as the most important and the most inestimable of all connections.

Describing the characteristics of the believers, the Holy Quran affirms:

"They will not find folk who believe in Allah and the Last Day loving those who oppose Allah and His Messenger even though they be their fathers or their sons or their brothers or their clan." *(58: 22)*

4. Extend support and counsel to your colleagues in the party and keep alive the spirit of mutual guidance and advice in your party life, for this is the real key to success.

"By the time, surely man is ever in a state of loss except those who believe and do righteous deeds and exhort one another to preach Truth and exhort one another to be steadfast."

5. Observe party discipline with full care, and do not consider it only a means of strengthening your party, but deem it as a religious duty.

Allah affirms:

"They only are true believers who believe in Allah and His Messenger and when they are with him on some common errand go not away until they have asked leave of him. Lo! those who ask leave of thee, those are they who believe in Allah and His Messenger." *(24: 62)*

Party discipline and loyalty and devotion to the leader is not only a legal point, but an important issue. The Holy Quran has affirmed the true faith of those who are loyal to party discipline and in no case abandon their party duty without leave of their leader.

6. Extend sincere cooperation in all the good works that are being carried out by the party and exert yourself to the maximum in this effort. Do not stain the purity of your moral character by entertaining any evil sentiments such as selfishness, or personal motives and self-glorification.

The Holy Quran enjoins upon the believers:

"And cooperate with each other in good works of piety and Allah-fearing."

7. Maintain cordial relations with your colleagues. If at times a difference of opinion arises, resolve the dispute at once and keep your heart clear of any feelings of grudge.

"So fear Allah and maintain cordial relations among yourselves."

8. Obey the Amir of the Islamic Party with all sincerity and in good spirit and remain loyal and devoted to him.

The Holy Prophet (S.A.W.) has observed:

"It is the duty of the Muslims to listen to and obey the order of their leader, regardless of the consideration whether such an order is agreeable or disagreeable to them, provided such an order does not constitute a transgression of Allah's law. In case no such order is issued as is repugnant to Allah's law, it should not be listened to, nor obeyed. *(Bukhari, Muslim)*

Hadrat Tamim Dari reports that the Holy Prophet [S.A.W.] observed:

> *"Religion means devotion and loyalty." The Holy Prophet [S.A.W.] repeated this observation three times. Thereupon we submitted: "Devotion and loyalty to whom?" The Holy Prophet [S.A.W.] observed: "Devotion and loyalty to Allah, His Messenger, His Book, the leaders of Muslims and the mass of Muslims."* *(Muslim)*

9. Avoid party chauvinism, bigotry and factionalism. Cooperate with everyone with an open heart and in good cheer. Esteem those who are working for the cause of religion. Deal with them in good faith and sincerity and consider them as your colleagues and comrades. All those who work for the cause of religion are in reality supporters and helpers of one another. The goal of everyone of them is the glory of religion and all of them wish to serve religion according to their lights. It is auspicious and fruitful to point out each other's faults in a spirit of friendship and understanding and to focus attention on correct mode of thought and action. On the other hand, it is below the dignity and office of the preachers of religion to indulge in such despicable conduct as hatred, friction, envy, grudge, confrontation and hostile propaganda against each other. The character of the preachers must be clear of all these blemishes who sincerely and truly wish to expend their energies and talents in the way of Allah and to render some service to the cause of Islam during their lifetime.

LEADING LIGHTS

1. To lead and guide the Islamic party choose a person who excels others in piety and fear of Allah. Heritage nor wealth is the basis of leadership or eminence in Islam. The best person in Islam is he who fears Allah most.

The Holy Quran affirms:

"O mankind! Lo! We have created you male and female, and have made you nations and tribes so that ye may

know one another. Lo! the noblest of you in the sight of Allah, is the best in conduct." *(49: 13)*

2. Regard the election of a leader as a sacred duty and use your vote as a trust from Allah only in favour of person who in your view is best qualified to discharge the onerous responsibility of leadership.

Allah affirms:

"Lo! Allah Commandeth you that you restore deposits to their owners," *(4: 58)*

This is a precise principle which encompasses all kinds of trusts. In the context of this Chapter 'trusts denote the responsibilities of an Islamic Party i.e. the duty of leadership should be vested by open choice in such a person who is the best qualified among you to discharge the onerous responsibility of leadership. To cast your vote in this case in a partisan spirit or to show undue favour or to act under the influence of other extraneous factors is a breach of trust. The character of a believer must be free from the taint of breach of trust.

3. If you are to lead an Islamic Party, you should be fully conscious of your responsibilities and should discharge your duty with complete honesty, diligence, sense of responsibility and energy.

The Holy Prophet [S.A.W.] observed:

"Allah shall ban the entry of that person into Paradise who is entrusted the duty of administering the affairs of Muslim society and he betrays their trust." *(Bukhari, Muslim)*

The Holy Prophet [S.A.W.] also observed:

"The person who accepts the charge of administering the affairs of Muslims and then does not serve their interests and does not tire himself out in their service to the same extent that he tires himself out to fulfil his own personal needs, Allah shall throw such a man headlong into the fire of Hell." *(Tibrani)*

4. Treat your subordinates with tenderness, affection, fairness and large heartedness so that they may

cooperate with you willingly and Allah may grant your Party the favour of rendering some service to Islam. Describing the virtues of the Holy Prophet [S.A.W.] the Holy Quran says: "It was by the mercy of Allah that thou west lenient with them (O, Muhammad). for if thou hadst been stern and fierce of heart they would have dispersed from round about thee." (3: 159)

Moreover, Allah has urged the Holy Prophet [S.A.W.]: "And lower thy wing (in tenderness) unto these believers who follow thee." (26: 215)

In the course of a speech, Hadrat 'Umar b. Khattab [R.A.A.] remarked: "O people! You owe us a duty to support us sincerely in our absence and assist us in performing deeds of piety." Furthermore he observed: "Officers of the government! No tenderness is greater before Allah and more profitable than the tenderness and leniency shown by the head of the executive. Similarly, no lack of wisdom and ineptness is more damaging, dangerous and despicable than the indiscretion, whimsical nature and haphazard actions of the executive head."

5. Realise the importance of your colleagues. Respect their sentiments and pay due regard to their needs. Treat them in such a fraternal way that they should look upon you as their greatest well-wisher.

Hadrat Malik ibn Hawarith relates: "Once some of us young men who were of the same age group went to stay with the Holy Prophet [S.A.W.] and lived in his auspicious company for twenty days. The Holy Apostle of Allah was no doubt extremely kind and tenderhearted. When the Holy Prophet [S.A.W.] felt that we were homesick, he [S.A.W.] enquired from us: "What relations have you left behind at home?" We submitted details, whereupon the Holy Prophet [S.A.W.] advised us: "You should now return home and live with them and teach them what you have learnt and propagate good deeds among them. Tell them the exact hours of prayers and when the time of prayer approaches, one of you should announce the call and he who excels all others in learning and character among you should lead the prayers."

6. Appreciate the worth and importance of your colleagues and considering them your real assets, take pains to

train them in right earnest. Do not underrate them as poor and destitute nor covet those upon whom Allah has bestowed worldly pomp, grandeur and wealth.

"Restrain thyself along with those who cry unto their Lord at morning and evening, seeking His countenances and let nor thine eyes overlook them desiring the pomp of the life of the world." *(18:29)*

In fact the people who have devoted their lives and resources to the propagation and preaching of religion are the veritable assets of a religious party. The duty of the party leader is to realise the value of these people and concentrate all his attention on their education and training.

7. Settle and execute all party matters in consultation with your colleagues. Try to develop their interest in the party and consolidate their support for the activities of the party. Allah, in praise of the believers, also affirms that they settle their affairs by mutual consultation. "And their affairs are (settled) by mutual consultation."

Allah has urged the Holy Prophet [S.A.W.] to consult his companions in matters of special importance. "And consult them in (important) matters."

8. Display generosity and selflessness in party matters. Do not seek to advance your own or your family's interests in any party matter. On the other hand, show a liberal and unselfish conduct so that your colleagues may always be prepared to make all sacrifices with a willing heart and may not feel disillusioned with the party or severe their connection with it or may not be moved to act with selfish and interested motives. Hadrat Abu Bakr [R.A.A.] once observed to Hadrat 'Umar [R.A.A.]:

"O son of Khattab! I have chosen you and appointed you over Muslims so that you may deal with them with kindness. You have been a companion of the Holy Prophet [S.A.W.]. You know how the Holy Prophet [S.A.W.] used to prefer our interests to his own interest and that of our family to his family, so much so that we often returned as a gift to the Prophet's family whatever we

received from him in excess of our needs and requirements." *(Kitab ul-Khard)*

9. Always avoid partiality and nepotism and never show undue regard and toleration. Hadrat Yazid b. Sufyan [R.A.A.] relates: "When Hadrat Abu Bakr [R.A.A.] appointed me chief of the army and sent me towards Syria, he gave me the following instructions:

'O Yazid! You have some kinsmen and relations. It is possible that you may feel tempted to prefer them to others for appointment to offices of trust. This is what I fear most about you."

The Holy Prophet [S.A.W.] observed: "Allah will accept no compensation or consideration from a person who is responsible for the affairs of the Muslims and appoints a man to an office of authority over Muslims merely on the basis of kinship or friendship, so much so that Allah shall consign the guilty person to Hell." *(Kitab ul-Khard)*

10. Maintain strict party discipline as far as is possible and do not show weakness or leniency in matters of discipline.

Allah affirms:

"So, if they ask thy leave for some affair of theirs, give leave to whom thou wilt of them, and ask for them forgiveness of Allah." *(24: 62)*

In other words, when the members of the party assemble to attend to some party business and later some members begin to seek permission to leave on account of their personal needs or disabilities, it behoves the leader of the party to accept the requests of those people only whose personal needs are really more pressing than the matters confronting them in the meeting or of those whose disabilities justify their leave by canonical law and, therefore, must be considered and conceded.

5

Muslim Festivals

MUHARRAM

Muharram is the first month of the Islamic calendar. It is one of the four sanctified months of the year. Fighting in this month is looked down upon and is often put to the side in respect for Islam. Since the Islamic calendar is lunar, Muharram moves from year to year when compared to the Gregorian calendar. The first day of Muharram is the start of the Islamic New Year. The Festival of Muharram takes place during this month in which Shia Muslims especially commemorate the Battle of Karbala. The commemoration reaches its climax on the tenth day of Muharram, known as Ashurah.

This day is related to the time of Moses when he crossed the Red Sea escaping from the Pharaoh. Sunni Muslims often fast on this sacred day. Later, in the month of Ramadan it is recommended to fast so the day of Ashura is optional. This month of Muharram also has traditions which have no support from Islamic teachings. For example, the celebration of the Muslim new year, and the partying and card giving, etc, associated with it is considered to be a bidah and even haraam to some.

Muharram is so called because it was unlawful to fight during this month; the word is derived from the word 'haram' meaning forbidden. It is held to be the most sacred of all the months. This months is most sacred to the Shi'a community and the fast on the first ten days of the month to commemorate the slaying of Hussain, a grandson of Muhammed, by the

Sunnis. The tenth day is called Ashura, meaning, 'the tenth', and it is a day of voluntary fasting. The Sunnis also fast on the tenth day because they believe that Adam and Eve, heaven and hell, life and death, fate and the pen were created on this day.

The Remembrance of Muharram is an important period of mourning in the Shiaite branch of Islam.

A banner (*aalam*) being carried in a procession during the Remembrance of Muharram in Bahrain. For the duration of the remembrance, it is customary for mosques to provide free meals (*nazar*) on certain nights of the month to all people. These meals are viewed as being special and holy, as they have been consecrated in the name of Husayn, and thus partaking of them is considered an act of communion with God, Husayn, and humanity. In Trinidad and Tobago all ethnic and religious communities participate in the event, locally known as "Hosay".

Many of the events associated with the remembrance take place in congregation halls known as "Hussainia".

The Tenth of Muharram and Ashurah

The Islamic year begins with Muharram ul Haram, the first month of the Hijri Calendar. While followers of other religions spend their opening month in worthless merriment, the first month of Islam teaches us lessons of admonition, good counselling, knowledge of Allah Ta'ala, sacrifice, selflessness, patience and seeking the pleasure of Allah Ta'ala.

The tenth day of Muharram (Ashurah) has many distinctive qualities and features. Allah Ta'ala created the heavens and the earth on this blessed day. On this day He gave His infinite blessings and bounties to many of His Prophets and delivered them from the clutches of their enemies.

Allah Ta'ala created Hazrat Adam (Alaihis-Salam) in this month, pardoned him of his mistake, and Hazrat Noah's (Alaihis-Salam) Ark landed successfully on Mount Judi, and he saved Hazrat Ibrahim (Alaihis-Salam) from fire and rescued Hazrat Musa (Alaihis-Salam) from Pharaoh. On the first of Muharram offer 2 rakats Nafl prayer. In each rakat after Surah Fateha recite Surah Ikhlas 3 times. After the Salam pray to Allah Ta'ala for all your needs and desires. From the blessing of this prayer, Allah Ta'ala will appoint an angel for such a person. The angel will guide him or her to do only good deeds and prevent them in engaging in sinful acts.

On the eve of "Ashurah" offer 100 rakats Nafl. In each rakat recite Surah Ikhlas 3 times after Surah Fateha. After Salam recite first 'Kalimah' 100 times. Allah Ta'ala will forgive all the sins of such a person.

Dua-e-Ashurah-An Insurance for a Year's Life: Hazrat Imam Zainul Abidain (Radi Allah Anhu) reports that who ever recites this dua on the tenth of Muharram, any time after sunrise and before sunset, or listens to its recitation from someone else, Allah Ta'ala will certainly make it an insurance for a years' life for him, by keeping death away from him. However, if one is to become the victim of death in that year, they will by some strange coincidence not remember to recite it.

Nafl Salat for the Eve of Ashurah: On the eve of Ashurah offer 4 rakats Nafl Salat as follows: In every rakat after Surah Fateha recite "Ayetul Kursi" once and Surah Ikhlas 3 times. After completing this Namaz recite Surah Ikhlas 100 times. Allah Ta'ala will purify such a person of all their sins and grant them endless bounties and blessings in paradise.

The Fast of Ashurah: On the 9th and 10th of Muharram, one should fast. If it is not possible to fast on both days, then every effort should be made to fast on the 10th day of Muharram, as there is great reward for this fast. (Muslim Shareef).

The following are some of the desirable acts one should do on the day of Ashurah:

1. To observe fast on this day.
2. To give as much charity as you can afford.
3. To perform Nafl Salat prayers.
4. To recite Surah Ikhlas 1000 times.
5. To visit and be in the company of pious Ulema.
6. To place a hand of affection on an orphan's head.
7. To give generously to one's relatives.

8. To put surma in one's eyes.
9. To take a bath.
10. To cut one's nails.
11. To visit the sick.
12. To establish friendly ties with one's enemies.
13. To recite Dua-e-Ashurah
14. To visit the shrines of Awliyas and the graves of Muslims.

Hazrat Abdullah bin Masood (Radi Allah Anhu), a Companion of the Holy Prophet Muhammad (Sall Allahu Alaihi wa Sallam) reports the following saying of the Messenger of Allah Ta'ala, "Whosoever prepares ample food and drink for his family on this sacred day and delights in feeding them generously, Allah Ta'ala will increase His provisions for that year and place much blessings and good therein."

Imam Hussain (Radi Allah Anhu) and his companions were martyred on the tenth of this month. Like any month in the Islamic Calendar there are in this first Islamic month, many anniversaries which are celebrated every where in the world.

Muharram festival commemorates the martyrdom of Hazrat Imam Hussain, the grandson of the Holy Prophet (peace be upon him). This festival starts at the 1st day of Muharram and lasts for 10 days until 10th of Muharram. Muharram is the first month of Islamic calendar.

During this month, while on a journey, Hazrat Imam Hussain, his family members and a number of his followers were surrounded by the forces of Yazid, the Muslim ruler of the time. During the siege, they were deprived of food and water and many of them were put to death. The incident happened at a place called Karbala in Iraq in 61st year after Hijra. This dispute was result of a disagreement among Muslims on the question of succession after the demise of Hazrat Ali, the fourth caliph.

Some sects of Muslims hold meetings where speeches are made on the happenings of Karbala and on the lives of martyrs. The Shias, however, observe this festival in a different fasion. As Muharram, the first month of the Muslim year, approaches, they put on black clothes, as black is regarded as a color of mourning. Majalis (assemblies) are held every day during the first nine days where shia orators relate the incident of the martyrdom of Hazrat Imam Hussain and his party in a great detail. On the 10th day of Muharram, large processions are formed and the devoted followers parade the streets holding banners and carrying models of the mausoleum of Hazrat Imam Hussain and his people, who fell at Karbala. They show their grief and sorrow by inflicting wounds on their own bodies with sharp metal tied to chain with which they scourge themselves. This is done in order to depict the sufferings of the martyrs. It is a sad occasion and everyone in the procession chants "Ya Hussain", with loud wails of lamentation. Generally a white horse beautifully decorated for the occasion, is also included in the procession, to mark the empty mount of Hazrat Imam Husain after his martyrdom.

During these first ten days of Muharram, drinking posts are also set up temporarily by the Shia community where water and juices are served to all, free of charge.

The 1st of Muharram is New Year's Day, and with it marks the beginning of the Islamic (Hijri) Calendar. Its real significance lies in the major turning point in the course of Islam. As told in the Noble Qur'ân: "Verily the number of months with Allah is twelve months (in a year), so was it ordained by Allah on the Day when He created the heavens and the earth; of them four are Sacred. That is the right religion, so wrong not yourselves therein ...".

Today itself, as we usher in the new year, many of us take the time to at least briefly reflect on the major lessons in the past year and anticipate new experiences in the fresh year of 1422 Hijrah. This is also the day that we should be reminded of the Prophet's last pilgrimage and the message that he wants us to carry in our hearts.

The prophet offered the noon and afternoon prayers in Arafah along with 100,000 worshippers, and the victory of Islaam over blasphemy became decisive and final. Thereafter, the Prophet mounted his camel, and delivered the historical sermon. In it, he had said: "... All mankind is from Adam and

Eve, an Arab has no superiority over a non-Arab nor a non-Arab has any superiority over an Arab, also a white has no superiority over black nor a black has any superiority over white except by piety and good action. Learn that every Muslim is a brother to every Muslim and that the Muslims constitute one brotherhood. Nothing shall be legitimate to a Muslim which belongs to a fellow Muslim unless it was given freely and willingly. Do not, therefore, do injustice to yourselves...".

The Period of mourning is observed in the first month of the Islamic calendar, and it commemorates the death of Hazrat Imam Hussain in the battle of Karbala. Muharram means 'respected'. It is the first month of the Islamic calendar.The first ten days of this month are observed as a period of mourning by Muslims, particularly by those belonging to the Shiah sect, in memory of the tragedy of 680 AD. Hazrat Imam Hussain, the grandson of Muhammad the Prophet was killed in the battle of Karbala. This event, called Muharram, is named after the month in which it took place. The tenth day, called Ashura, is observed as the day for a public expression of their grief and is the most important day of the month.

During the pre-Islamic period in the Arabian penninsula, fighting was prohibited in four months of the year.These months, of which Muharram was one, were considered sacred. This period of inactivity was a necessity in heavily decorated replicas of the tomb of the Imam and his family are made for Muharram the era of warring tribes. The tradition was maintained even after the advent of Islam, though provisions to accommodate and accept war in special situations, like a threat to the sovereignty of an empire, were introduced. The gory battle of Karbala was fought against this law and tradition of Islam. The inhabitants on the banks of rivers Euphrates and Tigris were traditional rivals. Their animosity was contained to some extent by Muhammad. But when his son-in-law Hazrat Ali was the Caliph, the old enmity re-surfaced. Hazrat Ali had two descendants, Hazrat Imam Hussain and Hazrat Imam Hassan. Hussain was the ruler of the part of the empire known today as Iran. The other part in modern Iraq was ruled by the Umayyads. Hussain was called upon by the Shiahs of Kufa, a small town in the Umayyad kingdom, to accept their allegiance and claim his place as the leader of the Islamic community. This was against the wishes of the ruler of Kufa, Yazid, who instructed his governor, Ibn-e-Ziad to take appropriate action. Meanwhile, in response to the call of the Shiahs, Hussain accompanied by his family members, headed for Kufa. When they reached Karbala, enroute to Kufa, the forces of the governor surrounded them and their 70 men. Hussain, his family and his troops were tortured and killed, and Hussain's head was severed and presented to the king. They received no help from the Shiahs of Kufa. This happened on the tenth day of Muharram and it was called Ashura.

To commemorate this tragedy, the 40 days starting from the first day of Muharram to Chehalum, are observedas a period of mourning by the Shiahs. During this period, women foresake alladornments, even their bangles. All kinds of celebration like marriage are disallowed during this period. Shiah Muslims are celibate for these 40 days. The first 10 days however, are the most important and are passionately observed asa period of mourning. During the first nine days of the month, majlish (enacted grief-stricken scenes from the battle of Karbala) are organised in Shiah mosques. Huge Shiah crowds wearing black assemble at imambaras, where plaintive verses in memory of Imam Hussain are recited. These nine days are also spent in making Taziahs. On Ashura, the most important day, processions with Taziahs are taken out in commemoration of the sad event. The procession also includes a well-decorated horse, representing the horse of Imam Hussain. Emotional plays, enacting scenes from the battle of Karbala, are performed by bare-chested Shiah men. They strike their body with chains while some walk with bare feeton burning coals. Crying "hai Hussain hum na rahe", meaning 'Oh Hussain, we were not there', they express their anguish at their in ability to have prevented him from being tortured. By beating themselves, the Shiahs relive the pain Hussain suffered and thus express their sorrow. They also distribute water, soft drinks and fruit juices to passers-by in an effort to quench the thirst of the six-month old son of Hazrat Imam Hussain and many others who are believed to have died asking for water. The Taziah processions from allover the town terminate at the Karbala of the city. Most old habitations with a Muslim tradition have a specially marked place to represent the original Karbala.

The Taziahs are buried there. Sometimes they are dismantled so that they can be used again. Often they are immersed in a river. According to a popular belief among the Shiahs, the mud on the grave of Hazrat Imam Hussain turns blood red on Ashura. Muharram is also a time for making vows. People pledge their promises to the Taziah of Hussain. They can do this in two ways. The first is by sending milk,a soft drink, dates or refined sugar to the craftsman who is making the Taziahs. The craftsman recites the Al-Fatiha breaks a coconut and distributesits water with the soft drink or milk in small cups to those present. The second method of making a vow is by performing an act of penance or self-torture before the Taziah. This is generally practiced by woman who volunteer to stand and watch over the Taziahs for a night or more. They go to the place where it is built, and accompany it through its route to the Karbala. This commitment is performed on the ninth night of the month of Muharram. Some people offer to roll on the ground for a certain distance in front of the Taziah as thanksgiving for favours that have been granted or for wish fulfillment. Though the 10 days of Muharram are a period of mourning for the Sunni sect too, they do not indulge in passion plays and nor do they cry out Hussain Hussain because their tradition stipulates grieving in silence. They keep a two-day roja on the ninth and tenth of the month, wear only black clothes and read the Namaz and AlFatiha five times a day.

Contrary to popular belief, Muharram is not a particular day, but the name of a month that marks the beginning of the year according to the Islamic calendar. Muharram is one of four months that have been designated as holy according to the Islamic calendar, the other three being – Dhul-Qa'adah, Dhul-Hijjah and Rajab.

Fasting in the Month of Muharram: Fasting is advocated in the month of Muharram. The Prophet is believed to have said: "The best fasts after the fasts of Ramadan are those of the month of Muharram." Although the fasts of the month of Muharram are not obligatory, yet one who fasts in these days out of his own will is entitled to a great reward by Allah Almighty. Fasting on the tenth day of Muharram, called Ashura, is particularly important, as it supposed to lead to great rewards. A person does not have to fast for the whole month. On the contrary, each fast during this month has merit.

Muharram – an Auspicious Time: The month of Muharram is also associated with many auspicious events in Islamic history. Allah is supposed to have created the heavens and the earth on this blessed day. On this day He give His infinite blessings and bounties to many of His Prophets and delivered them from the clutches of their enemies.

Allah created Hazrat Adam in this month and pardoned him of his mistake. Hazrat Noah's Ark landed successfully on Mount Judi during this time centuries ago. God is also said to have saved Hazrat Ibrahim from fire and rescued Hazrat Musa from the Pharaoh during the month of Muharram.

You must be wondering what there is to mourn about then? The tenth day of Muharram or Ashura is of supreme importance for Shia Muslims as they celebrate the death anniversary of Hussain, the grandson of the Prophet Muhammad.

The Tragedy at Kerbala: In the month of Muharram many centuries ago, (approximately October 20th 680 A.D.), an event took place in Iraq at a place known as Kerbala on the bank of the river Euphrates.

A large army, which had been mobilised by the Umayyad regime, besieged a group of persons numbering less than a hundred and put them under pressure to pay allegiance to the Caliph of the time and submit to his authority. The Caliph was a man much taken with earthly pleasures that deviated from the Islamic way of life. The small group resisted and a severe battle took place in which they were all killed. The leader of the small band of men who were martyred in Kerbala was none other than Imam Husain, the grandson of the Holy Prophet.

Imam Husain's martyrdom at Kerbala represents a conscious confrontation with anti-Islamic forces and a courageous resistance for a sacred cause. The tragedy was that the one who stood up to defend Islam was cut down in so cruel a manner. It is for this reason that the death of Imam Husain is mourned annually in the Muslim world.

The Observances: "Among the Shias in India the following ceremonies are common, although considerable differences in detail may be observed according to regions. As soon as the new moon appears, people assemble in the imam bara (lit, enclosure of imam), a permanent meeting place built in stone or, as mostly in southern India, they assemble in the 'ashur khanah (lit, ten-day house), a temporary structure. There they recite thefatihah over some sherbat (sweetened, cool drink), rice or sugar in Husain's name. The cool drink is meant to remind the faithful of the terrible thirst Husain and his family and retinue had to suffer. Food and drink are later distributed to the public, especially to the poor. In some places a pit is dug in which a fire is lighted every evening of the festival, and young and old people fence across it with sticks or swords. Or they run around it calling out: Ya'Ali! Ya'Ali! Shah Hasan! Shah Husain! Dulha! Hae Dost! Rahiyo! Oh 'Ali! (Noble Hasan! Noble Husain! Bride-groom! Friend! Stay! Stay!)

"The'ashur khanah is usually draped with black cloth on which texts of the Quran are written. The imam bara, too, will be decorated. Inside are placed the tazian-s or tabuts, wooden structures covered with silver paper, coloured paper and tinsel fringes. They are made with imagination and artistic sense and are meant to represent Husain's mausoleum, erected on the plains of Karbala, or else the Prophet's tomb at Medina or even the Taj Mahal of Agra. Nearby are placed imitations of articles which Husain is supposed to have used at Karbala, e.g., a turban of gold, a sword, a shield, a bow and arrow. There are also'alam-s or standards of different shapes, each one having its own special name and history. Often the 'a lam has the form of a human hand (panjab) fixed on top of the pole. This is the popular emblem representing the five members of the prophet's family: Muhammad, Fatima, 'Au, Hasan and Husain."

Processions and Other Ceremonies: "From the seventh to the tenth of Muharram processions are held to commemorate the martyrdom of Hasan's son, Qasim, who was slain shortly after his wedding, as well as the martyrdom of Husain. Along with the procession goes a white horse (duldul or dhu'l-janah) which represents the horse on which Husain rode, or it refers to the bridal horse of Qasim, who was married to Husain's favourite daughter Fatimat-us-sughra (as distinguished from Fatimah, the daughter of Muhammad), just before the battle of Karbala. With this in mind the people shout at intervals: Bride-groom! Bridegroom! On the eighth day a lance or spear is carried to represent Husain's head, which was carried on the point of a javelin by order of Yazid. In addition to these representations ta 'ziya h-s or tabut-s and standards of Hasan, Husain and Qasim are carried. All the time people beat their breasts, saying: Hasan, Husain! Sometimes the pro-cession halts, and then a group of men and boys, naked from the waist, beat themselves with a bundle of sharp blades so that the blood streams down their backs or, forming a large group, they beat their breasts in a uniform rhythm crying all together: Ya Hasan! Ya Husain! The tenth day is 'ashara 'ashurah. On this day the tabut-s or ta 'ziah-s are either stripped and thrown into the water, or they are taken to a ground set apart for this purpose (called Karbala) and literally buried in specially dug graves.

On the evening of the twelfth day people sit up all night, reading the Quran and reciting marsiyah-s and verses in honour of Husain. On the thirtieth day a quantity of food is cooked and, after saying the fatihah over it, it is given to the poor. With this act of charity the Muharram celebrations end."

The Memory of Karbala: Husain was the second son of Ali ibn Abu Talib and Fatimah bint Muhammad, the last Prophet. He was born in the 4th year after the hijra. His older brother, Hasan was named as the successor to his father, after Ali was murdered in the mosque in Kufah, Iraq. After Ali's death, people pledged their allegiance to Hasan as the khalifa (successor). Soon after he took office, however, Mu'awiyah, who had fought with Ali over the caliphate, formed an army to attack Hasan. In the interests of peace and unity, Hasan handed over the position of khalifa to Mu'awiyah who ruled until his death and passing of the caliphate to his son, Yazid.

Mu'awiyah, who was the son of Abu Sufyan (the arch enemy of Islam until he accepted Islam after the Muslims returned to Makkah), was not well liked among the "religious" Muslims. They disliked his son, Yazid, even more. Yazid's open disregard for Islamic law (shariah) and practices made many Muslims cringe at the thought of him taking the caliphate. Mu'awiyah, however, who insisted on turning the caliphate into a monarchy, pushed people to pledge allegiance to his son. On his deathbed, Mu'awiyah told Yazid not to try to force Imam Husayn to give allegiance to him because this would cause too much trouble. Soon after, in 60 A.H., Mu'awiyah died.

Little time passed before Yazid made it clear to his governors in Madinah that they were to force Imam Husayn to pledge allegiance to him or send Imam Husayn's head to him in Damascus. Representatives of Yazid came to Husayn in Madinah and asked for his allegiance. Imam Husayn asked for some time before he made his decision. In the meantime, he was able to move his family to Makkah where they were protected by the Sacred Precincts, Masjid-al-Haraam. It is forbidden in Islam to harm anything within these precincts.

Many people in the Ummah at that time who were already dissatisfied with the caliphate began to send letters to Imam Husayn urging him to join them in the city of Kufah in Iraq. They swore to defend him to the death and gave their allegiance to him.

To investigate the situation, Imam Husayn sent his cousin, Muslim ibn Aqil to Kufah. After discussing the situation with the people of Kufah, he was killed and beheaded by supporters of Yazid on Wednesday, 9th of Dhul-Hijja, the Day of Arafat, in the year 60 A.H. (680).

It was the time of pilgrimage in Makkah, and Imam Husayn had begun to perform the pilgrimage rites. When he learned that some of Yazid's men had come dressed as pilgrims to kill him in Makkah, he gathered his people together to leave for Iraq. He did not want his blood to be spilled within the sacred precincts and to have the sacred rite of Hajj dishonored by that violence. Thus, he, some members of his family, and a group of followers set out towards Kufah on 8th of Dhul-Hijjah.

As the Imam approached Iraq, he was informed that many of the people who had voiced their support for him had turned and now supported the reign of Yazid, possibly to save their own lives. It was then that many of his representatives, including Muslim Ibn Aqil were abused and killed.

As he and his followers marched closer to Iraq, a person that he met along the way who learned where he was going urged and pleaded with him not to continue his journey towards Kufah, but the Imam replied:

"Servant of God," he answered, "wise decisions are not hidden from me. yet the commands of God, the Exalted, cannot be resisted. By God, (my enemies) will not leave me till they have torn the very heart from the depths of my guts. If they do that, God will cause them to be dominated and humiliated until they become the most humiliated of the factions among nations."

Before the Imam and his followers were able to reach Kufah, Yazid's army surrounded them about 44 miles outside of Kufah in a desert called Karbala. At this point, Yazid's army cut off Imam Husayn's water supply, and his followers began to suffer from extreme thirst. Among these people were members of the Prophet's family, companions, and some women and children.

As the days passed in the month of Muharram, the first month of the new year on the Islamic calendar, Yazid's army, numbering 30,000, closed the circle around Imam Husayn's followers who were suffering from dehydration.

On the tenth day of Muharram, called Ashura, Imam Husayn and his followers went out with less than 100 people to meet the army of 30,000.

Ali Zayn al Abidin, son of Imam Husayn, peace be upon them, reported: When the cavalry began to approach al-Husayn, he raised his hands and said:

"O God, it is You in Whom I trust amid all grief. You are my hope amid all violence. You are my trust and provision in everything that happens to me, (no matter) how much the heart may seem to weaken in it, trickery may seem to diminish (my hope) in it, the friend may seem to desert (me) in it, and the enemy may seem to rejoice in it. It comes upon me through You and when I complain to You of it, it is because of my desire for You, You alone. You have comforted me in (everything) and have revealed its (significance to me). You are the Master of all grace, the Possessor of all goodness and the Ultimate Resort of all desire."

The Imam and his followers fought all day and fell to their deaths fighting in the cause of Allah. That day, all who fought were martyred. Among them were two children of Imam Hasan, and Imam Husayn's five year old child.

"When the Imam himself was ready to fight, he saw his six-month-old baby was dying from thirst. The Imam brought his infant near to the enemy and demanded some water for baby, saying: You want me but not this baby so take him and give him some water. The words of the Imam had not been finished that the thirst of the baby was quenched by a deadly poisoned arrow from the enemy which pinned the baby's neck to the arm of his father. The Imam threw some of his blood toward the sky saying: "O' Lord! Your Husayn has offered whatever You have given him. Bless me by acceptance of this sacrifice." Finally Imam came to the field and fought for a long time and was finally martyred. The army of Yazid having killed Imam Husayn, cut his head and raised it on a lance.

"The army of the enemy, after ending the war, burned the tents of the women and children accompanying the Imam and his companions, and plundered those helpless women. They decapitated the bodies of the martyrs, denuded them and threw them to the ground without burial. Then they moved women and children along with the heads of the martyrs to Kufah. They took with them the daughters and sisters of al-Husayn, peace be on him, together with 'Ali b. al-Husayn, peace be on him. The latter was still sick with a dysentery and was almost on the point of death. The bodies of the martyrs were under the sunshine for three days till a tribe passing that place found them and performed the burial.

"The event of Karbala, the capture of women and children of the Household of Prophet, their being taken as prisoners from town to town, and the speeches made by Zaynab, the daughter of Ali, who was one of the prisoners, became a scandal for the Umayyad Kingdom. Such abuse of the Household of Prophet nullified the propaganda which Muawiyah had built up for years. The scandal reached to the extent that Yazid denounced the actions of his agents in public. That was exactly what Imam Husain wanted to do, otherwise he would not bring women and children with him and sacrifice some, and let the rest to become captives. That was the only way to make a wave in order to awaken the Muslim nation.

"The event of Karbala was a major factor in the overthrow of Umayyad kingdom though its effect was delayed. Among its immediate results were the revolts and rebellions combined with bloody wars which continued for twelve years. During those riots none of the important elements in Karbala could escape revenge and punishment, including Yazid.

The Fast of Aashoorah The tenth day of this sacred month, Muharram is known as Aashoorah. It is one of the most important and blessed days of Allah in the Islaamic calendar. Some ulamaa (scholars) are of the opinion that before the fasts of Ramadhaan were made compulsory, the fast of the day of Aashoorah was compulsory upon the ummah. This is stated in a hadeeth reported by Aaishah radhiyallahu anha that the Holy Prophet sallallahu alayhi wasallam ordered the observance of the fast of Aashoorah. However, when the fast of Ramadhaan became compulsory, then whosoever wished, kept this fast and whosoever desired did not observe this fast. Bukhari Vol.1 Page 268 But, nevertheless the Prophet sallallahu alayhi wasallam continued to fast this day and encouraged his Companions to do the same.

Ibne Abbas radhiyallahu anhu says: I did not see Rasulullah sallallahu alayhi wasallam anxiously await the fast of any day, which he gave preference to over other days, but this day, the day of Aashoorah. Bukhari Vol.1 Page 268 Humayd Ibne Abdur Rahamaan narrates that he heard Muaawiyah Ibne Abi Sufyaan radhiyallahu anhu on the day of 'Aashoorah, during the year he performed hajj, saying on the pulpit: "O the people of Madinah! Where are your ulamaa (scholars)? I heard Rasullullah sallallahu alayhi wasallam saying: This is the day of 'Aashoorah. Allah has not enjoined its fasting on you but I am fasting it. Whosoever wish, keep (this) fast and whosoever desires do not observe (this fast)." Bukhari Vol.1 Page 268. In another hadeeth, Ibne Abbas raahiyallahu anhu narrates that the Holy Prophet sallallaha alayhi wasallam came to Madinah and found the Jews fasting on the day of 'Aashoorah. Hence the Holy Prophet sallallahu alayhi wasallam inquired of them, "What is (the significance of) this day on which you fast?"

They replied, "This is a great day. On this day Allah saved Moosa and his people and drowned Fir'awn and his nation. Thus Moosa alayhis salaam fasted on this day as a token of thanksgiving, therefore we too fast on this day." The Messenger of Allah sallallahu alayhi wasallam said, "We are more worthy of Moosa and nearer to him than you." Thereafter, the Holy Prophet sallallahu alayhi wasallam fasted on this day and ordered (his Companions) that a fast be kept on this day. Muharram is observed by the Shia community of Muslims in commemoration of the martyrdom of Prophet Mohammed's grandson, Imam Hussain, who was killed in the Battle of Karbala in AD 680. The prophet's son-in-law Ali, and Ali's elder son Hassan, are also remembered during this period as having suffered and died for righteous causes.

The word muharram also means respect. The first ten days of the month are observed as a period of mourning. After the death of the Prophet Mohammed, the Quran was considered the final word. The Prophet had named no successor. One faction of his followers believed that succession should remain within Mohammed's family, while another disagreed. After a long dispute, Abu Bakr, a loyal follower of Mohammed, was elected his successor. His reign was peaceful, as was that of his successors.

However, during the reign of Ali, the Prophet's son-in-law, there was opposition from the masses. Ali was assassinated and his elder son Hassan was poisoned. His younger son Hussain, his family and his troops, were tortured and killed, and Hussain's head was severed and presented to the king. The killing of Hussain happened on the tenth day of month of Muharram, and the event was called Ashura. It is now observed as a day for public expression of grief. These circumstances divided the Muslim community into the Shias and the Sunnis. The Shias consider Ali, Hassan and Hussain the rightful successors of Prophet Mohammed and mourn their death during Muharram.

The Shias observe the entire month as a period of mass mourning. There is no celebration or expression of joy of any kind. Women are expected to forsake all adornments. Public enactments of grief, depicting scenes from the Battle of Karbala, are carried out in Shia mosques on the first ten days.

The Shias in India observe certain ceremonies in common, though the details differ considerably. As soon as the new moon appears, people clad in black assemble and recite plaintive verses over sweetened cold drink, in memory of Imam Hussain.

The cool drink is meant to remind people of the terrible thirst Hussain and his family had to suffer. Food and drink are later distributed to the public, especially to the poor. The first nine days are also spent in making bamboo and paper replicas of the martyr's tomb. On Ashura, the tenth day, decorated taziyas, or tombs embellished with precious metals, are carried through the city streets. A horse is led in procession in memory of Hussain's horse, Dul Dul.

Wrestlers and dancers enact scenes depicting the Battle of Karbala. Bare-chested Shia men strike their body with chains or walk barefoot over burning coal while uttering cries of anguish for the torture that Hussain suffered. Apart from reliving his suffering, it is also an expression of the people's inability to save Hussain from the brutalities.

Muharram or the 'sacred month' is the first month of the Islamic or Hegira calendar. The Hadith instructs to observe fasting on the 9th and 10th of this month. Fasting on *Ashura* (the 10th of Muharram) was a *faraz* (obligatory) until fasting in ramadan was made faraz. Both in pre-Islamic times as well as at the time of the Prophet *Muhammad* (Sm), it was *haram* (forbidden) to be in war in this month. Muslims of the Shiah group observe the first ten days of the month as a period of mourning for the death of Imam Husain (R), the grandson of

Hazrat Muhammad (Sm). The tenth day of Muharram is called Ashura. Imam Husain (R) was killed on this day at the hands of the troops of Yazid, the son of Muawiyah, the Umaiyya caliph. Shiahs take out processions with tazia, the replica of the tomb of Imam Husain (R) and they show their grief by clapping on their chests or flagellating themselves with knives or chains. The mourning continues for forty days till the first ten days of the next month Safar. Muharram had been observed since the 10th century. In Bengal also it has been observed for the last few centuries.

The centre of observances of Muharram in Dhaka is the *Husaini* dalan Imambara. As mark of mourning, Shiahs dress in black for at least ten days of Muharram. During this time, they refrain from merrymaking, listening to music, or seeing plays or movies. They also do not arrange weddings during this month. Keeping in mind that Imam Husain (R) and his followers suffered from unavailability of water, some Shiahs refrain from eating fish. During these first ten days of the month, *majlis* (mourning assemblies), are held at the imambaras, separately for men and women.

The story of the martyrdom of Hazrat Husain (R) is told and *marsiyas* (elegies) are sung or recited in the assemblies. At the end of the service, food is distributed to the people. On the seventh of Muharram, *shirni* (special offerings) are made and the people pray for Allah's blessings. Food and fruits in large quantities and varieties are distributed on the occasion. Those who pray for Allah's blessings, pick out a food item, and make a *manat*, or promise, not to eat that food for a year. In case the prayer is deemed accepted, they promise to offer shirni the next year. Along with the shirni, some also offer silver *panja*, the model of an open palm with five fingers that represent the five holy figures, the Prophet Muhammad (Sm), his daughter Fatima (R), his son-in-law Ali (R), and his two grandsons Hassan (R) and Husain (R).Muharram processions were common in Bengal in the 18th century. Horses and elephants were also used in the processions. Processions nowadays are much smaller. In Dhaka, the procession begins at Husaini Dalan and, after winding its way through the streets, terminates at a place designated Karbala on the banks of the Dhanmandi Lake. The replica of *Duldul*, the horse of Imam Husain (R) and the flags in the procession show a symbolic presence of Imam Husain (R). Also latikhela (stick fights) are organised to remind of the battle between the troops of Imam Husain (R) and Yazid. As with other festivals in Bangladesh, Muharram has become an occasion for fairs at various places.

ID-UL-ZUHA

Also called Bakrid, Id-ul-Zuha, is a festival of great rejoice. Special prayers and exchange of greetings and gifts marked the Id-ul-Zuha (Bakrid), the festival of sacrifice, celebrated with traditional fervour and gaiety in India. Id-ul-Zuha is a reminder of Prophet Ibrahim's readiness to sacrifice his son for God's sake. It also marks the completion of Haj (pilgrimage to Mecca). On this day, special 'Dua' is recited by thousands of muslims for peace and prosperity.

It is a commemoration of Hazrat Ibrahim's great test of obedience to Allah, who ordered him to sacrifice the person dearest to him. Ibrahim decided to sacrifice his son Ismail, at Mina, near Mecca. As the great religious leader was on the point of applying the sword to the throat of his dear son, it was revealed to him that the exercise was merely a test of his faith in Allah, and that he could sacrifice a ram instead. On Bakrid, the Muslims go to the mosques in the morning to offer prayers to Allah. and then sacrifice the animal at home. Bakr means 'sheep', and on Bakrid, the affluent sacrifice one animal per member of the family, and distribute two-thirds of the meat among the poor. A full-grown camel, cow, goat or sheep, free from any disease, is sacrificed. Bakrid is also a day for feasting and visiting friends to say Id Mubarak.

It is one of the grandest Muslim festivals, and is also known as *Bakrid*. It fails on the 10th day of the Muslim month Zil-Hijja. There is an interesting story about the celebration. Once Hazrat Ibrahim was ordered by Allah in a dream to sacrifice his dearest thing. To Ibrahim his son was the dearest, So, he decided to sacrifice his son on the altar of Allah. He sought the permission of the members of the family and blindfolded himself so that at the time of sacrifice his love for the son may not deter him from the act. He struck with his sword, but when he removed the fold from his eyes, to his great pleasure and surprise, he found that he had sacrificed a ram instead of his son. Since, then a ram, or goat or a camel is sacrificed and distributed among the neighbours and relatives.

The sacrifice of a ram or goat also symbolizes that man's position in the creation is far more high than any beast, and any sacrifice, however great, is a small thing for the sake of religion and Allah. The sacrificial ram or goat is reared with great care and is kept quite healthy and fat And the man who does the sacrifice must. be a man of a character and deeply religious.

This Muslim festival of sacrifice, Id-ul-Zuha (Arabic) or Bakrid in India is celebrated all over the country. On this day Muslims sacrifice a goat or Bakr (Urdu) to commemorate the sacrifice of Prophet Ibrahim, who willingly agreed to kill his son at the behest of God.

According to Islamic belief, to test Ibrahim's faith, Allah commanded him to sacrifice his son Ismail. He agreed to do it but found his paternal feelings hard to suppress. So he blindfolded himself before putting Ismail on the altar at the mount of Mina near Mecca. When he removed his bandage after performing the act, he saw his son standing in front of him, alive. On the altar lay a slaughtered lamb. This festival coincides with the Haj pilgrimage in Mecca.

Prayers are offered in the mosques and the sacrificial meat is then distributed after the Id prayers. Special delicacies are prepared and served among family and friends on the occasion.

Bakr-Id: The feast of Bakr-Id is an occasion to give and to sacrifice. It is a day to thank the Almighty for one's good fortune and to share it with the less fortunate brethren.

Legend has it that Allah commanded Hazrat Ibrahim (Abraham) to sacrifice his son Ismail on Mount Mina near Mecca. Ibrahim, unable to see himself kill his son, blindfolded himself and carried out the pronouncement of God. When he took off the blindfold, a lamb lay slaughtered on the altar and his son stood there unharmed. Ibrahim understood then that this willingness on Ibrahim's part to give up his only son was what God sought, and not the sacrifice of human flesh and blood. The legend ascertains that all God requires of man is a surrender of his will and self. Like Ibrahim, who willingly surrenders his beloved son to God, a true follower of Islam is expected to sacrifice something that is dear to him.

The animal sacrifices made during Bakr-Id are mainly to provide food to the poor and to commemorate the noble act of Ibrahim. This spirit of sacrifice is what truly underlines the spirit of Bakr-Id. Incidentally, the day also coincides with the day when the holy Quran was declared complete. Bakr-Id is celebrated from the tenth to the twelfth day in the Islamic month of Dhul Hijjah. Every year, while pilgrims to the Mount of Mina make animal sacrifices as part of the pilgrimage rituals, Muslims the world over celebrate Bakr-Id in a similar fashion.

Every true Muslim who possesses wealth equal to or more than 400 grams of gold or is capable of affording two square meals a day, is expected to sacrifice an animal. A goat (also called bakri, hence Bakr-Id), sheep, camel or any other four-legged animal is slaughtered during one of the three days of the festival, and the meat is distributed. The sacrificial offering is divided in three parts-one for the self, another for friends, and the third, most importantly, for the needy. The sacrifice can be offered at any time before the afternoon of the third day.

Festivities mark the first day, when people wear new clothes, offer prayers at the mosque, and greet friends and relatives. Special prayers are offered on all three days. It is said that the celebrations are carried on over three days to ensure that the entire Muslim community partakes in the noble of act of giving and sharing.

Bakr-Id is celebrated all over India with much fervour, as it is in the rest of Islamic world. The name Bakr-Id, however, is most popular in India. In Arabic, the feast is usually referred to as Id-ul-Azha or Id-ul-Zuha.

Besides Hinduism, India is also the home of innumerable other faiths and the religious and cultural diversity of this nation is manifested in the large number of non-Hindu festivals. The sizeable Muslim communities have their Ids in common with Muslims across the world. *Id-ul-Fitr, Id-ul-Zuha* and *Id-i-Milad* are the three festive occasions widely celebrated by Muslims in India.

Id is celebrated with great enthusiasm all over the country, and one can see Muslims of all age groups and from all stratas of society attired in new clothes, visiting mosques to offer *namaaz.*

The tombs of many Sufi saints attract devotees of all religious persuasions, especially during the urs or death anniversaries. The best known urs are centred at tombs in towns like Ajmer, Delhi, Manakpur, Nagore and Dongri.

The Id-ul-Azha commemorates the ordeal of Hazrat Ibrahim, who had been put to a terrible test by God when he was asked to sacrifice whatever was dearest to him and he decided to sacrifice the life of his son. As he was on the point of applying the sword to his son's throat, it was revealed to him that this was meant only to test his faith, and it was enough, if instead he sacrifices only a ram in the name of *Allah*. This is celebrated on the tenth day of *Zilhijja,* when the *Haj* celebrations at Mecca are rounded off by the sacrifice of goats or camels. In India, too, goats and sheep are sacrificed all over the country and prayers are offered.

ID-UL-FITR (RAMZAN ID)

Coming with the new moon, this festival marks the end of Ramzan, the ninth month of the Muslim year. It was during this month that the holy Koran was revealed. Muslims keep a fast every day during this month and on the completion of the period, which is decided by the appearance of the new moon, Id-ul-Fitr is celebrated with great eclat. Prayers are offered in mosques and *Idgahs* and elaborate festivities are held.

ID-I-MILAD (BARAH-WAFAT)

The Prophet was born on the twelfth day of *Rabi-ul-Awwal,* the third month of the Muslim year. His death anniversary also falls on the same day, the word '*barah*' standing for the twelve days of the Prophet's sickness. During these days, sermons are delivered in mosques by learned men, focusing on the life and noble deeds of the Prophet.

In some parts of the country, a ceremony known as *sandal* rite is performed over the symbolic footprints of the Prophet engraved in stone. A representation of '*buraq*', a horse on which the Prophet is believed to have ascended to heaven, is kept near the footprints and anointed with sandal paste or scented powder, and the house and casket containing these are elaborately decorated. Elegies or '*marsiyas*' are sung in memory of the last days of the Prophet. The 12th day or the *Urs* proper is observed quietly, in prayers and alms giving

Id-uz-Zuha or Id-ud-Dhua popularly caller Bakri Id or Id Ebaqr ia a day of thanksgiving to God by means of sacrificing some animal like a goat, sheep, camel or bull. This month of the year which is considered propitious for pilgrimage to Mecca. Id-ul-Zuha or Id-ud-Duha are essential muslim festivals when thousands gather at mosques all over the country to offer prayers.

Id-ul-Fitr popularly known as Id is a festival celebrated on the first day of Shawwal, the tenth month of the Hijmi year since the time of Prophet Mohammed. Fitr means breaking the fast of refraining from fasting, while Id means happiness. The festical thus marks the end of the fast during the preceding month of Ramzan. Muslims regard this month as one of the great bounty from God.

Id-ul-Zuha, the festival of sacrifice popularly known as Bakr Id, is celebrated by Muslims in April/May. It marks the end of Ramzan, the month of fasting. Bakr Id celebrates the devotion of Prophet Abraham (Hazrat Ibrahim), who was willing to sacrifice his only son Ishmael at the behest of God. On this day Muslims sacrifice a goat (bakr in Urdu) to commemorate Hazrat Ibrahim's sacrifice. Two-thirds of the meat is kept by the family and one-third is distributed to the poor after Id prayers. The day is marked with family get-togethers, exchange of gifts and feasting on specially prepared delicacies like biryani, kebabs and kulfi. Id coincides with the Haj pilgrimage at Mecca.

JAMSHED NAVROZ

Over 3000 years ago, Shah Jamshed of the Peshadian dynasty ascended the throne on the Spring Equinox. His descendants, the Parsi community, celebrate it as the New Year, the dawn of a new day (Navroz literally means "new day"). It is celebrated, even today, with prayers and feasting.

In homes, a special spread, Haft-Sinn-the seven S's-is prepared. Seven is considered to be a lucky number and the spread contains seven items that begin with "s" in farsi: sabzeh (home grown sprouts), samanou (wheat germ), sib (apples), sonbol (hyacinth), senjed (sorb tree berry), seer (garlic), somagh (sumac). The table also holds seven foods beginning with 'sh' in Persian, sharab (wine), shakkar (sugar), shir (milk), shirinberej (sweet meat), shirin (sweet), shira (syrup) and shahad (honey); a copy of the Gathas (scriptures); a lit lamp; a mirror; a bowl of water with live fish; a shallow earthenware plate with sprouted wheat or beans (for prosperity); flowers (for colour); a gold or silver coin (for wealth); painted eggs (for productivity); and sweets and rosewater in bowls (for sweetness and happiness). These are meant to symbolize creation and to welcome spring.

Visitors to the house are first led to this table. They are asked to smile into the mirror, so that they may smile throughout the year. They are asked to look at the coin, so that they may have wealth the whole year round. They are sprinkled with rosewater so that they stay fragrant and healthy. After that, they are led to another table for a meal.

6

Islamic Religion and Routine

The Muslims rightfully maintain that Islam is not simply an abstract ideal which is conceived of just for nominal adoration or a stagnant idol to be frequented by admirers every now and then. Islam is a code of life, a living force which is manifest in every aspect of human life. The Muslims also maintain that the individual is the center of gravity and the launching instrument which can put Islam, or any other system for that matter, into full action on a full scale. This is why Islam always begins with the individual and invariably prefers quality to quantity. Let us begin, where Islam begins, with the individual. Let us examine the nature of the individual and find out how Islam views this nature. To clarify things as much as possible, and without getting entangled in philosophical disputes or abstract controversy, we can define man as having two complementary natures which are very intimately interrelated and continually interacting with each other.

These are the inner nature and the outer nature. Or one might say that man has one nature, but with two bridged sections which are hardly separable from each other. One is internal and another external. The internal nature of man refers to the *Ruh* (soul or self or heart) and *'Aql* (mind or power of reasoning or intelligence). In our illustration of the internal nature of man we shall have to deal with two aspects: (1) the spiritual or moral aspect and (2) the intellectual aspect. The rest of man's activities and transactions will have to be classified as the external or outer nature of man. After all, it is a universally admitted fact that man does not live by bread alone.

SPIRITUAL ASPECTS

Islam organizes the spiritual or moral life of man in such a way as to provide him with all the spiritual nourishment needed for piety and righteousness, for safety and peace. The Islamic prescription for the spiritual life of man grants, when faithfully applied, maximum positive results as far as man's spiritual growth and maturity are concerned. The main items in this Islamic prescription are:

1. Prayers (Salah);
2. Zakat or Almsgiving;
3. Fasting (Sawm);
4. Pilgrimage (Hajj);
5. Love for God and His Messenger, love for truth and humanity for the sake of God;
6. Hope and trust in God at all times; and
7. Sacrifice for the sake of God by virtue of actual unselfishness.

Various aspects of these items have already been discussed in some detail, and here we have only to add that without these fundamental elements there can be no true Faith as far as Islam is concerned. The reader is advised to refer to the previous sections of this work.

ACADEMIC ASPECTS

The intellectual nature of man is made up, as already mentioned, of mind or intelligence or reasoning power. To this aspect Islam pays extraordinary attention and builds the intellectual structure of man on the most sound foundations, which may be classified as follows:

1. True knowledge based on clear proofs and indisputable evidence acquired by "experience" or experiment or by both. In this connection it is safe to say, beyond doubt, that the Quran is the first authority to enjoin the zealous quest for knowledge through "experience" as well as experiment, meditation and observation. In fact, it is a Divine injunction incumbent upon every Muslim, male

and female, to seek knowledge in the broadest sense of the word and to search for truth. Nature and the whole universe are open and ever- revealing treasures of knowledge and truth, and the Quran was the first book to point to these rich sources of knowledge. It does not accept inherited "truths" or claimed facts which have no proof or evidence to substantiate them. As far as we know, the Quran was the first Scripture to say intelligently: "Why" and to demand proof in support of any conviction or contention. (Quran 2:111 and 21:24).

The Quran itself is an outstanding intellectual challenge, and it challenges the human intellect to dispute any Quranic truth or to produce anything similar to it. Open any chapter of the Quran and you will find the warmest appeal to the search for knowledge through the infinite sources of nature. Devotion to true knowledge is regarded by Islam as devotion to God in the most compensating sense.

2. The second part of this point is faith in God, an ever-revealing source of knowledge and a spiritual insight into countless fields of thought. In Islam, Faith in God is the cornerstone of the whole religious structure. But in order to make Faith in God valid, Islam requires that it should be founded on unshakable certainty and conviction. These, in turn, cannot be acquired without the proper investment of the intellect. Any stagnant or indifferent mind and any limited vision cannot possibly reach the height of the Most Supreme Truth—God—nor can it attain the real depth of Faith.

Islam does not recognize faith when it is attained through blind imitation, when it is accepted blindly or unquestioningly. This fact is very important as far as the intellectual life of man is concerned. Islam requires Faith in God, and the Quran makes numerous statements calling for Faith in God. But the significance of such statements is not in shelving them in the study room or even in the mind. The significance of such statements is that they constitute a warm invitation and an urgent appeal to the intellect to wake up and think, to ponder and meditate. It is true that the Quran reveals the essential truth and facts about God, yet it is equally true that it does not want man to behave like a lazy heir who makes no effort of his own. It wants man to enrich his intellectual wealth through serious endeavour and honest earning, so that he may become intellectually secure. "Easy come, easy go," and Islam disapproves of easy-coming faith which is bound to be easy-going. Islam wants Faith in God to be effective and permanent, to light every corner in man's heart and to prevail in every aspect of his life. Easy-coming faith cannot possibly do that, and Islam will not accept anything less.

When Islam demands Faith in God on the basis of knowledge and research, it leaves wide open all fields of thought before the intellect to penetrate as far as it can reach. It lays down no restrictions against the free thinker who is seeking knowledge to widen his vision and broaden his mind. It urges him to resort to all methods of knowledge, be they purely rational or experimental. By calling on the intellect in this way, Islam shows its high regard for and confidence in the intellectual abilities of man and wishes to free his mind from the tight shackles and limits of tangibility. It wants to elevate the individual and empower him with self-confidence and Heavenly authority to expand the domain of his mind into all fields of thought: physical and metaphysical, scientific and philosophical, intuitive and experimental, organic and otherwise. That is how Faith in God nourishes the intellect and makes the intellectual life prosperous and productive. When the spiritual and intellectual activities of man are organized according to the teachings of Islam as mentioned above, the internal nature of man becomes sound and healthy. And when man is internally secure and sound, his external life will be of the same nature.

APPARENT ASPECTS

The external nature of man is as complex, subtle and wide as his internal nature. We need to re-emphasize the fact that the soundness of the former is greatly dependent upon that of the latter and vice-versa, because man's complete nature is made up of both aspects. For the sake of clarification, once more, we have to classify the external nature of man into divisions and subdivisions. But we should always bear in mind that any imbalance in the system of human nature may become destructive and fatal. The fact of the matter is that both the internal and external natures of man act and interact responsively, and that Islam has extended its Divine touch to the internal as well as the external aspects of life.

Individual Aspects

Islam deals with the very personal life of man in such a way as to insure his purity and cleanliness and to give him a healthy diet and show him the proper manners of clothing, behaviour, adornment, sports and so on.

Purity and Cleanliness : It is an Islamic injunction that before offering the prayer the Muslim must perform an ablution, unless he has done one earlier and kept it valid. This obligatory ablution is sometimes partial and sometimes complete, depending on his or her condition. If we remember that a Muslim has to offer at least five obligatory prayers every day with a pure heart and mind, a clean body and clothes, on pure ground and with pure intention—we can very well realize the vital effect and beneficial results of this single act for man (cf. Quran 4:43, 5:7).

Diet : To maintain a pure heart and a sound mind, to nourish an aspiring soul and a clean healthy body, special attention should be given to the diet on which man lives. And this is exactly what Islam does. Some superficial or self-deceived persons may imagine that the food and beverages consumed have no direct or important effect on the general condition of the person who fills his stomach regularly. But this is certainly not the viewpoint of Islam, which takes the matter in a most serious way. The general principle of Islam in this respect is this: All substances which are pure in themselves and good for man are lawful for consumption as long as they are taken in moderate quantities. And all substances which are impure and badd or harmful are unlawful under all ordinary circumstances. There is always room and flexibility for exceptions to meet cases of absolute necessity (Quran 7:157; see the section on Islamic Morals above).

Beyond this general principle, there are certain foods and drinks that God has specifically forbidden. Among these are: the meat of dead animals and birds, the flesh of swine an anything slaughtered after the invocation of any name other than that of God (2:173; 5:4). The drinks which Islam considers harmful and destructive to the human spirit and morality, as well as to the physique and morale of man, are included in the Quranic verse which forbids all intoxicants and all forms of gambling or games of chance (5:93-94).

The prohibition of these foods and drinks is not by any means an arbitrary action or a dictatorial decree of God. It is first and foremost a Divine intention in the best interest of man and for his own sake. When the Quran describes these forbidden things as bad, impure and harmful, it has a vigilant eye on man's morality and wisdom, on his health and wealth, on his piety and common behaviour—all of which are invaluable assets in the estimation of Islam. The reasons behind this Divine intention are numerous. They are of a nature that is intellectual and spiritual, moral and mental, physical and economical. The sole purpose is to show man how to develop himself according to an upright course of life in order to be a healthy unit in the structure of the family, then of society, and eventually of humanity at large. Reliable medical doctors and social scientists should be able now to verify the benefits of this Islamic legislation.

Islam is as orthodox and uncompromising on the quality of the organic nourishment of man as it is on his spiritual soundness and intellectual growth. This point is brought to light by the fact that some dietary items are forbidden in kind, as mentioned above, and some in degree. The things which are lawful for the Muslim should be taken in moderate quantities without indulgence or excess (Quran 7:31). After shunning all forbidden items in kind and degree, the Muslim is invited by God to enjoy His gracious provisions and to experience gratitude to the Merciful Provider (2:168, 172; 5:90-91)

Clothing and Adornment : As regards man's clothing and adornment, Islam takes into serious consideration the principles of decency, modesty, chastity and manliness. Anything in clothing or adornment which is incompatible with the attainment, maintenance and development of these qualities is not allowed by Islam. Those materials and fashion which may stimulate arrogance or false pride and vanity are strictly prohibited. So are the adornments which may weaken the morality of man or undermine his manliness. Man should remain loyal to his manly nature, which God has chosen for him, and keep away from that which is likely to weaken or endanger his character. This is the reason why Islam warns men not to use certain clothing materials (i.e., pure silk) and certain precious metals (i.e., gold) for the purpose of adornment. These are things which suit the feminine nature alone. The handsomeness of man is not in wearing precious metals or flaunting pure and natural silken clothes, but in high morality, sweet nature and sound conduct. ' While Islam allows women to use the things which are forbidden for men and which are suitable for the feminine nature alone, Islam does not let them go loose or wander unrestricted. It allows women the things which suit the female nature and, at the same time, cautions them against anything that might abuse or upset that nature. The manner in which women should dress up, beautify themselves, walk and even look is a very delicate question, and Islam pays special attention to this matter. The vision of Islam in this respect is focused on the general welfare of women. Islam has given advice to both men and women to help women in particular retain and develop their dignity and chastity and so be safe from being the subject of idle gossip or vicious rumors and suspicious thoughts. The advice is imparted in these Quranic verses:

> *Say to the believing men that they should lower their gaze and guard their modesty; that will make for greater purity for them. And God is well-acquainted with all that they do. And say to the believing women that they should lower their gaze and guard their modesty; that they should not display their beauty and ornaments except what (must ordinarily) appear thereof; that they should draw their veils over their bosoms and not display their beauty except before their husbands, their fathers . . . (and certain other members of the household); and that*

they should not strike their feet in order to draw attention to their hidden ornaments (24:30-31).

Islam is very sensitive to the manners of clothing and ornamentation. It makes it crystal clear that both men and women should be confined to their respective natures to safeguard their natural instincts and to endow them with modesty and high morality. Prophet Muhammad is reported as having said that God condemns those men who behave or act like women and those women who behave or act like men. Nevertheless, it should be borne in mind that Islam lays no restrictions on the harmless or proper items of clothing and ornaments. In fact, the Quran calls such things the beautiful gifts of God and reproaches those who look upon them as forbidden (7:32-33).

Sports and Amusements : It is gratifying to notice that most of the Islamic forms of worship, such as Prayers, Fasting, Pilgrimage, display some sports-related characteristics, although they are basically and by nature meant for spiritual purposes. But who would deny the constant interaction between the physique and morale of man? Yet that is not all that Islam has to say on the subject of sports and amusements. Anything that provokes sound thinking or refreshes the mind and revitalizes the body with the aim of keeping an individual healthy is encouraged by Islam as long as it does not anticipate or involve any sin, or cause any harm or delay and hamper the fulfilments of other obligations. The general precept in this matter is the statement in which the Prophet said that all believers in God have good qualities but that the strong one is better than the weak one. It is also reported that he approved of those sports and amusements which build up the enduring physique and strengthen the morale.

It is a regrettable mistake to associate with sports and amusements things which are not really sports-related or amusing. Some people consider gambling and drinking as sports and amusements, but this is not the viewpoint of Islam. Life is worth living and is granted to us for a definite purpose. No one is supposed to abuse it by letting it go loose or becoming dependent entirely on luck and chance. So it is no intrusion on or violation of the personal rights of man when Islam extends its Divine touch to organize life even in its very personal aspects. Because life is man's most valuable asset and is designed for noble purposes, Islam has shown man the way to live it properly and enjoyably. Among the measures taken in this respect is the prohibition of gambling, which is really more tension-accelerating than tension-reducing. It is a grave abuse of life to make it subject to luck and mere chance. It is a deviation from the normal course of life if one entrusts his lot to the mad wheel of games and invests his abilities in the most unpredictable moves on a gambling table. To protect man from all of these unnecessary mental strains and shattering of nerves and to enable him to lead a natural life in means as well as in ends, Islam has forbidden all forms of gambling.

Similarly, it is a shameful retreat from reality and an irresponsible insult to the best quality in man—his mind—to get entangled in the tight strands of intoxication or cornered in the vicious whirl of alcohol. The menaces and tragedies of intoxication are too obvious to be elaborated. Many lives are being lost every day on this account. Many families break up because of this menace. Many billions of dollars are swallowed in the drinking channels every year. Countless doors are closed by the misery and unhappiness arising from the consumption of intoxicants. Besides the destruction of health, the depression of mind, the dullness of soul, the absorption of wealth, the disintegration of families, the abuse of human dignity, the sabotage of morality, the humiliating retreat from reality, every so-called social drinker is a highly potential alcoholic.

Islam cannot tolerate these menaces or let man abuse the very sense of life in this tragic way. That is why it does not associate gambling and drinking with good sports and refreshing amusements and has banned them forever. To appreciate this view, one has only to check any news medium, read any medical report, visit any social service agency, or watch any court proceedings. Of all the agonizing social problems, alcoholism is by far the most serious. More than half a million Americans become alcoholics every year. One in every ten to twelve people who take their first drink in any given year is destined to become alcoholic. All of these painful tragedies and real losses speak much louder than any theological or trade arguments.

FAMILIAL ASPECTS

There have been many definitions and descriptions of the family. For our purpose, we shall adopt the following simplified definition. The family is a human social group whose members are bound together by the bond of blood ties and/or the marital relationship. The family bond entails mutual expectations of rights and obligations that are prescribed by religion, enforced by law, and observed by the group members. Accordingly, the family members share certain mutual commitments pertaining to identity and provision, inheritance and counsel, affection for the young and security for the aged, and maximization of effort to ensure the family's continuity in peace.

Thus the foundations of the family in Islam are blood ties and/or marital commitments. Adoption, mutual alliance, clientage, private consent to sexual intimacy, and "common law" or "trial" marriages do not institute an Islamic family. Islam builds the family on solid grounds capable of providing reasonable continuity, true security, and mature intimacy. Its foundations have to be as firm and natural as possible in order to nurture sincere reciprocity and moral gratification. Islam recognizes that there is no more natural relationship than that of blood, and no more wholesome pattern of sexual intimacy than one in which morality and gratification are joined.

Islam recognizes marriage's religious virtue, social necessity, and the social advantages. The normal course of behaviour for the Muslim is to be family oriented and to seek a family of his own. Marriage and the family are central in the Islamic system. There are many passages in the Quran and statements by the Prophet which go as far as to say that when a Muslim marries, he has" perfected half his religion; so let him be God-minded and careful with the other half."

Muslim scholars have interpreted the Quran to mean that marriage is a religious duty, a moral safeguard, and a social commitment. As a religious duty, it must be fulfilled; but like all other duties in Islam, it is enjoined only upon those who are capable of meeting the responsibilities involved.

The Meaning of Marriage : Whatever meanings people assign to marriage, Islam views it as a strong bond *(meethaaqun ghaleez),* a challenging commitment in the fullest sense of the word. It is a commitment to life itself, to society, and to the dignified, meaningful survival of the human race. It is a commitment that married partners make to one another as well as to God. It is the kind of commitment in which they find mutual fulfilments and self-realization, love and peace, compassion and serenity, comfort and hope. All of this is because marriage in Islam is regarded first and foremost as a righteous act, an act of responsible devotion. Sexual control may be a moral triumph, reproduction a social necessity or service, and sound health a gratifying state of mind. Yet these values and purposes of marriage would take on a special meaning and be reinforced if they are intertwined with the idea of God, conceived also as religious commitments, and internalized as divine blessings. And this seems to be the focal point of marriage in Islam. To paraphrase some Quranic verses, the call is addressed to mankind to be dutiful to God, Who "created them from a single soul, and from it or of it created its mate, and from the two of them scattered abroad many men and women" (4:1). It was God Who "created mankind out of one living soul, and created of that soul a spouse so that he might find comfort and rest in her" (7:107). And it is a sign of God that He has "created for men, of themselves, mates to seek in their company peace and tranquillity, and has set between them mutual love and mercy. Surely, in that are signs for those who contemplate" (30:21). Even during the most trying times of married life, and in the midst of legal disputes and litigation, the Quran reminds the parties of God's law by commanding them to be kind to one another, truly charitable toward one another, and, above all, dutiful to God.

It is noteworthy that the Islamic provisions of marriage apply to men and women equally. For example, if celibacy is not recommended for men, it is equally so for women. This is in recognition of the fact that women's needs are equally legitimate and are seriously taken into consideration. In fact, Islam regards marriage to be the normal, natural course for women just as it is for men. It may even be more so for women because it assures them, among other things, of relative economic security. This significant additional advantage for women does not, however, characterize marriage as a purely economic transaction. In fact, the least focal aspect of marriage in Islam is the economic factor, no matter how powerful this may be. The Prophet is reported to have said that a woman is ordinarily sought as wife for her wealth, for her beauty, for the nobility of her stock, or for her religious qualities, but that he who chooses his mate for piety in preference to everything else is blessed and fortunate. The Quran commands marriage to those who are single and the pious even though they may be poor and slaves (24:32). On the other hand, whatever dowry (marriage gifts) a man gives his prospective wife belongs to her, and whatever she may have acquired prior to or after marriage is hers alone. There is no necessary community of the property held by the husband and the wife. Furthermore, it is the husband who is responsible for the maintenance and economic security of the family. He must even provide his wife with the kind of help and service to which she was accustomed before marriage, and, according to some scholars, she is under no *legal* obligation to do the routine housework, although she may do so, and usually does, for some reason or other (i.e., cooperation, economy, etc.)

The Permanence of Marriage : Because Islam considers marriage a very serious commitment, it has prescribed certain measures to make the marital bond as permanent as humanly possible. The parties must strive to meet the conditions of proper age, general compatibility, reasonable dowry, good will, free consent, unselfish guardianship, honourable intentions, and judicious discretion. When they enter into a marital contract, the intention must be clear to make the bond permanent and free of all casual and temporary designations. Thus, trial marriages, term marriages, and all marriages that appear experimental, casual, or temporary are forbidden. In one of his most unequivocal statements, the Prophet said that men and women who relish the frequent change of marital partners, that is, the "tasters" who enjoy one partner for a while and then shift to another, then to a third, and so on, are condemned.

However, to insist on the permanent character of marriage does not mean that the marital contract is absolutely indissoluble. Muslims are designated by the Quran as a Middle Nation and Islam is truly a religion of the "Golden Mean"—a well-balanced and well-integrated system. This is particularly clear in the case of marriage, which Islam regards as neither a sacrament nor a simple civil contract. Rather, marriage in Islam is something unique and possessing very special features of both a sacramental and a contractual nature. It is equally true that the alternative to this casual or temporary extremity is not the other extreme of absolute indissolubility of the marital contract. The Islamic course is one of equitable and realistic moderation. The marriage contract should be taken as a serious, permanent bond. But if it does not work well for any valid reason, it may be terminated in kindness and honour, with equity and peace.

The Husband-Wife Relationship : With piety as the basis of spouse selection, and with the earnest satisfaction of the conditions of marriage, the parties should be well on the way to a happy and fulfilling married life. However, Islam goes much further than this in setting the behaviour for husbands and wives. Many are the statements in the Quran and the Sunnah that prescribe kindness and equity, compassion and love, sympathy and consideration, patience and good will. The Prophet even declares that the best Muslim is the one who is the best to his family, and the greatest, most blessed joy in life is a good, righteous wife.

The consummation of marriage creates new roles for the parties concerned. Each role is a set of equitable, proportionate rights and obligations. The role of the husband evolves around the moral principle that it is his solemn duty to God to treat his wife with kindness, honour, and patience, to keep her honourably or free her from the marital bond honourably, and to cause her no harm or grief (Quran 2:229-232; 4:19). The role of the wife is summarized in the verse that women have rights even as they have duties, according to what is equitable, but that men have a degree over them (2:228). This degree is usually interpreted by Muslim scholars in conjunction with another passage which states, among other things, that men are trustees, guardians, and protectors of women because God has made some of them excel others and because men expend of their means (Quran 4:34). This degree may be likened to what sociologists call "instrumental leadership" or external authority in the household due to the division of labour and role differentiation. It does not, however, mean any categorical discrimination or superiority of one sex *to* the other.

The Wife's Rights: The Husband's Obligations. Translated into rules of behaviour, these ethical principles allocate to the wife certain rights and corresponding obligations. Because the Quran and the Sunnah of the Prophet have commanded kindness to women, it is the husband's duty to consort with his wife in an equitable and kind manner. One specific consequence of this Divine command is his responsibility for the full maintenance of the wife, a duty which he must discharge cheerfully, without reproach, injury, or condescendence.

Components of Maintenance : Maintenance entails the wife's incontestable right to lodging, clothing, nourishing, and general care and well-being. The wife's residence must be adequate so as to provide her with a reasonable level of privacy, comfort, and independence. Foremost is the welfare of the wife and the stability of the marriage. What is true of the residence is true of clothing, food, and general care. The wife has the right to be clothed, fed, and cared for by the husband, in accordance with his means and her style of life. These rights are to be exercised without extravagance or miserliness.

Nonmaterial Rights : The wife's material rights are not her only assurances and securities. She has other rights of a moral nature, and they are equally binding and specific. A husband is commanded by the law of God to treat his wife with equity, to respect her feelings, and to show her kindness and consideration. She is not to be shown any aversion by the husband or subjected to suspense and uncertainty. A corollary of this rule is that no man is allowed to keep his wife with the intention of inflicting harm on her or hindering her freedom. If he has no love or sympathy for her, she has the right to demand freedom from the marital bond, and no one may stand in her way to a new life.

The Wife's Obligations: The Husband's Rights. The main obligation of the wife as a partner in a marital relationship is to contribute to the success and blissfulness of the marriage as much as possible. She must be attentive to the comfort and well-being of her husband. She may neither offend him nor hurt his feelings. Perhaps nothing can illustrate the point better than the Quranic statement which describes the righteous people as those who pray:

> *Our Lord! Grant us wives and offspring who will be the joy and the comfort of our eyes, and guide us to be models of righteousness (Quran 25:74).*

This is the basis on which all of the wife's obligations rest and from which they flow. To fulfil this basic obligation, the wife must be faithful, trustworthy, and honest. More specifically, she must not deceive her husband by deliberately avoiding conception lest it deprive him of legitimate progeny. Nor must she allow any other person to have access to that which is exclusively the husband's right (i.e., sexual intimacy). A corollary of this is that she must not receive or entertain other men in her home without his knowledge and consent, and that she may not accept their gifts without his approval. This is probably meant to avoid jealousy, suspicion, gossip, etc., and also to maintain the integrity of all parties concerned. The husband's possessions are her trust. If she has access to any portion thereof, or if she is entrusted with any fund, she must discharge her duty wisely and thriftily. She may not tend or dispose of any of his belongings without his permission.

With respect to intimacy, the wife is to make herself desirable, attractive, responsive, and cooperative. A wife may not deny herself to her husband, for the Quran speaks of them as a comfort 'to each other. Due consideration is, of course, given to health and decency. Moreover, the wife is not permitted to do anything that may render her companionship less desirable or less gratifying. If she does any such thing or neglects herself, the husband has the right to interfere with her freedom to rectify the situation. To insure maximum self-fulfillments for both partners, he is not permitted to do anything on his part that may impede her gratification.

The Parent-Child Relationship

The Child's Rights : The Parent's Duties. Islam's general approach to children may be summarized in a few principles. First, it is a divine injunction that no child may become the cause of harm to the parents (Quran 2:233). Secondly, by implication, the parents should reciprocate and cause the child no harm. The Quran recognizes very' clearly that parents are not always immune from over-protectiveness or negligence. On the basis of this recognition, it has established certain guidelines and pointed out certain facts with respect to children. It points out that children are joys of life as well as sources of pride, seeds of vanity and false security, fountains of distress and temptation. But it hastens to stress the greater joys of the spirit and caution parents against over-confidence, false pride, or misdeeds that might be caused by children. The religious and moral principle of this position is that every individual, parent or child, relates to God directly and is independently responsible for his deeds. No child can absolve the parent on the Day of Judgement, and no parent can intercede on behalf of his child. Finally, Islam is strongly sensitive to the crucial dependence of the child on the parents. Their decisive role in forming the child's personality is clearly recognized in Islam. In a very suggestive statement, the Prophet declared that every child is born into the true malleable nature of *fitrah* (i.e., the pure natural state of *Islam),* its parents later on make it into a Jew, a Christian, or a pagan.

According to these guidelines, and more specifically, one of the most inalienable rights of the child in Islam is the right to life and equal life chances. Preservation of the child's life is the third commandment in Islam (6:151, cf. 17:23 *if).*

Another equally inalienable right is the right of legitimacy, which holds that every child shall have a father, and one father only. A third set of rights comes under socialisation, upbringing, and general care. To take good care of children is one of the most commendable deeds in Islam. The Prophet was fond of children and he expressed his conviction that his Muslim community would be noted among other communities for its kindness to children. It is charity of a higher order to attend to their spiritual welfare, educational needs, and general well-being. Interest in and responsibility for the child's welfare are questions of first priority. According to the Prophet's instructions, by the seventh day the child should be given a good, pleasant name and its head should be shaved, along with all the other hygienic measures required for healthy growing. This should be made a festive occasion marked with joy and charity.

Responsibility for and compassion toward the child is a matter of religious importance as well as social concern. Whether the parents are alive or deceased, present or absent, known or unknown, the child is to be provided with optimum care. Whenever there are guardians or relatives close enough to be held responsible for the child's welfare, they shall be directed to discharge this duty. But if there is no next of kin, care for the child becomes a joint responsibility of the entire Muslim community, designated officials and commoners alike.

The Child's Duties : The Parent's Rights. The parent-child relationship is complementary. Parents and children in Islam are bound together by mutual obligations and reciprocal commitments. But the age differential is sometimes so wide as to cause parents to grow physically weak and mentally feeble. This is often accompanied by impatience, the gradual decline of energy, heightened sensitivity, and perhaps bad judgment. It may also result in abuses of parental authority or inter generational estrangement and uneasiness, something similar to what is now called the "generation gap." It was probably in view of these considerations that Islam has taken cognizance of certain facts and made basic provisions to govern the individual's relationship to his parents.

> *The fact that parents are advanced in age and are generally believed to be more experienced does not by itself validate their views or certify their standards. Similarly, youth per se is not the sole fountain of energy,*

idealism, or wisdom. In various contexts, the Quran cites instances where the parents were proven wrong in their encounter with their children and also where children misjudged the positions of their parents (see Quran 6:74; 11:42-46; 19:42-48).

More significant, perhaps, is the fact that customs, folkways, traditions, or the parents' value system and standards do not in themselves constitute truth and brightness. In several passages the Quran strongly reproaches those who may stray away from the truth just because it is new to them, or contrary to the familiar, or incompatible with their parents' values. Furthermore, it focusses on the fact that if loyalty or obedience to the parents is likely to alienate the individual from God, he must side with God. It is true that parents merit consideration, love, compassion and mercy. But if they step out of their proper line to intrude upon the rights of God, a demarcation line must be drawn and maintained. The Quran sums up the whole question in the master concept of *ihsan,* which denotes what is right, good, and beautiful. The practical implications of the concept of observing *ihsan* to one's parents entail active empathy and patience, gratitude and compassion, respect for them and prayers for their souls, honouring their legitimate commitments and providing them with sincere counsel.

One basic dimension of *ihsan is* deference. Parents have the right to expect obedience from their children, if only in partial return for what they have done for them. But if parents demand something wrong or ask for something improper, disobedience becomes not only justifiable but also imperative. Obey or disobey, the children's attitude toward parents may not be categorical submissiveness or irresponsible defiance.

The last integral part of *ihsan* to be mentioned here is that children are responsible for the support and maintenance of their parents. It is an absolute religious duty to provide for the parents in case of need and to help them make their lives as comfortable as possible.

Other Aspects of the Family Life : Closely connected with the family life is the treatment of "servants," other family members, relations, and neighbours. To those who keep permanent maids, Prophet Muhammad has given advice and good tidings. "Masters" are enjoined to treat their servants like brothers and not like slaves, because whoever treats his servant well, said the Prophet, God will make his death easy and pleasant, a moment which is ordinarily painful and difficult. Servants are entitled to justice, kindness, mercy, food, clothing, accommodation and other personal expenses. The Prophet even says that/they should be fed and dressed from the same food and materials as used by their masters, and that this is to be provided by the masters themselves as a part of their obligations to his servants. They are not to be persecuted or disdained or overworked. This stipulation is designed to show how Islam dignifies humanity and honours labour without inviting the class warfare or the despotic authority of the proletariat. Being a servant or a labourer does not deprive any person of his rights or affect his dignity as a human being. Nor does it make him addicted to the opium of the Utopian proletariat. All citizens of a real Muslim society stand on an equal footing, because Islam does not recognize a caste system or a second-class citizenship. The only superiority acknowledged by Islam is that of piety and good deeds in the service of God (Quran 9:105; 49:13).

Man is ordained by God to extend his utmost help and kindness to other family members and relations, to show them true feelings of love and care. It might be interesting to note that the word "kinship" in Arabic is derived from a root word which means mercy (Rahim and Rahman). Kindness to one's kinsfolk is a short cut to Paradise, which is otherwise forbidden for those who neglect their duties in this respect. The extension of kind treatment to relatives is described by the Prophet as a Divine blessing of one's life and provisions. It is a sacred duty to be good to one's kin, even though they may not respond in a similar way. The duty is enjoined by God and should be observed for the sake of God regardless of the kin's response (Quran 2:177; 4:36; 16:90; 17:23-26).

The status of neighbours is very high in the viewpoint of Islam. Neighbours of all kinds enjoy a great number of privileges conferred on them by Islam. In his elaboration on the Quranic teachings relevant to this point, Prophet Muhammad is reported as saying that nobody can be a true Believer unless his neighbours feel secure and safe from his side. Also, nobody can be a true Believer, if his neighbours pass the night hungry and he has eaten his fill. He who is best to his neighbours, stated the Prophet, will enjoy the neighbourhood of God on the Day of Resurrection.

Presents, gifts and sharing of joys and sorrows should be exchanged between neighbours. In another declaration the Prophet said: "Do you know what the rights of a neighbour are? Help him if he asks your help; give him relief if he seeks your relief; lend him if he needs a loan; show him concern if he is distressed; nurse him when he is ill; attend his funeral if he dies; congratulate him if he meets with any good; sympathize with him if any calamity befalls him; do not block his air by raising your building high without his permission; do not harass; give him a share when you buy fruits, and if you do not give him, bring your purchases right to your house quietly and do not let your children take them out to excite the anger of his children." Moreover, the Prophet is reported as having said that the rights of the neighbours were so much emphasized by the angel Gabriel that he thought neighbours would perhaps be entitled to partake of one's inheritance.

SOCIETAL ASPECTS

The social life of the true Muslim is based upon supreme principles and is designed to secure happiness with prosperity for the individual and the society. Class warfare, social castes and domination of the individual over society or vice versa are alien idea. Nowhere in the Quran or the Traditions of the Prophet can one find any mention of superiority due to class or origin or wealth. On the contrary, there are many Quranic verses and sayings of Muhammad to remind mankind of the vital facts of life, facts which serve at the same time as principles of the social structure of the Islamic life. Among these is the fact that humanity represents one family springing from one and the same father and mother and aspiring to the same ultimate goals.

> *The unity of mankind is conceived in the light of the common parentage of Adam and Eve. Every human being is a member of the universal family established by the First Father and the First Mother, and therefore is entitled to enjoy the common benefits just as he is enjoined to share the common responsibilities. When people realize that they all belong to Adam and Eve and that these two individuals were the creation of God, there will be no room for racial prejudice or social injustice or second-class citizenship. People will be united in their social behaviour just as they are united in nature by the bond of common parentage. In the Quran and the Traditions of Muhammad there is a constant reminder of this important fact: the unity of humanity by nature and origin. This is to eliminate racial pride and claims to national or ethnic superiority, and pave the way for genuine brotherhood*
>
> *(Quran 4:1; 7:189; 49:13).*
>
> *The unity of humanity is not only in its origin but also in its ultimate aims. According to Islam, the final goal of humanity is God. From Him we come, for Him we live and to Him we shall all return. In fact, the sole purpose of creation as described by the Quran is to worship God and serve His cause, the cause of truth and justice, of love and mercy, of brotherhood and morality*
>
> *(Quran 51:56-58).*

The relations between the individual and society are based on this unity of origin and ultimate goal as the background of the social life in Islam. The role of the individual is complementary to that of society. Between the two there is social solidarity and mutual responsibility. The individual is responsible for the common welfare and prosperity of his society. This responsibility is not only to the society but also to God. In this way the individual works with a sound social-mindedness and a genuine feeling of inescapable responsibility. It is his role to do the utmost for his society and to contribute to its common welfare. On the other hand, the society is also responsible to God for the welfare of the individual. When the individual is able, he is the contributor and society is the beneficiary. In return he is entitled to security and care should he become disabled. In this case, he is the beneficiary and society is the contributor. Thus duties and rights correspond harmoniously. Responsibility and concern are mutual. There is no state to dominate the individual and abrogate his personal existence. Likewise, there is no individual or class of individuals to exploit the society and corrupt the State. There is harmony with peace and mutual security. There is a constructive interaction between the individual and the society.

In addition to the unity of humanity as regards its origin and ultimate goal, and along with this mutual responsibility and concern, the social life of Islam is characterized by cooperation in goodness and piety. It is marked with full recognition of the individual and his sacred rights to life, property and honour. It is also marked with an effective role played by the individual in the domain of social morals and ethics.

In an Islamic society the individual cannot be indifferent. He is enjoined to play an active part in the establishment of sound social morals by way of inviting to the good and combating the evil in any form and with all lawful means at his disposal. In so doing, not only does he eschew evil and do good but he also helps others to do the same. The individual who feels indifferent to his society is a selfish sinner, his morals are in trouble, his conscience is in disorder, and his faith is undernourished.

The structure of social life in Islam is very lofty, sound and comprehensive. Among the substantial elements of this structure are sincere love for one's fellow human beings, mercy for the young, respect for the elders, comfort and consolation for the distressed, visiting the sick, relieving the grieved, genuine feelings of brotherhood and social solidarity, respect for the rights of other people to life, property, and honour; and mutual responsibility between the individual and society. It is a common thing to come across Prophetic statements like these:

> *Whoever relieves a human being from a grief of this world, God will relieve him from a grief on the Day of Judgement.*

> *Anyone who has no mercy on the juniors and respect for the seniors is not one of us Muslims.*
>
> *None of you is a true believer in Islam until and unless he loves for his fellow man what he loves for his own self.*
>
> *Whoever invites others to good is like the doer of good and will be rewarded accordingly, and whoever instigates evil is like the doer of evil and will be punished accordingly.*

In the Quran, on the other hand, one finds numerous Divine instructions like these:

> *O you who believe! Mind God as He should be minded, and die not except in a state of Islam. And hold fast, all together, by the Rope of God, and be not divided among yourselves. And remember with gratitude God's favour on you; for you were enemies and He joined your hearts in love, so that by His Grace you have become brethren; and you were on the brink of the Pit of Fire and He saved you from it. Thus does God make His Signs clear to you that you may be guided. Let there arise out of you a band of people inviting to all that is good, enjoining what is right, and forbidding what is wrong. They are the ones to attain felicity. (3:102-104).*
>
> *O you who believe! Fulfil all obligations ... and help one another in righteousness and piety, but do not help another in sin and rancor. Mind God; for God is strict in punishment (5:1-3).*

In addition to what has already been said, the social patterns of Islam can also be seen in the Prophet's last sermon, which he gave during the course of his final pilgrimage. Addressing the tens of thousands of pilgrims, he said, among other things:

> *O people! Listen to my words, for I know not whether I will be granted another year after this to find myself amongst you at this place. Your lives and properties are sacred and inviolable amongst one another until you appear before the Lord, as this day of this month is sacred for all. And remember that you will have to*

appear before your Lord, Who will demand from you an account of all of your actions. O people! You have rights over your wives and your wives have rights over you. Treat your wives with love and kindness. Verily you have taken them as the trust of God, and have made their persons lawful unto you by the words of God. Keep always faithful to the trust reposed in you, and avoid sins. Henceforth, the vengeance of blood practiced in the days of ignorance and paganism is prohibited and all blood feud abolished. And your slaves! See that you feed them with the same food as you eat yourselves, and clothe them as you clothe yourselves; and if they commit a fault which you are not inclined to forgive, then part from them, for they are the servants of the Lord, and are not to be harshly treated. O people! Listen to my words and understand the same. Know that all Muslims are brothers unto one another. You are One Brotherhood. Nothing which belongs to another is lawful unto his brother unless freely given out of good will. Guard yourselves from committing in justice. Like this day of this month, in this territory sacred and inviolable, God has made the life and property and honour of each of you unto the other, until you meet your Lord. Let him that is present tell it to him that is absent. Maybe he that shall be told will remember better than he who has heard it. Verily. I have fulfilled my mission. I have left that amongst you, a plain command, the Book of God, and anifest Ordinances which if you hold fast, you shall never go astray.

ECONOMIC ASPECTS

The economic life of Islam is also based upon solid foundations and Divine instructions. Earning one's living through decent labor is not only a duty but a great virtue as well. Dependence of any able effortless person on somebody else for a livelihood is a religious sin, a social stigma and disgraceful humility. A Muslim is enjoined by God to be self-supporting and to avoid being a liability on anybody. Islam respects all kinds of work for earning one's livelihood so long as there is no indecency or wrong involved. With a clear conscience and due respect from society, the Muslim can roll up his sleeves and undertake any kind of work available in order to provide for himself and his dependents. Prophet Muhammad is reported as having said that it is far better for one even to take his rope, cut wood, pile it up and sell it in order to eat and give charity than to beg for sustenance from others. According to Islam, the status of honest working men cannot be lowered on account of the kind of work they are doing for a living. Yet the laboring workers have no limited scope for improving their lots and raising their standards as high as possible. They have equal opportunities at their disposal and enjoy freedom of enterprise.

Whatever the individual makes or earns through lawful means is his private possession, which neither the State nor anybody else can justifiably claim. In return for this right of private possession, he has only to fulfill certain obligations to the society and pay certain taxes to the State. When this is done, he has full rights to protection by the State, and his freedom of enterprise is secure and guaranteed. Under the Islamic system the menace of greedy capitalism and destructive communism never arises. The enterprising individual is responsible for the prosperity of the State, and the State, in turn, is responsible for the security of the individual. Class conflicts are replaced by cooperation and harmony; fear and suspicion are remedied by mutual security and confidence.

The economic system of Islam is not drawn in the light of arithmetical calculations and capacities of production alone. Rather, it is drawn and conceived in the light of a comprehensive system of morals and principles. The person who is working for another person or for a firm or an institution is ordained by God to do his work with efficiency and honesty. The Prophet said that if any of you undertakes to do any work, God loves to see him do it well and with efficiency. Once the work is done, the worker is entitled to a fair wage for his services. Failure by the employer to pay the just wage or attempts to cut it down and waver on it is a punishable act, according to the Law of God.

Business transactions enjoy a great deal of attention in Islam. Honest trade is permitted and blessed by God. This may be carried out through individuals, companies, agencies and the like. But all business deals should be concluded with frankness and honesty. Cheating, hiding defects of merchandise from the dealers, exploiting the needs of customers, and engendering a monopoly of stocks in order to increase one's own prices are all sinful acts and punishable by the Islamic Law. If one is to make a decent living, it has to be made through honest ways and hard endeavour.

Otherwise, easy come, easy go. But it is not only that, for anybody that is bred with unlawful provisions will be, according to the Prophet, a burning fuel for the Hell Fire on the Day of Judgement. To combat cheating and exploitation, Islam demands honesty in business,, warns the cheaters, encourages decent work and forbids usury or the taking of interest in return for lending money to those who are in need of it. This is to show man that he rightfully owns only what he works for, and that any exploitation of other people's pressing needs is irreligious, inhuman and immoral. In the Quran God says:

> *Those who devour usury will not stand except as one stands whom the Evil One by his touch has driven mad. That is because they say: "trade is like usury." But God has permitted trade and forbidden usury. Those who, after receiving direction from their Lord, desist, shall be pardoned for the past; their case is for God (to judge). But those who repeat (the offence) are Companions of the Fire; they will abide therein (for ever). God will deprive usury of all blessing, but will give increase for deeds of charity; for He loves not creatures ungrateful and wicked* *(2:274-276).*

> *And the Firmament has He raised high, and He has set up the Balance (of Justice) in order that you may not transgress (due) balance. So establish weight with justice and fall not short in the balance* *(55:7-9).*

This is to guide man to resort to justice and straight forwardness in all of his dealings and transactions. The future of cheaters is grim and their doom is awful. Here is how the Quran looks into the matter:

> *Woe to those who deal in fraud, those who, when they have to receive by measure from men, exact full measure, but when they have to give by measure or weight to men give less than due. Do they not think that they will be called to account on a Mighty Day, a Day when (all) mankind will stand before the Lord of the Worlds (83:1 -6)?*

Besides that, there are numerous Traditions of Prophet Muhammad excluding the cheaters, exploiters, monopolizers and dishonest business people from the band of the true Muslims. Any business deal that involves injustice or cheating or exploitation is strictly prohibited and can be voided by the Law even after it is concluded. The main purpose of the Islamic legislation that deals with economic and commercial matters is to secure the rights of the individual and to maintain the solidarity of society, to introduce high morality to the world of business and to enforce the Law of God in that sphere of enterprise. It is logical and consistent that Islam should be concerned with such aspects as these, because it is not merely a spiritual formula but a complete system of life in all of its aspects.

Proprietors are constantly reminded of the fact that they are in reality mere agents appointed by God to administer their holdings. There is nothing in Islam to stop the Muslim from attaining wealth and striving for material improvement through lawful means and decent channels. Yet the fact remains that man comes to this world empty-handed and departs from it likewise. The actual and real owner of things is God alone, of Whom any proprietor is simply an appointed agent, a mere trustee. This is not only a fact of life but also has a significant bearing on human behaviour. It makes the proprietor always ready to spend in the way of God and to contribute to worthy causes. It makes him responsive to the needs of his society and gives him an important role to play, a sacred mission to fulfil. It saves him from the pit of selfishness, greed and injustice. This is the true conception of property in Islam, and that is the actual status of proprietors. The Quran considers possession of wealth a trying test, and not a token of virtuous excellence or privileged nobility or a means of exploitation. God says:

> *It is He Who has made you (His) agents, inheritors of the earth: He has raised you in ranks, some above others; that He may try you in the gifts He has given you. Verily, your Lord is quick in punishment, yet He is indeed Oft-Forgiving, Most Merciful* *(6:165).*

Moreover, the Quran reports to mankind an interesting discourse between Moses and his people. It runs as follows:

> *Said Moses to his people: "Pray for help from God, and wait in patience and constancy; for the earth is God's. He gives it as a heritage to such of His servants as He pleases; and the end is best for the righteous." They said: "We have had nothing but trouble, both before and after you came to us." He said: "It may be that your Lord will destroy your enemies and make you inheritors in the earth; that so He may try you by your deeds"*
>
> *(7:128-129).*

This discourse between Moses and his people does not imply in any sense a recognition of any privileged genus of mankind due to racial origin or ethnic identity. Nor does it mean that the Quran approves completely of the conduct and conceptions of the followers of Moses in later centuries. The tone of the text is rather reproachful and critical of the doubters and reassuring of the fact that everything in the earth belongs to God, Who distributes it among His servants in the form of inherited trusts and objects of trial. The point is brought home time and again throughout the Quran. For example, it says:

> *To Him belongs the dominion of the heavens and the earth, and all affairs are referred back to God ... Believe in God and His Messenger, and spend (in charity) out of the (substance) whereof He has made you heirs. For, those of you who believe and spend (in charity)—for them there is a great reward. And what cause have you why you should not spend in the cause of God? For to God belongs the heritage of the heavens and the earth*
>
> *(57:5, 7, 10).*

Unlike Communism, Islam replaces the totalitarian artificial supremacy of the Communist State by the beneficial supremacy of God, and the Communist theory of class warfare by sound morals, mutual responsibilities and cooperation. On the other hand, it provides the utmost assurance against greedy capitalism and ruthless exploitation by proprietors. The economic system of Islam grants full recognition to the "independent" entity of the individual and to his natural aspirations to work and possessions. Yet it does not conceive of him as absolutely independent of God or of the universe. It does not deify man or his capital, nor does it deify the proletariat and abolish free enterprise. It accepts man the way he is created and deals with him accordingly, making allowances for his instinctive aspirations and limited power. Man is a man, and he should be accepted and dealt with as such. He is not a god or a semi-god who can arrogate to himself absolute powers and unquestionable infallibility. Nor is he a countless or insignificant entity.

He is someone to be recognized, but in his real status and not in an exaggerated or belittled nature. He is not above or out of the rest of the universe but a part of a whole system, an element in the total foundation of the universe.

Although man is encouraged to work, is free to engage in enterprise, is entitled to earn and possess, the fact that he is a mere trustee provides the necessary measure to insure the proper handling of his possessions, which are his trusts.

He has the authority to earn, to invest and to spend. Yet in so doing he is guided by high principles which save him from going astray. An example may be sufficient to illustrate the point. Proprietors are not unreservedly free to spend their money or handle their properties the way they please. There are certain rules of expenditure to be followed.

In the words of the Quran, God enjoins upon the proprietor to fulfill his financial obligations towards his fellow men, and to be moderate in his private spending. He is always reminded of the fact that God is the Real Provider and Actual Possessor. Here is the declaration of the Quran:

And render to the kindred their due rights, as (also) to those in want, and to the wayfarer. But squander not (your wealth) in the manner of a spendthrift. Verily, spendthrifts are brothers of the Evil Ones, and the Evil One is to his Lord (Himself) ungrateful. Make not your hand tied (like a niggard's) to your neck, nor stretch it forth to its utmost reach (like a foolish spendthrift); lest you become rebuked and destitute. Verily your Lord does provide sustenance in abundance for whom He pleases, and He provides in a just measure. For He does know and regard all of His servants. (17: 26-27, 29-30).

POLITICAL ASPECTS

Like the social and economic life, the political life of Islam is based on sound spiritual and moral foundations and is guided by Divine instructions. The political system of Islam is unique in its structure, its function, and its purpose. It is not pragmatic or instrumentalistic. It is not a theocracy, whereby a certain class of people assumes divine rights (hereditary or otherwise) and places itself above other citizens and beyond accountability. Nor is it a proletariat, whereby some revengeful laborers capture power. It is not even democracy in its popular sense. It is something different from all that. To appreciate the political outlook of Islam one has only to know that it is based on the following principles:

1. Every deed of the Muslim individual or group of individuals must be inspired and guided by the Law of God, the Quran, which is the constitution chosen by God for His true servants. "And if any do fail to judge (or rule) according to what God has revealed, they are the unbelievers ... they are the wrong-doers ... they are the rebels (5:47-50)" and "Verily this Quran does guide to that which is most right and best (17:9)."
2. Sovereignty in the Islamic State does not belong to the ruler or even to the people themselves. It belongs to God, and the people as a whole exercise it by trust from Him to enforce His law and enact His will. The ruler, any ruler, is only an acting executive chosen by the

people to serve them according to the Law of God. This is the foundation of the Islamic State and is consistent with the general outlook of Islam on the universe, of which God is the Creator and in which He is the Sole Sovereign. In the Quran, one comes across statements like these: "Authority, power and sovereignty belong to none but God" (Quran 12:40), or "Blessed be He in Whose hands is dominion, and He has power over all things" (Quran 67:1), or "Verily God does command you to render back your trusts to those to whom they are due; and when you judge (or rule) between people that you judge with justice. Verily how excellent is the teaching which He gives you!" (4:58), or "And to God belongs the dominion of the heavens and the earth, and all that is between; and unto Him is the final goal (of all)" (5:18).

3. The aim of the Islamic State is to administer justice and provide security and protection for all citizens, regardless of colour or race or creed, in conformity with the stipulations of God in His constitution: the Quran. The question of religious or racial minorities does not arise so long as they are law-abiding and peaceful citizens. The Quran says:

   O you who believe! Stand out firmly for justice, as witnesses to fair dealing, and let not the hatred of others to you make you swerve to wrong and depart from justice. Be just: that is most close to piety, and mind God, for God is well-acquainted with all that you do. (5:9; cf. 4:135).

   Verily God will defend those who believe ... those who, if We establish them in the Land, establish regular prayers and give regular charity, enjoin the right and forbid the wrong. With God rests the end (and decision) of all affairs (22:38, 41).

4. Formed for the above-mentioned purposes and established to enforce the Law of God, the Islamic State cannot be controlled by any political party of a non-Islamic platform or subjected to foreign powers. It has

to be independent so that it can exercise its due authority on behalf of God and in His cause. This originates from the principle that a Muslim is one who submits to God alone and pledges loyalty to His Law, offering his utmost cooperation and support to those who administer the Law and observe its stipulations. It is incompatible with Islam, therefore, for a Muslim nation to pledge support to any political party of a non-Islamic platform or to yield to a non- Islamic government of alien origins and aims: "And never will God grant to the unbelievers a way (to triumph or rule) over the believers" (4:141). The answer of the Believers, when summoned to God and His Messenger, in order that He may judge (or rule) between them, is no other than this:

They say: "We hear and we obey" ... God has promised, to those among you who believe and work righteous deeds, that He will, of a surety, make them His vicegerents in the land, as He made those before them; that He will establish in authority their religion—the one which He has chosen for them; and that He will change (their state), after the fear in which they (lived), to one of security and peace: "They will worship Me (alone) and not associate any partner with Me" (24:51, 55).

God has decreed: It is I and My apostles who must prevail. Verily God is One full of strength, able to enforce His will. You will not find any people who believe in God and the Last Day loving those who resist God and His apostles, even though they be their fathers or their sons, or their brothers or their kindred. For such believers He has written Faith in their hearts and strengthened them with a spirit from Himself (58:21-22).

5. The ruler, any ruler, is not a sovereign over the people. He is a representative employee chosen by the people and derives his authority from his obedience to the Law of God, the Law which binds the rulers and the ruled alike by a solemn contract over which God is the Supervisor. The political contract of Islam is not

concluded between the administration and the public alone. It is between these combined on one side and God on the other, and it is morally valid and binding only as long as the human sides fulfil their obligations to the Divine. The rulers who are chosen by their people to administer the words of God are entitled to support and cooperation from the public inasmuch as they observe the very words of God. Should the public or any member of society fail to render support to and cooperation with such administrators, their act would be considered an irresponsible offense against the administration as well as against God Himself. Likewise, if the administration swerves from the Path of God or fails to observe His Law, it is not only committing a like offense but also has no right to the support and loyalty of the public. The Quran says:

> O you who believe! Obey God, and obey (he Messenger (of God) and those charged with authority among you. If you differ in anything among yourselves, refer it to God and His Messenger, if you do believe in God and the Last Day. That is best, and most suitable for final determination (4:59).

Obedience to those charged with authority is conditioned by their own obedience to the Law of God and the Traditions of His Messenger. Prophet Muhammad said that there is no obedience or loyalty to any human being, ruler or otherwise, who is not himself obedient to God and bound by His Law. The early successors of Muhammad understood this principle very clearly and declared in their first statements of policy that they were to be obeyed and helped by the public as long as they themselves obeyed God, and that they had no claims to obedience from the people if they were to depart from the way of God.

6. The rulers and administrators must be chosen from among the best qualified citizens on the basis of their own merits of virtue, fitness and competence. Racial origin or family prestige and financial status do not in

themselves make any potential candidate more or less qualified for high public offices. They neither promote nor hinder the merits of the individual. Each candidate must be judged on his own merits, of which family prestige, wealth, race and age as such constitute no significant part. The candidates may be chosen by public consent through general elections, or they may be selected and authorized by public leaders, who are, in turn, entrusted with leadership by the free accord of the various sections of society. Thus, an Islamic State can have as many representative councils or municipal governments as desired. The right of election or selection and the conduct of administration are governed by the Law of God and must be aimed at achieving the best interest of society as a whole. The Prophet said: "Whoever entrusts a man to a public office where in his society there is a better man than this trustee, he has betrayed the trust of God and His Messenger and the Muslims." In a political sense this means that the electorate cannot, morally speaking, be indifferent to public events and that they, whenever they cast ballots, must vote after careful investigation and premeditated choice. In this way the State could have the best possible safeguard of security and responsible citizenship, something which many contemporary democratic states lack.

7. After the people make their choice through election or selection of their ruler, every citizen is enjoined to supervise, with his means, the conduct of the administration and question its handling of public affairs whenever he sees anything wrong with it. If the administration betrays the trust of God and the public, it has no right to continue in office. It must be ousted and replaced by another, and it is the responsibility of every citizen to see to it that this is done in the public interest. The question of hereditary power or lifetime government is therefore inapplicable to an Islamic State.
8. Although the ruler is chosen and appointed by the people, his first responsibility is to God and only then to the

people. His office is not just symbolic nor is his role simply abstract. He is not a helpless puppet whose function is to sign papers or execute the public will invariably, i.e., whether it is right or wrong. He must exercise actual power on behalf of the people for their best interest in accordance with the Law of God, because he has a dual responsibility. On the one hand, he is accountable to God for his conduct and, on the other, he is responsible to the people who have put their trust in him. He will have to give a full account before God of how he treated his people (i.e., either on an individual basis or through representatives). But both the ruler and his people will also have to give a full account before God of how they treated the Quran, how they regarded the Law of God which He has given as a binding force. It is because of his responsibility to the people that he should handle their affairs in the best common interest, and it is because of his accountability to God that he should do so according to the Law of God. Thus, the political system of Islam is fundamentally different from all other political systems and doctrines known to mankind. In addition, the ruler is not to govern the people according to their own desires. Rather, he is to serve them by making justice a common law, by making their genuine obedience to the Sovereign Lord of the universe a regular function of the state, and by making sound morality a noble undertaking of the administration.

9. Although the Quran is the Constitution of the Islamic State, Muslims are ordained by God to handle their common affairs through consultative methods. This makes room for legislative councils and consultative bodies on the local as well as on the national and international levels. Every citizen in the Islamic State is enjoined to offer his best advice on common matters and must be entitled to do so. To insure fulfillment of this obligation in a practical and useful way, the rulers must seek the advice of the learned and experienced people in the state. But this does not in any sense deny the

right of average citizens who must speak out whenever the occasion arises.

In this way every citizen of the Islamic State has an obligation, in one capacity or another, to fulfill and is deeply concerned, directly or otherwise, about the conduct of public affairs. Islamic history provides authentic records of how the chief rulers and Caliphs were questioned, advised, and corrected by common people, men and women alike. The principle of mutual consultation is so fundamental in Islâm that one must not only speak his mind, but do so in the sincerest and most effective manner, for the best interest of society. Consultative methods in politics, or in any other field for that matter, are not only a democratic formula of government, but a religious injunction and a moral duty enjoined upon the rulers as well as the ruled. In addition to his constant observance of this principle, the Prophet said that it is an essential part of religion to give good counsel. The purpose of such counsel is to insure that the Law of God is observed, and that the rights of citizens are honoured and their obligations fulfilled. To prevent the rise of professional politics and to counteract any underground politicians who are running on opportunistic platforms, the Prophet, speaking on God's authority, said that whoever speaks, be it in a form of counsel or any other form, must say the right and good things or else keep silent. This is to warn counsellors and advisers against selfish inclinations or egotistic temptations and to guarantee that counsel is given with the since rest intention and in the public's best interest, because it is authorized by God, carried on His behalf and aimed at the common welfare. A ruler's seeking of counsel and then rendering it on the part of the public is not a matter of choice or a voluntary measure: it is an article of Faith, a religious ordinance. Muhammad himself, although wise, "infallible" and unselfish, was not above the maxim or an exception to the rule. God instructs him in this way:

> It is by the mercy of God that you dealt gently with them (your people). Were you severe or harsh-hearted, they would have broken away from about you. So pass over their faults, and ask for (God's) forgiveness for them; and consult them in affairs (of moment). Then, when you have taken a decision, put your trust (in Him) (3:159).

Enumerating the characteristics of the Believers, the Quran makes clear mention of mutual counsel as an article of Faith: The Believers are those who believe in God and put their trust in their Lord, those who avoid the greater crimes and shameful deeds, and, when they are angry even then forgive; those who hearken to their Lord, and establish regular prayer, and conduct their affairs by mutual consultation and spend out of what We bestow on them for sustenance (by way of charity); and those who, when an oppressive wrong is inflicted on them, (are not cowed, but) help and defend themselves (42:36-39).

10. Under the political system of Islam, every citizen is entitled to enjoy freedom of belief and conscience, and freedom of thought and expression. He is free to develop his potentialities and improve his lot, to work and compete, to earn and possess, to approve and disapprove of things—all according to his honest judgment. But his freedom is not, and cannot be, absolute, for then it would amount to chaos and anarchy. It is guaranteed by the Law of God and governed by the very same Law. As long as it is in line with this Law it is the rightful privilege of every individual citizen, but if it transgresses the limits of the Law or conflicts with the common interest, it becomes a violation of God's Law. It must therefore be controlled. The individual is part of the whole universe, so he must adjust himself to the Law and order of God, the Law by which the entire universe is administered. On the other hand, he is a member of his community or nation, and must adapt his own rights and interests to those of others in a mutually beneficial

manner. If the individual takes an independent attitude on a certain matter of public concern and finds the majority taking a different attitude, he must in the end side with the majority in order to maintain solidarity and cooperation, provided that the majority's decision is not contrary to the Law of God. Yet in the process of forming a public opinion he is fully entitled to express his own opinion and persuade others of his convictions without disturbance or distortion. When it becomes clear that the majority has chosen a different course, then he is bound to go along, because the matter in question is no longer under individual consideration or deliberation but is undergoing public implementation (3:102-105; 8:46).

11. The governorship of the Islamic State is a public trust with which the administrators have been entrusted by the word of God as well as by the common consent of the people. With God being the Supreme Sovereign of the State, whoever represents Him in the top office must be faithful to the Entrusting Authority and must be a believer in God. And with the majority of the people being Muslims, whoever assumes the office of Presidency or Caliphate must be a true Muslim. These measures are taken in order to serve the common interest and to fulfil all of the obligations of the State to God as well as to the citizens. They are also to secure and honour the rights of the so-called religious or racial minorities.

It is unfortunate for humanity that this ruling of Islam has been poorly understood and badly distorted. The fact of the matter is that this ruling does not discriminate against minorities but is rather protective and assertive of their rights. Whoever wishes to be a law-abiding citizen of the Islamic State is welcome to it, and shares with others the duties and prerogatives of responsible citizenship. His being a non-Muslim does not lower his status or drop him down to second-class citizenship, as long as he obeys the common Law of the State and exercises his rights in a responsible manner. If he wishes, for example, to pay the religious tax (Zakat) and other state taxes like the Muslim citizens in order to maintain the State and in return for his own security and welfare, he may do so. But if he thinks that paying the Islamic Tax (Zakat) is humiliating to his dignity or injurious to his feelings on account of his being a non-Muslim, he may pay his taxes in a different form, one known as "tributes" or Zizya—so he in fact enjoys a choice which Muslims of the same state do not enjoy. In return for his contributions to the State, he is fully entitled to protection and security by the State officials and the society.

Similarly, if such a citizen wants to administer his personal life of marriage, divorce, foods, inheritance, and so on according to the Islamic Law, his desire must be recognized and his rights must be respected. But if he wishes to administer these affairs according to his own religious teachings, he is absolutely free to do so and no one can hamper the exercise of his rights in that respect. So in personal or sentimental matters, he may resort to his own teachings or to the public regulations. But in matters of public interest and common affairs he must abide by the Law of the State, the Law of God. No matter what he chooses, he is no less entitled to protection and security than any other citizen. All of this is not a dream of a heavenly kingdom yet to come. It is the teaching of the Quran, the practice of Muhammad and the record of Islamic history. It is reported, for example, that 'Umar ibn al-Khattab, the second Caliph after Muhammad, was once passing by a place where he found an old Jew in a pitiful condition. 'Umar inquired about the man and found out what state he was in. In a regretful tone he said to the man: "We collected tributes (taxes) from you when you were able. Now you are deserted and neglected. How unjust to you 'Umar has been." After he finished his remark, a regular pension for the old man was ordered and made effective immediately. 'Umar and other rulers received their political orientation at the hands of Muhammad, who, in turn, had been taught by God. These teachings are recorded in the Quran in such verses as the one below:

> *God forbids you not, with regard to those who do not fight you for (your) Faith nor drive you out of your homes, from dealing kindly and justly with them. For*

> *God loves those who are just. God only forbids you with regard to those who fight you for (your) Faith, and drive you out of your homes, and support others in driving you out, from turning to them for friendship and protection. Those who turn to them for friendship and protection are the wrongdoers (60:8-9).*

Finally, it is a categorical error to compare the Islamic State and its need for a Muslim head with the secular state where it is, theoretically, conceivable to have a head of state who may belong to a minority group. The comparison is fallacious and misleading for several reasons. First, it assumes that secularism, however superficial, is sounder than the Islamic ideology. Such an assumption or premise is pretentious. Second, the duties and rights of a head of state under Islam are quite different from those of his counterpart in a secular order, as outlined above. Third, the modern secular spirit is for the most part a redemptive, apologetic restitution, a case which does not apply to Islam. Moreover, a head of a secular state, if there can be a real one, may belong to a racial, ethnic, or religious minority. But he almost invariably has to join a majority party. What this does, in fact, is to substitute a political majority for a religious one, which is hardly an improvement of the minority status as such. Furthermore, the secular argument presupposes that the leadership of the state is a right or a privilege that may be conferred upon or denied to a particular individual. The Islamic position is radically different. In Islam, leadership of the state is first and foremost an obligation, a trying commitment and an awesome responsibility. It would be inequitable, therefore, if Islam imposed such responsibilities upon non-Muslims.

GLOBAL ASPECTS

The international life in Islam is the pattern of relationships between an Islamic state or nation and other states or nations. Like the other aspects of the Islamic life, this one stems from Divine guidance and follows the Godly pattern. It is laid down on the following foundations:

1. An unshakable belief in the unity of mankind in origin, in human status, and in aims. (Quran 4:1; 7:189; 49:13);

2. Due respect for other people's interests and rights to life, honour and property, as long as they do not encroach upon the rights of Muslims. This is because usurpation, transgression and wrong of all kinds are strictly forbidden (2:190-193; 42:42);
3. Peace as the normal course of relations, with the exchange of goodwill missions and mutually honest endeavours for the sake of humanity in which all people share equally (see above and Quran 8:61);
4. Intolerance of appeasement and encroachment in international relations. Should someone be tempted to violate the rights of the Islamic State, or disturb its peace, or endanger its security or exploit its peaceful policies, the State must hasten to defend itself and suppress all attempts of such a nature. Only here, under such circumstances, Islam justifies war. But even then there are moral principles to be followed in order to confine its scope to a minimum and to pursue it only as far as necessary. The Law of war and peace in Islam is highly moral and unique, comprehensive and sound. It deserves a special study by jurists and moralists alike, something which this work cannot cover. But it should be remarked, however, that Islam neither justifies an aggressive war nor makes destruction of crops, animals, homes, etc., an objective. It neither allows the killing of non-fighting women, children and aged people nor tolerates the torture of war prisoners and the imposition of its teachings on the defeated. It is only a defensive measure, justified by the practical principles of Islam, as long as wrong, injustice and aggression exist in the world (2:190-195, 216-218; 22:39-41; see also the discussion on Jihad below);
5. Fulfilling the obligations undertaken by the Islamic State and honouring the treaties concluded between the Islamic State and other states. This is only binding if the other parties remain faithful to their obligations and honour their treaties. Otherwise, there can be no validity of treaties or binding obligations (5:1; 8:55-56, 58; 9:3-4);

6. Maintaining internal peace and security, and making a genuine contribution to human understanding and universal brotherhood on the international level.

These are the inspiring sources in the making of the Islamic State's international life. The Islamic State does not live just for itself and its own subjects. It has a wide scope and an important mission in the international field. By the order of Islam it has to strive for the prosperity and advancement of its own citizens in every aspect of life, and by the same order it should make valuable contributions to humanity at large. This engenders friendly relations, in the broadest sense of the word, with friendly people and states. It enjoins the Islamic State to play a vital role in the interest of humanity on the international level in education, economics, industry, politics, and so on. This role was initiated by Muhammad himself and was maintained by his followers throughout the succeeding generations.

Before we conclude this chapter, it should be pointed out that whatever is discussed here is based on the sound, genuine and true principles of Islam as stated in the Quran and the Traditions of Muhammad. This is the Islam which Muhammad and his faithful followers practiced and exemplified in the most excellent manner. It is not the Islam of any particular theologian or any particular jurist or ruler. Rather, it is Islam, the writer believes, as it really is and as it is meant to be. It should also be borne in mind that the Islamic system of life is unique and different from all other systems and ideologies. Whether one looks at it from a spiritual or moral, intellectual or cultural, political or economic or any other point of view, one can readily see that it is marked with distinctive characteristics. To illustrate, one may cite a few examples:

1. The source of the Islamic ideology is different. It is not man made, or the production of subversive politicians or revengeful economists, or the work of pragmatic moralists or selfish industrialists. It is the work of God, the art of the Infinite One, created in the best interest of humanity as a whole. And by its nature it is binding and venerated by all of those who are faithful. It is intelligible to every sound mind for it is free of puzzling

mysteries, secret reservations and arrogated prerogatives.

2. The aims of the Islamic ideology are also different. It is not aimed at world domination or physical expansion, but rather at world submission to the Will of God and world confinement to the limits of God's Law. Its principal objectives are to please God and cultivate man in such a way as to help him to obey the Law of the Creator and be a faithful vicegerent of the Lord. To achieve this end, it deals with all aspects of life, and its purpose is to develop in man a clear mind, a pure spirit, a live conscience, a healthy body and responsive feelings. A person with these qualities cannot fail to obey God and adopt the most sound course of life. So the objectives of the Islamic ideology are far from being simply human or temporal.
3. The Islamic ideology has all the elements and forces that make it comprehensive and practical, moderate and flexible. Its Divine origin reveals only the fundamental and inviolable principles, leaving a due scope for the human intelligence to work out details and make the necessary adaptations. In whatever way one looks at it, one can see that the Islamic ideology is composed of comprehensive, practical and resourceful principles. It is comprehensive because it deals with all the major aspects of life; practical because it has been put into practice and translated into reality at one time or another; moderate because it does not favour the individual capitalist or the proletariat. In addition, it is not exclusively concerned with the mundane or with the spiritual and is confined neither to this world nor to the Future life. It marks a middle way between all extremes and is a guide to a moderate and stable life. Apart from these established principles, there is a great deal of flexibility allowed when it comes to working out details suitable to various regions and ages. This flexibility is a matter of fact and a necessity, because the ideology is the work of God and in it, as in all of His work, there is a wide scope for the human mind and human effort.

Bibliography

Abbas Hashmi : *Rasul (PBUH)*, Adam Pub., New Delhi, 2001.

Abdali, M.R. : *Scientific Thought in Islam*, Pious Publications, Hyderabad, 2001.

Abdul Qadir : *Criminal Law of Islam*, Kitab Bhavan, New Delhi, 1999.

Abdul, H.S.: *The Life of Muhammad (PBUH)*, Islamic Pub., New Delhi,1997.

Abdullah Enan : *Decisive Moments in the History of Islam*, Islamic Book Company, Delhi, 1996.

Adil, H. M. : *Letters of Hadrat Usman Ghani (R.A.A.)*, Kitab Bhavan, New Delhi, 1992

Ahmad, Ilyas : *Sovereignty, Islamic and Modern*, Allies Book Corporation, Karachi, 1965.

Ahmad, Imtiaz : *Ritual and Religion among Muslims in India*, Manohar Publishers, New Delhi, 1984.

Ahmed, Hasanuddin : *Islamic Economics*, Goodword Books Pvt. Ltd., New Delhi, 1991.

Ali, Ameer : *Muhammadan Law*, Kitab Bhavan, New Delhi, 1986.

Arnold, T. W. : *The Caliphate*, Routledge & Kegan Paul Ltd., London,1965.

Asghar, Ali : *Islam : Women and Gender Justice*, Gyan Books Pvt. Ltd., New Delhi, 2001.

Ataur-Rahim : *Jesus a Prophet of Islam*, Idara Ishaat-e-Diniyat Pvt. Ltd, New Delhi, 1995.

Azam, Zaki : *The Ideas of Arab Nationalism*, Cornell University Press, New York,1956.

Baral, Raj : *Regional Migrations : Ethnicity and Security*, Popular Prakashan, Bombay, 1995.

Beverly, Milton : *Islam and Politics in the Contemporary World*, Blackwell, New York, 1987.

Bosworth, C.E. : *The Legacy of Islam*, Oxford University Press, New York, 1979.

Carl, W. : *Teaching of Sufism*, Deep & Deep, New Delhi, 2000.

Charles Howard : *The Constitutionalism*, Great Seal Books, New York, 1947.

Chave F. : *Islamic Histroriography*, Cambridge University press, New York, 1990.

Daniel, N.A. : *Islam and the West : the Making of an Image*, University Press, Edinburgh, 1962.

De, Laet : *The Political Systems of Empire*, Oxford, New York, 1963.

Edwin, Elliot : *Worship in Islam*, University of Madras, Madras, 1925.

Fauzi M. : *The Islamic State : a Study in Traditional Politics*, Oxford, New York, 1967.

Gardet, Louis : *Mystique Musulmane*, Allen & Co., Paris, 1961.

Gellner, E. : *Post-Traditional Forms in Islam : the Turf and Trade*, Oxford, New York, 1982.

Ghulam Sarwar : *Muhammad (PBUH) the Holy Prophet*, Dar-ul Ishaat, Karachi, 1997.

Gibb, H.A.R : *Studies in the Civilization of Islam*, Beacon Press, Boston,1962.

Glubb : *The Story of Arab Legion*, Feroz Pub., Lahore, 2000.

Gulzar Ahmed : *The Prophets (PBUH) Concept of War*, Aziz Pub., Islamabad, 2000.

Herbert, Friedman : *The Amazing Universe*, National Geographic Society, Washington D.C., 1980.

Husaini, S.A.Q : *The Pantheistic Monism of Ibn al-Arabi*, Feroz Pub., Lahore, 1970.

Hussain, Ahanger : *Customary Succession among Muslims*, Uppal Publishibng House, New Delhi, 1997.

Hussain, M. : *Imam Abu Hanifah : Life and Work*, Kitab Bhavan, New Delhi, 2001.

Hussain, S. : *Human Rights in Islam*, Kitab Bhavan, New Delhi, 2001.

Ikbal Ali : *Islamic Sufism,* Idarah-I-Adbiyat-I-Delhi, Delhi, 1979.

Ikram, S.M. : *Muslim Civilization in India,* Oxford, New York, 1981.

Jafar Sharif : *Islam in India,* Atlantic Publishers, New Delhi, 1999.

Jafar, Sharif : *Islam in India,* Oxford, New Delhi, 1972.

James, Piscarton : *Islam in the World of National States,* Macmillan, New York, 1982.

Jean-Baptiste : *Travels in India,* W.Crooke, London, 1925.

Jha, V. : *Indian Society: Historical Probings,* Rawat Pub., Delhi, 1974.

John L. Esposite : *Islam in Transition,* Oxford, New York, 1969.

John Surowiecki : *The Pulse of the Planet,* Crown Publishers, U.S.A. 1972.

Kalim Bahadur : *Domestic Conflicts in South Asia,* South Asia Publishers, New Delhi, 1986.

Kalim, M. Siddiq : *Studies in Pakistan Culture : an International Perspective,* Manohar Publications, New Delhi, 1993.

Karnal, A. : *Islam : Today and Tomorrow,* Deep & Deep Pub., New Delhi, 1989.

Katharine, Scarfe : *Perception of the Islamic Word,* Cambridge University Press, New Delhi, 1992.

Kaur, R. : *Islamic Co-operation and Unity,* Deep & Deep Publications, New Delhi, 1993.

Kazim Munishi : *Alamgir-Nama,* A.B.C. & Co., Calcutta, 1865.

Khaduri, M. : *War and Peace in the Law of Islam,* Hopkins Press, Baltimore, 1955.

Landau, R. : *The Philosophy of the Ibn Arabi,* Century Pub., London, 1959.

Lewis, Richards : *Universe,* Harmony Books, New York, 1973.

Mac, Closky : *Pacts for Peace,* New Century Pub., London, 1980.

Margery Milne : *The Nature of Life,* Crown Publishers, New York, 1995.

Mathew, Thomas : *Political Economy of Etimic Conflict,* School of International Studies, Jawaharlal Nehru University, New Delhi, 2003.

Mayne, P. : *Saints of Sind,* New Century Pub., London, 1965.

Meer, Ali : *Observations on the Musulmauns of India,* Macmillan & Co., London, 1832.

Mohiuddin, Ahmad : *Saiyid Ahmad Shahid,* Modern Pub., Lucknow, 1975.

Moreland, W.H. : *From Akbar to Aurangzeb,* MacMillan & Co., London, 1923.

Mualana, Taqi : *Fundamentals of Ijtihad,* Idaara-I-Adabiyat, Delhi, 1986.

Muhammad, Asad : *Islam at the Crossroads,* Kitab Bhavan, New Delhi, 2003.

Murtaza, G. : *Judicial System of Islam,* Kitab Bhavan, New Delhi, 1994.

Muslehuddin, M. : *Islam : its Political System,* Kitab Bhavan, New Delhi, 1999.

Nabith, A. : *The Foundations of the Articles of Faith,* Feroz Pub., Lahore, 1963.

Nicholson, R.A. : *Studies in Islamic Mysticism,* Cambridge, New York, 1967.

Nikki, R. : *Saints and Sufis, Muslim Religious Institutions since 1500,* University of California Press, California, 1972.

Noomi, Kurtha : *Prisoners of War and War Crimes,* Deep Publications, Lacknow, 1980.

Padwick, C.E. : *Muslim Devotions,* MacMillan & Co., London, 1960.

Palamer, E.H. : *The Quran,* Atlantic Publishers, New Delhi, 1996.

Peter Lambron Wilson : *Traditional Modes of Contemplation and Action,* University Press, Tehran, 1977.

Qazi A. Qadir : *The Changing World of Islam,* Royal Pub., Lahore, 1992.

Richards, J.F. : *Mughal Administration in Golkonda,* Oxford, New York, 1975.

Robert, D. : *Exploring our Living Planet,* National Geographic Society, Washington, 1989.

Rodinson, Maxime : *Islam and Capitalism,* Penguin, London,1974.

Rosenthal, E.I.J. : *Islam in the Modern National State*, University Press, Cambridge,1965.

Sardar, Ziauddin : *The Future of Muslim Civilization*, Croom Helm, London, 1979.

Sarton, George : *Introduction to the History of Science*, Carnegie Institute, Washington, 1950

Saxena, K.P. : *Human Rights: Perspective and Challenges*, Lancers Books, New Delhi, 1996.

Saxena, V. K. : *Muslims and the Indian National Congress*, Discovery Publishing House, New Delhi, 1985.

Scarman, Leslie : *Law : the New Dimensions*, Stevens and Sons, London, 1974.

Schacht, J. : *The Origins of Muhammadan Jurisprudence*, Clarendon Press, Oxford, 1953.

Schwartz, E. : *Science and Civilization in Islam*, Cambridge, London, 1966.

Seervai, H. : *Constitutional Law of India*, N.M. Tripathi & Co., Bombay, 1967.

Setalvad : *War and Civil Liberties*, Feroz Pub., Lahore, 1992.

Sharif, M. : *Islamic Social Framework*, Islamic Book Foundation, Dacca, 1980.

Sharma, S.R. : *Women's Education in Ancient and Muslim Period*, Discovery Publishing House, New Delhi, 1996.

Siddiqi, M.Z. : *Hadith Literature*, Deepali Pub., Calcutta, 1961.

Singh, Nagendar : *Human Rights and International Cooperation*, S. Chand & Co., New Delhi, 1969.

Sir William : *The Caliphate, its Rise, Decline and Fall*, Oxford, Edinburgh, 1915.

Sir, Richard : *Sind and Races that Inhabit the Valley of the Indus*, Allen & Unwin, London, 1851.

Sir, Thomas : *The Caliphate*, MacMillan, London, 1965.

Smith, M. : *An Early Mystic of Baghdad*, Cambridge, New York, 1920.

Smith, M.: *The Mystic and her Fellow Saints in Islam*, Cambridge, London, 1929.

Smith, W. C. : *Modern Islam in India : a Social Analysis*, Manohar Publishers, New Delhi, 1985.

Suhrawardi, Umar : *Awarif al Maarif bin Muhammad*, Sheikh Ghulam Shahabuddin Ali & Sons, Lahore, 1964.

Syed Husain : *Three Muslim Sages*, Cambridge, New York, 1959.

Syed, Amir Ali : *The Spirit of Islam*, Royal Pub.,Lahore, 1979.

Taqi Muhammad : *An Introduction to Islamic Finance*, Idara Ishaat-e-Diniyat Pvt. Ltd., New Delhi, 1999.

Thompson, H.R. : *Sculptures and Inscriptions of Darius the Great on the Rock of Behistan*, Oxford, London, 1907.

Valliuddin, Mir : *The Quranic Sufism*, Motilal Banarsi Das Publishers, New Delhi, 1989.

Wahed, Husain : *Administration of Justice during the Muslim Rule in India*, Ashish Publishing House, New Delhi, 1977.

Waheed, Akhtar : *Sufi Approach to the Problem of Alienation*, Wilson & Co., New Delhi, 1975.

Waheed, Mirza : *The Life and Works of Amir Khusrau*, Kaveri Pub., Calcutta, 1935.

Walker, Benjamin : *Foundation of Islam : the Making of World Faith*, Rupa & Co., New Delhi, 2001.

Watt, M. : *The Faith and Practice of Al-Ghazzali*, MacMillan & Co., London, 1953.

Watt, W.M. : *Islam and the Integration of Society*, Routledge, London, 1961.

Yazbeck, Haddad : *Islamic Values in the United States*, Oxford, New York, 1997.

Yezbeck Haddad : *Islamic Values in the United States*, Oxford, New York, 1999.

Zafeeruddin, M.M. : *System of Modesty and Chastity in Islam*, Idara Ishaat-e-Diniyat Pvt. Ltd, New Delhi, 1995.

Zahid, Malik : *Subjects of Quran*, Kitab Bhavan, New Delhi, 1998.

Zahurul Hasan : *Tarikb-i-Sufiya-i-Gujarat*, Jamil Academy, Ahmadabad, 1981.

Zaydan, Jurji : *Umayyads and Abbasides*, Luzac & Co., London,1907.

Index

❑❑❑